Traveling in French C

MW01615322

Traveling in French Cinema

Sylvie Blum-Reid
University of Florida, USA

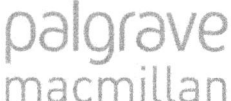

© Sylvie Blum-Reid 2016

First published 2016 by
PALGRAVE MACMILLAN

Palgrave Macmillan in the UK is an imprint of Macmillan Publishers Limited, registered in England, company number 785998, of Houndmills, Basingstoke, Hampshire RG21 6XS.

Palgrave Macmillan in the US is a division of St Martin's Press LLC, 175 Fifth Avenue, New York, NY 10010.

Palgrave Macmillan is the global academic imprint of the above companies and has companies and representatives throughout the world.

Palgrave® and Macmillan® are registered trademarks in the United States, the United Kingdom, Europe and other countries.

ISBN 978-1-349-57954-9   ISBN 978-1-137-55354-6 (eBook)
DOI 10.1057/9781137553546

This book is printed on paper suitable for recycling and made from fully managed and sustained forest sources. Logging, pulping and manufacturing processes are expected to conform to the environmental regulations of the country of origin.

A catalogue record for this book is available from the British Library.

Library of Congress Cataloging-in-Publication Data
Blum-Reid, Sylvie.
Traveling in French cinema / Sylvie Blum-Reid, University of Florida, USA.
pages cm
Includes bibliographical references and index.
1. Travel in motion pictures.   2. Motion pictures—France—History.
I. Title.

PN1993.5.F7B565 2015
791.43044—dc23   2015021817

Typeset by MPS Limited, Chennai, India.

Contents

List of Figures

Acknowledgements

I wish to thank all of those who came along for this trip: all of my family and friends. I am grateful to you for your guidance, patience, and support.

Special thanks to Khaled Gorbal who agreed to meet with me and discuss his film, *Un si beau voyage*, as well as Rabah Ameur-Zaïmeche, who I met in his film production house in 2009.

I acknowledge the formative importance of the NEH Seminar: Cinematic Images in Urban and Rural France, organized and directed by George Santoni (summer 1991, Albany), one of the best formative experiences one can have early in a career. I thank all of my film students for all of their stimulating exchanges and appreciation of French and European cinema and culture and intellectual ideas.

I am grateful to the College of Liberal Arts & Sciences at the University of Florida for the travel grants that have enabled me to present my research at various national and international conferences, and I am happy to have the long-standing support of my departmental chair Mary Watt and colleagues in Film Studies regarding teaching and research.

My sincere appreciation for the work of computer expert Ken Booth, the manager at the Applications Support Center of the University of Florida.

A very special thanks to the different librarians at the University of Florida, who have supported my research focus over the years: Frank di Trolio, John Van Hook, Matt Loving, Paul McDonough, Elaine Needelman, and Jim Stevens, as well as Judy Shoaf, director of the Language Learning Center, for all of her enthusiastic and tireless help with film material and film class support.

Conferences

Parts of this book were presented in earlier versions at the following conferences:

"Variations on the Euro-trip," 5th Annual Studies in French Cinema, French Institute, London, March 31, 2005.

"Going Home or Geographic Crossing in Contemporary French Cinema," SCMS, Chicago, March 2007.

"Away from Home: Two Directors in Search of Their Identity," Transnational Cinema session, MLA, 2005, Washington D.C.

"A Return to the Native Land: Rabah Ameur-Zaïmeche's *Bled Number One.*" *MESEA-*. The Society for Multi-Ethnic Studies: Europe and the Americas, Leiden- Summer 2008.

A segment of my interest in Romain Duris, the actor, was read at SCMS and appears in Chapter 4. "Le Corps/Coeur de Romain Duris," Society for Film and Media Studies, New Orleans, March 2011.

"Le Filmer Nomade – *Transylvania*" de Tony Gatlif, 20th–21st century French and Francophone Studies conference, "Crossings, Fictions, Fusions," Long Beach, March 2012.

"Filming the 'Bled' – Nostalgia for the Country in Diasporic Cinema," SCMS, Los Angeles, March 2010.

Publications

A section of this book was published in the form of the essay "Away from Home: Two Directors in Search of Their Identity," *Quarterly Review of Film and Video*. Volume 26, 1 (2009): 1–9.

Introduction

'A trip: Must be done quickly.'
'Voyage: Doit être fait rapidement.' (Flaubert,
Dictionnaire des idées reçues 435)
'One thinks one is going to take a trip, but soon the
trip makes you or unmakes you.' Nicolas Bouvier
(1929–1998). 'On croit qu'on va faire un voyage, mais
bientôt c'est le voyage qui vous fait ou vous défait.'

The book reflects on travel narratives in French fiction films from
the 1980s to the present. I plan to explore movement through the
various landscapes traversed in French films over the past twenty years.
Different modes, situations and perspectives will be examined. I borrow
from the fields of cultural studies, ethnography, film studies, gender
studies, philosophy, semiotics, tourism studies, and travel writing.

In the 19th century, 'flânerie' – a derivative of traveling – was commonly perceived as a masculine activity, observed in Baudelaire's writing about the Parisian *flâneur*, a street wanderer associated with the
act of looking. Going back to the 16th century, Montaigne, the ideal
European traveler, relays the dominant masculine activity of sightseeing and contemplation of women in Italian cities in his *Journal de voy-
age/The Journal of Montaigne's Travels in Italy by way of Switzerland and
Germany. 1850 and 1851*, a journal discovered 180 years after his death,

le plus commun exercice des Romains, c'est se promener par les
rues; ... A vrai dire, le plus grand fruit qui s'en retire, c'est de voir les
dames aux fenêtres, et notamment les courtisanes, qui se montrent à
leurs jalousies avec un art si traître que je me suis souvent émerveillé
comme elles piquent ainsi notre vue; et souvent, étant descendu de

1

cheval sur-le-champ et obtenu d'être ouvert, j'admirais cela, de combien elles se montraient plus belles qu'elles n'étaient. Elles savent se présenter par ce qu'elles ont de plus agréable ... Chacun est là à faire des bonnetades et inclinations profondes, et à recevoir quelque oeillade en passant. (131–132). ('The only pleasure you have in them is to see them passing before the place where you are ... In one part of the street where the ladies have a better view, the gentlemen, on fine horses, run the quintain, and exhibit some grace at it. On this day all the fair gentlewomen of Rome were seen at leisure, for in Italy they wear no mask as they do in France and show themselves quite openly.')[1]

The Surrealists emulated Arthur Rimbaud's call for the open space of the road. André Breton recounted that before the publication of *Le Manifeste du surréalisme/The Surrealist Manifesto* (1924), he and his friends wanted to follow Rimbaud's famous injunction to 'drop everything and hit the road' (Brassaï 6).

Walking (and traveling) as summoned by George Steiner in his essay *A Certain Idea of Europe* is an activity specific to the European identity. It is a part of its very fabric, before the advent of modern transportation routes. The nature of travel and work, as well as the relations between men and women, evolved. Several trades are based on the actual displacement of the worker, as the embroiderer and seamstress or midwife and country doctor, and even actors, singers, and filmmakers in the early part of the 20th century. Nicole Verdier's ethnographic study *Façons de dire, façons de faire* covers some of the women's practices in rural France. The film *Les Brodeuses/Sequins* (Eléonore Faucher 2004) magnificently retraces the seamstress's itinerary.

Women have traditionally been limited from traveling in the past. Few of them had the freedom to move and those who could move between spaces and places were usually designated as suspicious individuals. Vagabondage and charity were paired and frowned upon especially if a woman or young girl was involved, as in Hector Malot's *En Famille/Nobody's girl* (1893).[2] The book is a classic and was at one point distributed as a book prize at the end of the school year to meritorious French pupils.

Some female travelers (and writers) used male disguise in order to wander the world freely, as with Isabelle Eberhardt (born in Geneva) in Algeria and Alexandra David-Neel in Tibet, whereas most of the early male travelers openly recorded their impressions of nature, otherness, women, and exoticism in their 'relations de voyage.' Others deliberately picked their clothes according to their taste, and not as a disguise to avoid recognition (Maillart, Schwarzenbach).

A nascent tourist industry proposed to revolutionize tourism in the 19th century and packaged trips such as 'the discovery of Europe in a week'. Women and men became producers, distributors, and avid consumers of a more affordable tourism after a century of Grand Tours offered to mostly upper class male youth.

Travel literally designates 'the path to cover', the road. Several aspects participate in traveling. Walking is a dominant activity, an exercise in contemplation and thinking; it can be part of a daily regimen, designed to process different stages, as exemplified in the daily walks undertaken by the main protagonist in Karin Albou's *La petite Jérusalem* (2005), emulating philosopher Emmanuel Kant's daily promenades.

Travel is not necessarily a lucrative and pleasurable activity, limited to the enjoyment of a few, as described above. It points to traumatic experiences of displacement, forced migration, deportation, exile, and flight, or to necessary trips for work-related reasons. The migration flows to France, from within and without, developed new transportation routes and new laws that destabilize the fundamental notion of hospitality. Some of the films selected here speak to such conditions. Travel is a survival strategy for disenfranchised people, in order to secure a better job and a safer 'home' or in order to keep their jobs. At the end of the 20th century, and the beginning of the 21st century, the situation of guest workers and refugees from various countries has become a central preoccupation for western countries, sometimes threatening their longtime universal pledge to offer asylum. The fate of Eastern European Jews who migrated to France and other countries of Europe in the 1930s is a reminder of the predicament of refugees today. Their subsequent destiny destroyed the commonly held belief that one could settle down and live 'like god in France'. Presently the situation of Pakistani, Syrian, Turkish, Kurdish, Afghan, African, and Chinese asylum-seekers crossing France, Italy, Spain, and other European countries and the Mediterranean Sea in search of employment and refuge has become a political nightmare for European governments as documented in films such as *Inguélézi* by François Dupeyron (2003 France), or *Dirty Pretty Things* by Stephen Frears (2002 UK) and more recently *Welcome* by Philippe Lioret (2009 France) and *Le Havre* by Aki Kaurismäki (2012 Finland/France, Germany).

This book embraces several discourses and examines the meaning of 'routes' and circulation at the beginning of the 21st century channeled through recent movies and texts. It touches on the topic of departure point and destination. What are some of the European travel motifs, others than tourist hot spots? The existence of borders or boundaries is acknowledged. Despite attempts to cross and forego borders in a unified Europe, what was once true of western affluent countries no longer holds with the global threat of terrorism imposed on travelers and workers, as well as new policies established to promote a 'selective' immigration. Etienne Balibar's consideration of the phenomenon of 'vacillating borders' isolates the notion that established borders need to be revisited. What Balibar qualifies as a 'malady', the problematic circulation of people,

> has relativized the functions of the port of entry and by contrast revalorized internal controls, creating within each territory zones of transit and transition, populations 'awaiting' entry or exit ... individually engaged in a process of negotiation of their presence and their mode of presence with one or more states (218).

Of interest in the book will be the form and metaphors used in travel narratives and what they accomplish on a purely cinematic level. Away from packaged tourism, 20th-century writers used diary notes as the traveler's preferred format. Nicolas Bouvier draws on the diary form in his journey across Eastern Europe to Afghanistan in *L'Usage du Monde*, a book that has become a bible for studies in travel narratives and backpackers alike. Notes logging travel impressions rival journal entries, with the example of Ella Maillart in *Croisières et Caravanes*, a Francophone Swiss traveler whose travel narrative was first published in English.[3] Maillart toured through Asia, Russia, China, and Afghanistan in the 1930s. *Journey to Kafiristan/Die Reise nach Kafiristan* (Dubini brothers 2001) draws its inspiration from Annemarie Schwarzenbach's and Ella Maillart's road trip to Aghanistan in 1939 and their travel records.

Road movies, an emergent genre derivative of travel narratives usually paired with American cinema, are multiplying in Europe, although the concept derives from American films. They were present in the 1960s and 1970s with Chantal Akerman's *News from Home* (1977) juxtaposing scenes of New York life with the filmmaker's voiceover reading letters from her Belgian mother, or Jean-Luc Godard's fleeing characters in *A Bout de Souffle/Breathless* (1959) and *Pierrot le fou* (1964). Other texts are in the form of chronicles, manuals, how to guides, or epistolary chronicles. *Les Rendez-vous d'Anna* (1978), Akerman's most European film, crisscrossing different countries in the form of a travelogue, paves the way. A more recent version appears in Julie Delpy's *Two Days in Paris*

(2009), a comedic travelogue that addresses a Franco-American couple's relationship in one of their displacements abroad. Several recent books attest to the phenomenon, such as Michael Gott and Thibaut Schilt's *Open Roads, Closed Borders. The Contemporary French Language Road Movie*, and Neil Archer's *The French Road Movie Space, Mobility, Identity*. They are devoted to the road movie genre, as is Ewa Mazierska and Laura Rascaroli's *Crossing New Europe: Postmodern Travel and the European Road Movie*. Annie Goldmann's *L'Errance dans le cinéma contemporain*, an early study, established the notion of wandering, by encompassing films by Godard, Duras, Akerman, Jarmusch, and Wenders. According to Goldmann, who traces the emergence of travel narratives in the 1960s, these directors' films were the earliest ones to deal with a certain kind of wandering. Her study is not so much devoted to road movies but to the concept of wandering in films as Suzanne Liandrat-Guigues does in *Modernes Flâneries du Cinéma*.

I am interested in geographic displacements, crossings and sometimes transgressions. I do not focus solely on the road movie genre, except formally in one chapter. Each travel mode (buses, cars, trains, airplanes, tractors) points to the importance of speed, our reliance on such modes throughout the 20th century, and the counterpart to that reliance found in the growing importance attributed to slowness, here related to traveling, which acts as a resistance and an alternative to the effect of accelerated life-styles. In fact, a celebration of slowness (although the term in English has negative connotations) is paired with drifting (or wandering), an activity inherited from 18th-century philosopher Jean-Jacques Rousseau, in *Rêveries d'un promeneur solitaire/Reveries of a Solitary Walker* (1782) and 19th-century romanticism. Contemporary writers Pierre Sansot and Philippe Delerm advocate such a pace. Slowness emerges as an alternative lifestyle that is more necessary than ever at the beginning of the 21st century. While it may seem archaic and counter-productive in postmodern times consecrated to communication, hyper-speed and efficiency, to take time off assists us to listen to others and to our body, and to facilitate dreaming. Jacques Rozier and Jacques Tati as well as Aki Kaurismäki are avid proponents of leisure time, reevaluating pace and inner reflection. I consider some of the wandering displayed in films such as *Sansa* (Siegfried), *L'Arpenteur, Le lac et la rivière* (Sarah Petit), or *La légende du Saint-Buveur* (Ermanno Olmi).

Amidst these travel narratives, I distinguish healing tropes in *Un si beau voyage* (Khaled Ghorbal), *Nocturne Indien* (Alain Corneau), *Le Grand Voyage* (Ismaël Ferroukhi), and *Transylvania* and *Exils* (Tony Gatlif). By healing, I mean a form of return to wholeness and health, body, mind, and spirit that is accomplished through the travel process. The individual ends up at peace in his/her life and cleansed in the long run. Some films participate in different categories that are mutually interchangeable. For instance, a character may be nomadic, and a rebel, yet the trip in turn can unexpectedly become a healing one (Calle's *No sex last night*, or Gatlif's *Transylvania*).

Travel turns out to be a way of learning and of seeing. Marc Augé in *L'Impossible Voyage* urges us to 'learn how to travel again in order to learn how to see anew' (13–14). As a result, characters open to the Other. The journey transforms into a cleansing experience, or an inner voyage as with *Mr. Ibrahim*, or *Maine-Océan*.

Le monde existe encore dans sa diversité. Mais celle-ci a peu à voir avec le kaléïdoscope illusoire du tourisme. Peut-être une de nos tâches les plus urgentes est-elle de réapprendre à voyager, éventuellement au plus proche de chez nous, pour réapprendre à voir (Augé 14–15). ('The world still exists in its diversity. But this has little to do with the illusory kaleidoscope of tourism. Maybe one of our most urgent tasks is to learn to travel anew, eventually closer to home, in order to learn how to see again.')

Augé opposes tourism for its reinforcement of spatial divisions and constitution of tourism arenas, spas, and clubs, 'which turned nature into a product' (14).

Due to new technologies (the internet grid), as well as socio-political and sometimes religious emergencies, displacements and journeys undergo severe mutations. Paul Virilio observes that 'the transport revolution of last century had already quietly begun to eliminate delay and changes the nature of travel itself, arrival at one's destination remaining, however, a "limited arrival" due to the very time it took to get there.' The 'elimination of departure at the end of the twentieth' century is a radical notion that places the sole emphasis now on 'arrival' (16).

The archetypal traveler stands at the core of our societies, a notion supported by Michel Maffesoli's *Le Voyage ou la conquête des mondes*. Our culture is returning to the 'wandering' trope and that of the nomad. Maffesoli revisits the uncanny traveler as someone who resists the norms of society – a figure of desire for the sedentary type, but also a troublesome one. The dialectical poles of sedentarism and nomadism are raised as well as questions regarding the urge to travel: 'la frénésie des voyages étant une manière déguisée de vivre l'immobilité' ('the frenzy to travel is a new disguised way to live immobility') (50).

Travel, when not a necessity, consists of a journey into the self, an exploration of one's identity and one's past, singular or collective. Roma filmmaker Tony Gatlif's nomadic films address the notion of one's place within the world. Some of the narratives examined are self-centered and introspective. At that stage, it is not so much the act of traveling that matters but the subsequent personal transformations that are accomplished through travel. As illustrated by Xavier de Maistre's 18th-century parodic *Voyage autour de ma chambre/Voyage around my bedroom* (1794), the distance covered is not the most important matter. De Maistre playfully puts forward to the world a 'new way of traveling', one that would be affordable to all 18th-century classes.

Travelers (tourists) have the advantage – and luxury for some – to leave a place without delay and to pass from one relation to the next, thereby escaping scrutiny from their contemporaries. The traveler, being constantly on the move, is inconspicuous, far from people's gaze since he/she is never anchored and never forges long-time relations. Louis-Charles Fougeret de Monbron examined some of the characteristics of travelers and stated that 'le seul moyen de se rendre la vie gracieuse dans le commerce des hommes, c'est d'effleurer leur connaissance, et de les quitter, pour ainsi dire, sur la bonne bouche' ('the only way to make life gracious in the business of men, is to barely make their acquaintance, and leave them, more or less, before exhausting one's welcome') (168). The traveler has an advantage over the 'resident' in that there is no time to realize people's imperfections, nor for people to notice theirs either as they spend very little time in one place.

The book has many facets; it is limited mostly to French or French-speaking narratives (francophone films and texts) yet straddles other European-based narratives when they resort to travel motifs presented earlier. My conclusion will point to further paths to be examined that were not necessarily taken. It reflects on the expansion of travel literature and festivals that take place yearly and how travel modes, and as a result films, are changing with new technologies.

1
Departures

Variations on the Euro-trip

This chapter charts a two-prong approach to Cédric Klapisch and Tony Gatlif in their films *L'Auberge espagnole* (2002), *Gadjo Dilo* (1997) and *Exils* (2004). The second part examines Tony Gatlif, the Franco-Algerian-Gypsy filmmaker's background and his experience as a migrant and exile who left Algeria for France in the 1960s. I choose the trope of departure as well as the fabrication of a European travel film type as a motivating force. I borrow from Star Studies in order to analyze the performance of Romain Duris, an actor shared by the two filmmakers.

In what is unofficially entitled *La Trilogie des Voyages de Xavier/The Trilogy of Xavier's Trips*, Cédric Klapisch confirms his intention to place travel at the center of his protagonist's experience. The final installment, *Casse-tête chinois/Chinese Puzzle*, came out in 2013, eleven years after the first film *L'Auberge espagnole/The Spanish Inn* (2002). The first part of the chapter concentrates on the first two films of the trilogy. Klapisch follows a young twenty-five–year-old French man Xavier Rousseau (Romain Duris) who decides to study Spanish in Barcelona and complete his studies. Xavier's (auto)biographical account stretches roughly over twenty years of his life.

In the first part, Xavier leaves everyone and everything behind, his country, mother, girlfriend, and his maternal language/native tongue, and becomes an exchange student or, poetically speaking, 'a foreigner in a foreign land'. The entire story is projected against the ambitious backdrop of the constitution of the European community, harmoniously experienced at its most microcosmic level: Xavier shares an apartment with seven European roommates, a sort of tower of Babel at the heart of Barcelona. Europe is typecast by six members (out of twenty-five then) with Denmark, Italy, Germany, Belgium, Spain, Great Britain, and France, leaving out other nations. Xavier's future is carved out for him: he is to become a young technocrat or white-collar worker, a *cadre*, an insider of the new European financial elite, with headquarters at the Ministry of Finance in Bercy. The director even thanks minister Fabius in the final credit sequence.[1] Xavier secures an Erasmus grant that consists in [Erasmus is] a European Commission exchange programme that enables students in 31 European countries to study for part of their degree in another country and provides 'A fun challenging experience', as detailed by the following goals:

> The confidence to live in another country
> New or improved language skills
> New perspectives on an academic subject
> An international network of friends
> Travel opportunities throughout Europe
> Academic credits
> Transferable employment skills.[2]

However, in an unexpected twist, and after many tribulations, the experience abroad proves life changing for Xavier as he drops everything upon his return to France, unable to follow the plan. Stylistically, the escape figure culminates in one of the final scenes located at the Ministry of Finances when he turns his back on a diploma, runs away, and opts for a 'jobless future.' The implicit sequel *Les Poupées Russes/ Russian Dolls* (2005) is outlined at the end of the first film, preparing the spectator for the next phase. Xavier decides to return to his childhood dreams of becoming a writer. The end (of the film) formally constitutes the beginning of his living up to his true aspirations, and the recovery of self, shedding the path that was preordained by his father and father's (business) partner and dictated by class. Reaching this stage takes multiple trajectories that Xavier experiences physically and psychically, providing several false beginnings to the turn of events that he desperately wants to tell us/spectators.[3]

L'Auberge espagnole

The somewhat autobiographical plot transposes Klapisch's own trajectory following his failure to enter the French national film school and his decision to live in New York for two years and study filmmaking at New York University. In 2002 Spain, one of Europe's preferred tourist destinations, was at the height of its economic bubble. A long instructive review of *L'Auberge espagnole* found on a website for fun European vacations, displays alongside it information for travelers, bathroom decorations tips, and wardrobe advice for women.[4]

I read the film as a travel narrative, and will henceforth refer to it as part of the European-travel or euro-trip – a name that I adopt for lack of a better term. I attempt to situate and track the trend in contemporary French but also European cinema. Of course, this is an elastic label, as the notion of genre clearly demonstrated by Rick Altman's study is fluid rather than static, and with it the notion of national cinema. Raphaëlle Moine observes that genres are an abstract construct that serves to regroup films as well as a concrete construct (11). The Euro-travel genre is a minor genre, a direct heir to adventure films, branching off sometimes into comedy, but it is the beginning of a more serious trend that is born of transnational routes, displacement, migration, and expatriation scenarios that constitute one of the tropes of our postmodern era.

Genres are 'specific networks of formulas which deliver a certified product to the waiting customer. They ensure the production of meaning by regulating the viewer's relation to the images and narratives constructed for him or her. In fact, genres construct the proper spectator for their own consumption' (Andrew 110). *L'Auberge espagnole* parallels and mimics the advent of TV-reality shows that occurred at the beginning of the 1990s on French television. Programs such as *Loft Story* and *Nice People* were based on a formula that brought together a group of European roommates to test their skills at adaptation in a collective space.[5] *Loft Story* moved from French television channel M6 to TF1 in 2003 on the heels of the successful Klapisch film and its new European twist: 'M6 already had its "loft" presented by Benjamin Castaldi, TF1 will have its *Auberge espagnole* starting in May.'[6]

Altman explains genre as a 'complex concept with multiple meanings', some of which are determined by the industry and others by viewing positions (14). His study relies mostly on Hollywood classical cinema, but raises the possibility that genres are possibly teaching us something about a nation and may be codified by certain parameters shared by a nation. For the present chapter, I focus on the 'Europeanness' of the genre, as it ventures into the different nations constitutive of Europe. This way, the main character's learning experience passes through his adolescent-like state reflective of the state of Europe in its infancy, learning, vacillating, and charting something different, new and collective. The film of course cannot speak for the (then) twenty-five member countries of the European Union, nor can it speak for the future candidates to the Union that were standing by in 1996, for example Bulgaria, Croatia, Estonia, Poland, and Slovenia, that became European Union members after its release.

L'Auberge espagnole activates at least two types of travel: one is couched in the Bildungsroman type, or *roman d'apprentissage* inherent to the genre and the other is the escape. Both are not necessarily mutually exclusive. To travel, wrote Montaigne, is not only about learning but also about 'fleeing'.[7] Xavier has a nagging impulse to escape from France, his mother, and possibly his girlfriend. By the end of the trilogy, he has mastered the form and adapted to living as an exile.

Timothy Corrigan's analysis of road movies finds a few emerging traits in the 1950s that reflect a breakdown of the family structure, taken from an essentially male perspective as well as a quest.[8] The structure evolves in the 1960s and 1970s when the typical male-buddy system breaks down and loses its innocence. Eventually in the 1980s, the genre crashes, allowing for the appearance of women as in Ridley Scott's *Thelma and Louise* (1991) and Agnès Varda's *Sans toit ni loi* (1985). Through the example of Wim Wenders's *Paris Texas*, Corrigan takes us through the story of Travis,

> a wanderer who has not only lost a family and an identity but, more importantly in some ways, a road and a car. ... What Travis might have been searching for once is what most road questers invariably want: an authentic home, a lost origin where what you see is what you are (154).

L'Auberge espagnole retains some of the genre markers and confirms a quest for some lost origins that is the topic of yet another euro-travel movie, directed by Gatlif, *Gadjo Dilo/The Crazy Foreigner/L'Etranger fou* (1997). Although Klapisch's film is not a road movie in a strict classical sense, the filmmaker cast Xavier as a character in search of himself, who 'does not exist yet, who is on the path, [but] there is not yet a highway traced for him.'[9] The myth of the road erupts in the narrative, yet roads are symbolic as the character leaves for a metaphoric open road.

Xavier's strained relationship with his divorced mother (and his girlfriend) that is more or less resolved at the close of the film, if one accepts that sharing a steak with one's vegetarian mother and engaging in friendly conversation is a sign of conflict resolution. The father is absent from his life. Leaving France comes at a cost. The character breaks down several times.

Klapisch advocates the importance of erasing boundaries, walls, and stereotypes in order to recognize and embrace the multiplicity of identities that constitute not only Europe but also being French at this historical juncture. He moves away from the Franco-French concerns that plague much of French cinema, and opens up the perspective. Xavier's voice-over narration literally takes off when it tackles these issues. The image of an airport runway and jetty is inserted several times to illustrate the movement of the plot.

Paradoxically it is a young African student – a fleeting appearance in the film who claimed the importance of maintaining a Catalan language and identity at a time when the European Union is debated at an earlier point in the film – who explains the identity politics that Xavier adheres to during a group discussion. The man from Gambia argues in favor of Catalan: 'It's not about an identity, but about the respect of identities.' Xavier reconsiders his French identity from this point on and definitely lets go of the 'gaulois' shared heritage advocated by the French neurosurgeon comrade who resettled in Spain with his wife.[10] Interestingly, the film does not use Catalan as a means of communication once the somewhat radical call for a Catalan identity and language is made.

The story of a taking-off

Immersion in a foreign language and the encounter with Others contribute to building the narrative. Xavier would probably be on his way to a business career, complete with a business suit and life in a 'square' world. He turns his back on a nostalgic time when people would grow their own food and live on a farm, as in *Le Monde de Martine* or *Martine à la ferme*, a series of French children's books first published in 1954, which he shows to his more evolved girlfriend who rebels against the sexist image inherent to the story. His narrow world tumbles down very quickly with what he describes as the big *bordel* (the big mess), signifying the real world and especially Europe.

Xavier's real aspirations are not clearly defined. The film provokes a tension between a desire for simplicity or a return to a Rousseauesque natural world, and the desire for a big messy 'Euro-pudding.' It is in the big mess that Xavier finds himself. He becomes his own agent when he mediates with the landowner in Barcelona, avoiding eviction for the group.

The discovery of self passes through the filters of sexuality, eroticism, women, friendships, and travel. The film presents a relatively simple perspective that was not spared by *Cahiers du cinéma* critics. Thus some explain Klapisch's film(s) as,

Un petit cinéma de l'ingénuité post-adolescente dont Klapisch s'est fait le chantre depuis *Le péril jeune* ... *L'Auberge espagnole* ressemble à un *Loft* qui fonctionnerait non pas selon un principe d'exclusion et de resserrement progressif mais selon son exact contraire: un élargissement progressif (du cadre, des personnages) entraînant tout le monde dans un souci de boulimie euphorique et globalisant. (Malausa 86)[11] (A small cinema about post-adolescent ingenuity, of which Klapisch seems to be the master, since *School Daze* .... *L'Auberge* resembles the *Loft*, which would operate not only according to a principle of exclusion and a progressive tightening but its exact contrary, a widening (of the frame, or characters) bringing everyone into a euphoric and globalizing sense of bulimia.)

Yet, there is more depth to the film. Xavier does not resemble the prototypical traveler: once he arrives in Barcelona and settles in the 'Spanish inn', he becomes a sedentary student of a foreign culture. His urban wandering reveals a fascination for Barcelona, the city that the director views as mythical and that appears at times in a touristy, clichéd way (Gaudí's architecture, the port), sampling some of its tourist landmarks in one sequence and the less known Barcelona at other times. As he did in *Chacun cherche son chat/When the Cat is Away* (1996), Klapisch walks us through an architectural tour of the city, and maps out its geography first perceived through foreign eyes (most like those of the spectators). He exploits the notion of habitus and living in a city that at first is foreign, but will become natural once lived-in, echoing Georges Perec's notion of the city and the neighborhood. What does living in a foreign city mean at first? Xavier responds: 'After a while, all this belongs to you because you've lived there.'

Traveling through language, traveling through the city

Traveling is first and foremost traveling in a (foreign) language and being seduced by foreign names and words. Incidentally, the traveler is protected by the barrier of the foreign language, which can be beneficial to his ears in the way relayed by Roland Barthes of his own travel experience in Japan in *Empire of Signs*,

> The murmuring mass of an unknown language constitutes a delicate protection, envelops the foreigner (provided the country is not hostile to him) in an auditory film, which halts at his ears all the alienations of the mother tongue ... Hence, in foreign countries,

what a respite! Here I am protected against stupidity, vulgarity, vanity, worldliness, nationality, and normality (9).

The streets of Barcelona become a text, a grid on the screen, displaying Xavier lugging his bags, and spelling out foreign names like *Urquinaona*, and mixing world geography locations, while celebrating the pleasure of naming and the poetry of the text:

> Urquinaona s'est glissé doucement autour de Mouffetard, de Ponto Combo, de ... Knock le Zout.... Il est devenu normal et familier. ('Urquinaona slipped quietly around Mouffetard, Ponto Combo, and Knock le Zout ... It became normal and familiar.')

The traveler gets acquainted with space, a new geography and a new vocabulary in a visual crisscrossing of streets or roads. The foreign city in time becomes familiar, natural, and homelike, and upon return the home city (Paris) treats Xavier as a foreigner. Exile creates a distance in one's rapport with language, with one's nation and its inhabitants, one's parents, and one's self. Leïla Sebbar, in a letter exchange with Nancy Huston, summarizes the exilic state as 'residing in a border zone, always on the side, neither in nor out, but in a permanent state of imbalance' (Huston/Sebbar 28). A similar condition applies to Xavier, who ends up at the hospital as he suffers from visions of Erasmus, a 17th-century time traveler-scholar who visits him in his bedroom at night, or walks toward him on a pier. The hospital brain scan provides an accelerated montage of his experiences, real and fantasy. In one scene, he speaks only in Spanish and tells people that he has lost 'his mother's tongue.' The scan converts into a geographical map. The examination reveals nothing but fatigue and exhaustion and a large imagination, not to mention an excessive practice of foreign languages.

In one of the final sequences, Xavier's identity pictures scroll down the grid-like screen and negate uniqueness and individualism: 'he is neither this nor that'. The montage highlights the multifaceted European identities that he now embraces: 'He is this, and this one, and that one.' He is the young boy in the picture; Klapisch's son Pablo appears on a picture that becomes animated. He is at once French, Spanish, and Danish. He has also learned to incorporate his feminine side.

> I'm not one but multiple ... I'm like Europe. I'm all that, ... a bordello. I can now start to tell you all. ('Je suis pas un mais plusieurs

... je suis comme l'Europe, je suis tout ça ... un bordel. Je peux enfin commencer à tout vous raconter').

This awareness closes the joyful-painful year, and the budding econo-mist discards all prearranged plans to jump ahead at the possibility of a 'future without a job' or the life of the artist that he is to lead in *Les Poupées russes*, the sequel. The conversion implies that he may as well be a 'foreigner' and that he in fact has become a tourist in his own land, which he now views with a different eye. The recognition plays out in Montmartre, a tourist location by excellence. The voice-over narration waxes poetic as he is leaving Martine who broke up with him, and heads up the Montmartrois staircase towards Place du Tertre:

(Xavier's voice over): All these streets. Such a complex trajectory in order to get here! I found myself in the streets of Paris where Parisians never go. (script)

The camera tracks him up Montmartre, closing-up on his face in tears:

I was a foreigner among foreigners. ... Why was I there? I didn't know! I never quite knew why I was where I was. (script)

When a Japanese tourist takes a picture of him, he interjects:

I must be typical. (script)

In the same sequence Xavier spots a group of Erasmus exchange students, his doubles, and signals to them. The Erasmus exchange program becomes an instant password, a mantra into the shared com-munal values. He learns to speak the language of Barcelona's popular cafés, and develops an understanding of women's sexuality and the laws of seduction thanks to an intimate friendship with Isabelle, the Belgian lesbian. The synopsis, based on an economic pursuit of 'a bet-ter future', a fate anchored in the present reality of France and Europe, mandates the protagonist to 'experience the world, Europe, social life, autonomy, and sexuality',[12] a positive move disrupting one's cocoon and familiar prejudices (Klapisch).[13] By advocating the importance of breaking down boundaries, walls, and stereotypes, one is able to recognize and embrace the multiplicity of identities that constitute Europe.

The third space

Traveling away from home forces one to alter one's perceptions, to come out of one's reserve and open up to changes. Alain de Botton positions the traveler in a third space where 'journeys are the midwives of thought. Few places are more conducive to internal conversations than a moving plane, ship or train' (57). Airport scenes abound in the film just as they pop up in countless films from the 1970s until today, replacing the early rail/road models. They manifest instances when people are out of touch with each other, and miss each opportunity to share their feelings. An illustration of such a moment ensues in the scene when Xavier takes Martine back to the Barcelona airport, and they look away from each other. Xavier is no longer the same person by the end of the story, which now has a subject and an identity; he is in the process of writing his story. He is standing on the empty runway, the only 'open' road in the film, a runway made for planes.

The reception of *L'Auberge Espagnole* was overwhelmingly positive, especially among the young audience. The film generated so much acclaim that a sequel was produced, *Les Poupées russes*, projecting Xavier five years later in Russia (June 2005). Made on an estimated budget of €5,300,000, *L'Auberge espagnole* sold 2,957,487 tickets in France by August 2003. In the US, it grossed $3,895.664 in September 2003 after its May release. In France, the film ranked fourth on the list of national box office bestsellers.[14]

The travel concerns of *L'Auberge espagnole* are far-removed from the issues of displacement and migration found in the films covered in Chapter 5 of this book, such as François Dupeyron's *Inguélézi* (2004), Tony Gatlif's *Exils* (2004), Philippe Lioret's *Welcome* (2009), and Aki Kaurismäki's *Le Havre* (2011). *Inguélézi* follows Turkish Kurd immigrants illegally crossing France in order to reach England. Shot like a clandestine film, it was not widely distributed. The core of the film deals with the possible fate that awaits those illegally crossing Europe to reach the Promised Land – a pattern that characterizes the end of the 20th century and beginning of the 21st century. Afghan, Iraqi, Turkish, Kurdish, and Pakistani refugees have set camp at the French border near the Euro tunnel entrance, in Sangatte (Calais), awaiting some sort of transfer and acceptance into England. Apparently, 1,300 people were living at the refugee center in 2002 and 78,000 people would have crossed since 1999.[15] The narrative speaks of the urgency of the situation, disregarding any possibilities of conviviality and cultural exchanges. Dupeyron and Lioret denounce a situation that has taken place behind the scenes in France, a country that represses immigration and, like others in Europe, has suddenly become very protectionist as to who can stay legally within its borders without being chased away and who can legally shelter people freely. Similarly, Stephen Frears in *Dirty Pretty Things* (2002) enters the world of Turkish and Nigerian immigrants in London – communities that are invisible on most screens. The plot includes horror and thriller-like qualities.

All the films mentioned above are part of a growing list that bears witness to a surge of displacement and migration at the turn of the century. Of course, different concerns and practices are at stake. For some, based on national economy and politics, these narratives document the fear, alienation, and urgency of a situation. For others, surfing on the success and riches of the European community, travel and study experiences are enriching and sometimes enlightening and 'light' fares. *L'Auberge espagnole* effectively tries to speak the new language of Europe, a sort of tower of Babel, targeting cultural and linguistics exchanges among privileged youths as a supposedly new phenomenon of the postmodern era.

Away from home

Two French directors crossed the border to film on foreign land. Tony Gatlif's *Gadjo Dilo/The Crazy Stranger* (1997) planted his camera in Romania and Cédric Klapisch's *L'Auberge Espagnole/The Spanish Inn* (2002) was set in Cataloña, Spain. The experiment is not unique to French cinema of the late 1990s or early 2000s, nor to the careers of these two directors, since Klapisch released two sequels with *Les Poupées russes/Russian Dolls* (2005) and *Casse-tête chinois/Chinese Puzzle* (2013). Gatlif, who had previously shot in Spain for *Vengo* (2000), went further south of the French and Spanish borders in *Exils* (2004). Retracing his footsteps to his Algerian homeland after years of absence, Gatlif for the first time returned 'home', just as he returned to Romania, a country of adoption, for the earlier films *Gadjo Dilo* and *Transylvania* (2006).

These extra-'hexagonal' excursions give a vista onto the current landscape of French cinema, and the way it bridges other cultures, countries, and cultural practices.[16] The scripts produced are inextricably linked to the present state of Europe, its history, and its position in a Global North world as much as they are to the filmmakers' identity formation and philosophy. European borders have become 'porous' or open to a relatively free circulation of goods and people, with a coda: the free circulation depends on the migrants' ethnic and religious origins. For instance, a Turkish Kurd crossing France becomes illegal, unwelcome, and hunted down, as in *Inguélézi* (Dupeyron 2004). The notion of a national cinema restricted to a national space is in a flux. These travel narratives, placed within the genre of the European journey[17] – a visible trend in not only contemporary French but also European cinema and culture in late 20th century – go beyond national borders. The European travel film encompasses multiple travel or migratory motifs that can be located within the European borders, with attempts to move beyond them, mapping out unchartered territory outside of what constitutes Western Europe and venturing into Eastern or Central Europe and sometimes North Africa or the Middle East. Examples of such films as *Gadjo Dilo* (1997), *Exils* (2004) are discussed further.[18] Many of the films fall into a transnational category with the likes of Richard Linklater's *Before Sunrise* (1995) and *Before Sunset* (2004), the story of an intercontinental love affair that started on a train and involved travelers from two different continents, shot by an American director. Linklater's trilogy concludes with *Before Midnight* (2013), almost twenty years later in the lives of the two protagonists, who are now approaching middle age. Such films cross national boundaries and involve travels to/through a European country, as well as personal journeys away from home and sometimes within France.

L'Auberge espagnole rides on the enthusiastic cultural, social, and educational exchange amongst European youth that took place in Spain, France and elsewhere during the economic bubble. Klapisch is considered a 'Europtimist'. According to Sylvie Forbin, one of the key-players in the European film production system, *L'Auberge espagnole* strongly embodies a European film, advertising the European construction and the Erasmus program.[19] It speaks the new language of Europe, a sort of tower of Babel that privileges cultural and linguistic exchanges among 'hip' youths, with a marked emphasis on English as a *lingua franca*,

> An important strand in making Europe's political space more vibrant and relevant is the creation of cross-national networks and encouraging cross-border mobility. The Union budget is increasingly used to promote links and networks between groups or areas within the member states with student mobility, R&D networks, cross-border co-operation, and networks of diffuse social groups. The Commission sees this activity as critical to its legitimacy and the legitimacy of the Union as a whole. (Laffan)

Filming at the periphery, or the nation's borders and beyond, moving away from the inner sanctum (Paris), the film opts for the 'ballad-form' that Annie Goldmann observed as the 'wandering in contemporary cinema' present in 1960s cinema.

Les Poupées russes/Russian Dolls (2005) opened after the referendum on the European constitution was massively turned down in France in June 2005. However, the film programmatically addresses the need to spread a larger Europe as far East as Russia, expanding both East and South, with the debate on Turkey's inclusion the source of many arguments.[20] In September 2005, at the time Hurricane Katrina devastated Louisiana and Mississippi, the French weekly journal *Le Nouvel Observateur* featured a series of articles devoted to the all-time high migratory pattern of French people 'who want to change country'.[21] North America is by far the favorite destination of French expatriates who seek employment and education abroad when they are limited to accomplish this at home. The cover clipped a photograph from *Les Poupées russes* with Xavier, five years later, lugging a suitcase at a train station, accompanied by Wendy (Kelly Reilly), the English roommate from Barcelona; both are boarding the Eurostar train, a recurrent icon throughout the film. The narrative operates a triangulation between London, Paris, and St Petersburg, viewed as the European city par excellence in its architectural design, a combination of the old and modern Europe (Klaspich).[22] The journalist credits the Erasmus program for enabling 20,000 students to act 'à la Romain Duris in "L'Auberge Espagnole" while spending a year in a European university'.[23] Xavier jumps five years ahead in film time and turns thirty. In 2005, political gloom plagues the hero, critical at first of his ex-girlfriend Martine, who is totally invested in combating globalization on a large scale. They do not speak the same language, yet they have remained close friends. His childhood dream of becoming a writer comes at a price as he struggles to make a living by writing commercial scripts and being a ghostwriter. In so doing, he accepts work abroad, and shuffles back and forth between England and France in a pattern that is reminiscent of the film *Ma femme est une actrice* (Yvan Attal 2001). The protagonist is still very much disoriented but finds a balance and an identity amidst a newly created community of friends and girlfriends (not with his own family). The reunion in St Petersburg celebrates the wedding between Wendy's brother, an English man (Kevin Bishop), and his Russian fiancée. Klapisch continues with the Europeanization trend,

> *Les Poupées russes* is a film about the widening of Europe. The previous one was located in Barcelona: I wanted a 'new elsewhere' ... the idea was the same, to speak of Europe in what it has not yet become

... I believe in Europe, I am among those who believe that this idea is more important than one's national problems.[24]

Klapisch relies on the model of a euro-centered narrative, and distances himself from the familiar French geography,

In fact, I think that in all my films, I try to lose myself! I always try to surprise myself by choosing a very different topic from the previous film. Here, in order to surprise myself, there was the fact of going geographically far away and getting there through foreign languages, I manage to no longer know where I am. (Klapisch) ('En fait, je crois que sur tous mes films, je cherche à me perdre! J'essaie toujours de me surprendre en choisissant un sujet de film assez différent du précédent. Là, pour arriver à me surprendre, il y a le fait d'aller loin géographiquement et d'arriver par le biais de langues étrangères à ne plus savoir où j'en suis.')[25]

Both films are situated in the transitional places or *non-lieux* located in zones such as airport terminals, airport runways, train stations, and Eurostar for *Poupées Russes*, all spaces that question identity, even though the journey away from home does not imply a forced exile or migration. Klapisch toys with the notion of the individual embracing the (European) community as the new family formation and only viable project for the future. The concept of itinerary and trajectory lies deep in his films and touches on the iconography of the crossroad, the map, or the grid-like town all converging to an intersection of several roads offering a choice to one's identity, both symbolic and physical. This notion is picked up again in *Paris* (Klapisch 2008).

The last installment, *Casse-tête chinois/Chinese Puzzle* (2013), moves the character further away from home and turns him into a new immigrant in New York, following his breakup with Wendy, his English wife, who moved there. Nearing forty, Xavier is settling down and fights to stay close to his two children, now relocated to New York. He becomes a naturalized citizen through an arranged marriage with a Chinese-American woman. The narrative performs a reunion of all his (female) friends. In a rather elaborate plot he reunites with his best buddy, Isabelle, the Belgian woman, for whom he donates his sperm, his ex-wife Wendy, and his former girlfriend Martine. He finds a job as a courier and continues writing his novel, as he is a celebrated author in France. However, the last chapter remains in North America; all of them leave 'old' Europe behind. A span of twenty years between

Barcelona and New York has (fictionally) elapsed; Xavier, still a mess, struggles to find a balance and becomes an immigrant in a land of new immigrants, rubbing shoulders with hyphenated citizens. Ethnicity is now a stronger component of the narrative. The appeal of Europe is waning; Frenchness or Europeanness are no longer a discussion topic. On the other hand, the United States constitutes an attractive alternative, but Chinese businesses are also dominant on the world stage. By far the most expensive film to produce in the trilogy, with a budget of €17,300,000 and released in the USA in May 2013, its gross box office receipts amounted to $335,430 in July 2014. It is expected to be less successful than *L'Auberge espagnole*, which earned $3,895,664 in the five months after its May 2003 initial release.[26]

Healing narratives

Gatlif makes movies about the road, and places his actors (male and female) on a quest across space and time. His films are nomadic, travelogue-like, and cryptic. In the earlier *Mondo* (1997) a young ten-year-old boy (Ovidiu Balan) was found alone in Nice;[27] the camera follows him for a short time in a ballad through France where he is welcomed by those who practice the laws of hospitality or otherwise rejected. Very young, he appears already old and wise. He has no bearings, no precise origins. One day he disappears, just as he arrived. Mondo is the character of the eponymous short story by Jean-Marie Le Clézio and one of Gatlif's rare screen adaptations of a literary text as he usually writes his own scripts.[28] Mondo is the reincarnation of 'Le Petit Prince;' one knows nothing of him, of his family, or of his house.

> When he liked someone, he would stop him, and simply ask: Would you like to adopt me? ('Quand il y avait quelqu'un qui lui plaisait, il l'arrêtait et il lui demandait tout simplement: "Est-ce que vous voulez m'adopter?"') (11).

The narrator wonders if he arrived 'after having traveled a long time in the cargo of a ship, or on the last car of a merchandise train' (12).[29] Mondo comes from the other side of the sea, 'he is not from here' (12).[30] The character is a wanderer impacting those he meets on his path.

Gatlif is of Algerian Berber and Gypsy-Andalusian descent and personally familiar with displacement. The foreigner (*Gadjo Dilo/The Crazy Stranger* 1997) adapts to another country, language and culture, although it is commonly believed that Gypsies and the Rom language know no geographical boundaries and have no particular allegiance to nationalism (Fonseca 28).[31] The discovery of Gypsy culture is performed by a French man, a non-Gypsy, or a *gadje* (Duris) who happily sheds his own language and cultural identity to embrace Romani culture and Rom language. *Gadjo Dilo* transplants a young Parisian man in the middle of icy Romania in winter; *Exils* moves south across Spain and lands first in Morocco before making its way to Algeria. This inverts the familiar script of the south-north migratory pattern from Algeria or Morocco to France or to its other European partners such as Spain, Germany, Holland, Belgium, and England. The crane shot of a road traveled against the grain by a couple is a recurrent motif. When Zano buries his violin in a cement wall by the second sequence, the spectator feels the pain inflicted in the act of walling in an instrument that is attached to his life, his father, and his art (Zano is a musician and so was his father). The rituals enacted in the film connect it to *Gadjo Dilo* as part of the filmmaker's larger vision or *oeuvre*. Zano is in search of something that is not immediately made clear to the audience. The past he is excavating (in the act of burying) is tied to the colonial past of his parents and grandparents in Algeria; these were among the Europeans settled in Algeria called *pieds-noirs*. The film geographically casts through its displaced character a look back into the (colonial) ghost of the past. Naïma (Lubna Azabal), his companion, is a young French woman of Algerian descent who does not speak Arabic.[32] Naïma's assumed knowledge of Arabic is tested along with her religious orientation and hybrid identity. As a male traveler Zano does not encounter that problem and is free to roam around, with the declaration that 'music is my religion'. Several modes of transportation are used from trains to buses and boats when they are not walking. The director and his crew made the final portion of the itinerary of a return physically by foot from Morocco to Algeria made clandestinely, since the border had then been closed for years. On the same road, the travelers walk against the flow of a crowd going west, toward Morocco, leaving Algeria, one of the most compelling oneiric segments in the film. They are going cross-current, just as they did when they cross paths in Spain with two siblings, a Moroccan brother and sister who are slowly making their way north to Paris, and whose letter and message ('we have safely arrived in Europe') they deliver to their mother left behind in Algeria. Large Northern metropolises attract young migrants as magnets, as they try to make it in the industrial European north.

Gatlif implicates himself psychically and physically more than in his earlier films. He fled home at a young age in the 1960s, and returned to Algeria after a forty-three-year absence. His long filmography (some twenty films by the time of *Exils*) focuses on transplanted persons of various origins, the displaced, homeless, and people who have been uprooted. The return is lived as a pilgrimage. He self projects in the young adults Zano and Naïma and circles around different ideas, using music as the mode that best suits the exilic experience and the pain as well as the urgency of a 'return'.[33] It helps him heal his wounds. Figurative or literal scars reveal wounded personas that have survived some cruelties. Naïma reveals her scars, on her face and lower back to Zano, whose burned leg scar is a trace of his parents' fatal car accident, which he survived. The trip is a sensual experience but also testifies to what happens to migrants on their way to a better place. The sea journey brings a moment of joy and fresh air to some of the pain that lies ahead. Upon arriving in Algiers, Naïma does not feel well and is forced to wear the Muslim robe and scarf, which she quickly discards. She is in direct conflict with the culture of veiled women. Zano breaks down after seeing old pictures of his family, one of them showing his father with the violin, in an apartment that seems frozen in time. The director carefully weaves in the possible equivocal feelings one feels returning to one's displaced parents' home, left untouched. Zano's tears attract the empathy of the two Algerian women now living in his former family home. The last segment of the film presents a long night of Sufi dances conducive to a healing of one's wounds and scars, on a physical and spiritual level. Naïma is ushered in front of a female healer who tells her that her soul is lost, and begs her to find her bearings and her family. This leads to the extended final sequence of trance-healing. It is through the healing performed by women, and Sufi dances, trances, and music, that Naïma undergoes a symbolic rebirth and reconnects with the country of her ancestors.[34]

A certain sensibility comes to those who travel the world and appear as foreigners wherever they are. This is doubly articulated by Naïma once she is in Algiers: *'Je me sens étrangère de partout'* ('I feel like a foreigner from everywhere'). Her ambiguous statement emphasizes that she belongs nowhere, yet at the same time, she might be from everywhere. In a certain sense, Gatlif is not just a director who can be labeled a 'French director' in the narrow sense of the word. His work espouses multiple geographical spaces and pursues several identity quests that transcend the national, the transnational, and the European. Gatlif touches beyond the European space and national allegiances to embrace a Mediterranean and worldly dimension that borders a 'planetary' and 'nomadic' dimension in the sense proposed by Canadian writer Nancy

Huston in her discussion of Romain Gary.[35] His camera makes sweeping takes of the lush Spanish fruit plains and countryside.

At the close of the film, after a long night of trances, Zano deposits his music and headphones on the tomb of his grandfather (Gatlif inserts the tombstone of his grammar school teacher), summoning the ancestors again, and reenacts a celebration that concluded the earlier *Gadjo Dilo*. There, Stéphane buried his deceased father's tape recorder near a road milestone, and danced following Gypsy custom.[36] In both scenarios, ghosts or spirits are invoked and characters make peace with the past. They reconnect with their heritage in order to move on. They open up to each other and to the world. Naïma shares an orange with Zano, who abandons the earphones that constantly isolated him in his own world. The lyrics accompanying the act are entitled 'Those who have left us always come back to us' ('Ceux qui nous quittent').[37]

Romain Duris

Romain Duris's performances are atypical. Susan Hayward's formulation that the body of the 'star' is anchored in its national culture through its morphology, gestures, and intonations (among other signs) is important when reflecting on the casting of Duris. Cast as a foreigner, a nomadic character in search of lost origins or a lost identity, Duris plays Xavier or Stéphane or Zano, key roles in Klapisch's and Gatlif's films, not to mention Michel Audiard's thriller *De Battre mon coeur s'est arrêté/The Beat that my Heart Skipped* (2005). In 2006 the *New York Times Style Magazine* consecrated Duris as the prototypical French man/actor of the year (Hirschberg).[38] Among some of his recurrent roles, one finds the traveler, the interloper, and the man who is attracted to and initiated into a new culture. He is the gypsy-like wanderer, the fun-seeking Bohemian with long untamed hair and locks. He becomes the director's double for both Gatlif and Klapisch for whom he has acted over the years. He is their fetish actor. Duris first appears in Klapisch's early *Le Péril jeune/Good Old Daze* (1994).[39] Interestingly, the correspondence between François Truffaut and Jean-Pierre Léaud in their director-actor relationship (through the character of Antoine Doinel), began to circulate for the Klapisch/Duris tandem, not for Gatlif. *L'Auberge espagnole* manipulates the transformation and shock happening on a physical level for anyone accustomed to seeing Romain Duris in a Klapisch or Gatlif film. The characters of Xavier, Stéphane, or Zano illustrate a generational divide occurring in Europe and point to an acceleration of movement, displacement, migration, and exchanges – a shift that has taken place over the past twenty years mostly in the youth generation, through study abroad programs and work-related practices.

Gatlif is instrumental to the transformation of Duris, the actor, particularly in his work on the body. The filmmaker's approach, which most likely touches each and every actor he directs, is more physical in its dimension and inclusion of music and dance. In many ways, his films are viewed as choreographies. Similarly, the actor has to undress or disrobe in his films, showing the importance and naturalness of the body and skin in many frames as well as the importance of shedding the old (cultural) baggage for the new. *Exils* opens on an extreme close-up of Zano's naked back and skin. He is standing in front of a window that gives onto a complex urban highway system (the single exterior image of France with that of the brick wall). 'What if we left for Algeria?' the character asks as he turns to his female companion. The camera scans body scars up close. Duris had to practice dancing for *Gadjo Dilo* to prepare for the role. The filmmaker prides himself on initiating the actor into becoming a Gypsy. As in *Gadjo Dilo*, the character and the actor are open to multiple experiences and identities.[40]

My chapter does not attempt to contrast and compare these two filmmakers' work, as they are very distant from each other. Yet having evaluated their views on the world and/or Europe, one can read similarities in their openness to the Other, a geographically and racially different Other, and the way they cast a certain sensibility onto an actor of the moment, that happens to be one they share. Gatlif operates in a countercultural sphere and militates for oppressed, homeless and stateless people. Both auteurs expand on the notion of the hero as nomadic, open to other cultures, and ready to grow in that experience. They deconstruct their male protagonist, casting a sensitive individual on a quest, someone who is not a superhero or confident about himself, who does not have all the answers to life's questions, and who can never be construed as arrogant, territorial, and nationalistic. On the contrary, the main character struggles to understand himself and the world; in the process, he experiments with and is able to incorporate his feminine side.[41] On one level, the protagonist is more at ease elsewhere than at home, which has now become elusive.

In the films discussed, the question of 'home' is raised. Where is home, and is it where one was born, and/ or when one lives? Is the community of friends one makes not more important? Is this film community not totally located in an imaginary dreamlike mode? Is Europe one's new home? If so, shouldn't it extend East and South? In a certain sense, Stéphane is just as much an outsider to Roma culture as he is an outsider to France when he is in Romania; Xavier is more European than French and feels like an outsider upon his return home to France. Each time the protagonist travels, he builds a network of support and friendships. The same image does not quite play back when he is 'home.' Either way, both filmmakers bridge two or more cultures and downplay the notion of borders to playfully laugh at stereotypes that critics find in their films.

2
Rituals: The Unlikely Journey

I will now turn to a discussion of rituals in society and how individuals undertake a journey in order to find themselves. I examine several films that fall within this category. Alain Corneau's *Nocturne Indien* (1989) takes the spectator on a trip to India, casting a Western traveler in search of his lost friend, and losing himself in the process, only to find himself. Antonio Tabucchi's postmodern novel on which the script is based sheds a light on my interpretation of Corneau's film. Khaled Ghorbal's *Un si beau voyage* (2008) is featured in the second part of the chapter 'The Sacred', when an exiled worker journeys back to his home country of Tunisia and sheds all his material belongings. The next segment covers Emmanuel Finkiel's *Voyage/Tracks* (1999) as it maps out three different itineraries of discovery and travel in Europe, with France, Poland, and Israel, integrating the full weight of Jewish history and identity.

The mise en scène of movement, travel modes, and routes is a recurrent motif in films. A celebration of mobility and speed that has taken place from early in the 20th century up to the present time has in turn generated a reappraisal of slowness and immobility. Films become a stage where rituals of all sorts are enacted. A ritual implies a social rite done in accordance with a social custom or a religious ceremony. They are not linked to organized religion. Rituals enable people to congregate in groups and connect with a certain communal or tribal spirit that is lacking in a society where everyone is solitary and lonely (Maffesoli). Some modern-day rituals are rooted in the thought of moving itself, as in Chantal Akerman's *Demain on déménage/Tomorrow we move* (2004) or Sophie Calle's *No sex last night* (1996).

Summer vacation rituals involve hiking trails (*GR* or *Sentiers de Grandes Randonnées*) and mountain climbing in Corsica with *Les Randonneurs* (Philip Harel 1997). Renewed pilgrimage routes to Compostella arise in

St-Jacques ... La Mecque (Coline Serreau 2005) or new pilgrimage routes as with *Emmenez-moi* (Edmond Bensimon 2005), the latter a buddy movie in the shape of a musical. Four men from Northern France trek from Roubaix to Paris to thank the 'wizard of Oz', acclaimed singer Charles Aznavour. The members of the down-and-out group in *Emmenez-moi* find a goal to their otherwise depressed lives. Other rituals involve single individuals and their experience alone, in search of the sacred. These individuals are detached from group activities, and perform an interior voyage, looking into themselves for harmony and peace.

Nocturne Indien (1989), Alain Corneau's passage through India film, borrows the travel form as a means to find and lose oneself. The plot is not exactly untested,

> *Nocturne Indien* is a lyrical travelogue that tells the existential tale of Rossignol, a solemn Portuguese archival researcher who journeys through India in search of a missing friend named Xavier whose physical and psychological description curiously resembles his own image.[1]

The camera follows the protagonist, a Portuguese man called Rossignol (Jean-Hughes Anglade) in multiple close-up shots of his wide-eyed face, captured in semi-darkness. The character arrives in India for the first time looking for a friend who disappeared. His quest propels him to various cities and regions, forming a triangular shaped map between Bombay, Madras, and Goa, where the trip ends. A French website has digitally mapped the narrative's locations.[2] Crossing a total of five states, each major stop is visually captioned in a black frame with white lettering as in a silent movie. In the following pages I will examine the script and the original novel. The script is adapted from Antonio Tabucchi's short novel *Notturno Indiano/Nocturne Indien/Indian Nocturne* (1984) published first in Italian and translated into French in 1987.[3] Tabucchi (an Italian) studied in France, specializing in Portuguese literature, with an interest in the poet Fernando Pessoa.[4] Travel narratives fascinate him. He too traveled where the story takes us. In the incipit, he claims to be a traveler and views this narrative as insomnia as well as a journey (Tabucchi).[5]

> Cage District was much worse that I had imagined. I'd seen it in the photographs of a famous photographer and thought I was prepared for human misery, but photographs enclose the visible in a rectangle. The visible without a frame is always something else (5).

At its source, Tabucchi's writing is cinematographic and shapes itself around light, framing devices, and cinematic-like sequences. The reliance on photography and frames or 'off camera' (the *hors-champ*) contributes to his style, and the way the journey progresses and concludes. The story unfolds as in a dream (or a nightmare) that Corneau respects in his use of nighttime sequences, lighting, and shades. In many ways, this is a film noir that doubles as travel narrative. The protagonist in search of his 'lost' friend Xavier has very few leads and each one takes him to a different location, which suits him perfectly since he never stays in one hotel for more than one night. The 'Index of the Places in this book' mostly lists hotel names, railway stations, bus stops, the hospital, the Theosophical society, and the Bogmalo Beach in Goa. The last two stops occur in former Portuguese colonies – the state of Goa and the town of Madras, now renamed Chennai. The Portuguese colonizers landed there in the 16th century; their influence still lingers in the architecture and permeates both film and novel. Corneau's meeting with Tabucchi gave him the impression that the 'film was taking place in Lisbon as much as Bombay'.[6]

Starting in Bombay, Rossignol locates a young prostitute who requested his assistance in a letter. She knew and loved Xavier. Xavier Janata Pinto's portrait slowly emerges as someone who was sad, afflicted by some deep-rooted melancholia, and who may have taken his life. He is/was of Indo-Portuguese origins. He disappeared in India a year earlier yet his ghost haunts the search. Rossignol relies on very little information; he uses correspondence to track him down and his paths through different places. His description of Xavier is strikingly similar to his own: a man with dark hair, thin, and a long and sad face ... as if he is looking at his mirror image, unknowingly.

It is said, 'Many people get lost in India.' At the hospital archives, the traveler meets a doctor who he hopes saw his friend. However, the reality of India takes him aback: 'you can forget your European notions, they are an arrogant luxury', the doctor tells him, explaining that over one and a half million patients pass through the hospital during the Monsoon months.[7] It is not clear whether each traveler ever loses his/her European way. However, the traveler brings along his or her culture as baggage.

Tous les types de voyage, journaux, récits de conquêtes, carnets de notes, observations ethnologiques, récits de pèlerinage, (...) poème en direction du 'paradis perdu' ou de la 'terre promise' .... obéissent à la loi selon laquelle la vérité du voyage tient au dévoilement d'un sens de l'étranger accessible au voyageur et reconductible aux critères de sa propre culture (Derrida, Malabou 36). ('All types of travel, diaries, conquest narratives, notebooks, ethnological observations, pilgrimage narratives, poems about a 'lost paradise' or the 'promised land' ... obey a law according to which the truth of travel is held in the revealing of a foreign meaning accessible to the traveler and conducive to the criteria of his own culture.')

The search for Xavier becomes the search for the self. As Xavier's profile emerges, one learns that,

> He wrote stories ... they were about things that didn't work out, about mistakes; for example, one was about a man who spends his life dreaming about making a trip, and when one day he's finally able to make it, that very day he realizes that he doesn't want to go any more (17)

While visiting the hospital, the inquisitive Rossignol walks through the sick patients' ward, hoping to locate his friend. He seems rather out of place. His gaze is transfixed on native patients who are lying on their beds. The musical score starts then – the main theme is a piece by Franz Schubert, his String Quintet in C Major, D956, op. 163, composed in 1828, one of the last chamber works he composed. The adagio resonates at intervals throughout the film. Its first four minutes and the end of the movement play, but never the faster, angst-ridden middle section. The title *Nocturne Indien* implies a musical dimension yet the novel barely incorporates any music and definitely barely any Indian music. The Schubert score, the filmmaker's choice, inspired him during the scriptwriting.[8] It is not strictly speaking a film score. There is no diegetic source for it. If the film is quite scenic, due to the nature of the country – locations, people, legends, and expected sightseeing attractions (monuments) – the camera is rather withdrawn or shies from them; many sequences are 'interior' shots saturated in brown or reddish shades that are suited, like the music, to Rossignol's melancholy mood. Conversations take place indoors and/or at night. It aptly fits the criteria of film noir (Della Coletta 229). India is not postcard-like. The exteriors do not matter because the voyage is an interior one, yet the film proposes some deceptively iconic travel markers, such as a tour guide to India.

Incidentally, Tabucchi wrote two versions of a 'train ride' to Madras, the train turning out to be a pivotal episode in the film. One version appears in a book of short stories *Petits Malentendus sans importance/ Little Misunderstandings of no importance*, written around the same time as *Nocturne Indien*[9]; he is accustomed to echoing some of his stories. I will thus draw from both versions as they illuminate each other, and rely on each one as they each support my discussion of the film and inform Corneau's script. On top of the fact that trains are the preferred vehicles, they allow passengers to fully savor a place, in direct opposition to the plane journey, which transports one quickly from point A to B, but during which one loses touch with the country and its culture. The filmic sequence is configured slightly differently (by the director/ scriptwriter) and instead of borrowing from Tabucchi's novel, at the root of the film, it stages another of Tabucchi's travel narratives, in the short story form, *Les trains qui vont à Madras/The trains that go to Madras*. The result is still a Tabucchi adaptation yet slightly modified.[10]

The man encountered in the short novel's fourth chapter for the duration of the train ride to Madras is not a European Jew but a Jain with a heavy past who is captured in both short story and film. Jainism is an Indian religion that practices a philosophy of non-violence. The man is on his way to Madras to 'die.' This revelation comes at the end of the four-and-a-half page chapter, which otherwise contains a discussion of religion, spirituality, and linguistics.

The train ride consecrates slow speed travel and what is gained from such a mode of transportation – a trope that surfaces in many contemporary travel narratives, some of which I analyze later on (*Mr. Ibrahim, Le Grand Voyage, Maine-Océan, Trafic* etc.). On the night train to Madras (the one depicted in the film and the twelve-page short story), as part of the many chance encounters one experiences during travels, the main character rooms with a strange German fellow, who introduces himself as Peter and is on his way to Madras to check a statue. The two travelers have a long exchange and even share a meal. The German man is an avid specialist of Dravidian art and statues. He narrates his own past as a prisoner in a concentration camp, and the fact that he endured torture at the hands of Nazi doctors. A Nazi doctor once put his life into balance next to a dancing statue of Shiva. The name of this train companion, Peter Schlemihl, is heard during a police check as the train enters the Tamil Nadu state. Rossignol is perplexed; he is familiar with the German story written by Adelbert von Chamisso, a French aristocrat exiled in Germany (1814). *Peter Schlemihl's Miraculous Story* is about a man who sold his shadow to the devil and is in turn rejected by everyone and condemned to wander his entire life. Rossignol doubts the 'real' identity of the man since he is a known literary character; there 'can only be one' Peter Schlemil for him. Rossignol understands that the man has never been to Madras before; however, he is told the following important sophism: 'Pour connaître un lieu, on n'a pas forcément besoin d'y être allé.' ('In order to know a place, it is not necessary to go there') (Tabucchi 326).[11] Interestingly, the short story centers solely on the train ride to Madras, and the encounter with Peter Schlemil. There are no auxiliary searches, and the only question raised is about the narrator/traveler's imagination, and his fabrication of such an encounter.

In the film, Rossignol hears of the man again a day later as he is investigating his friend's disappearance, during a news bulletin announcing the murder of a German doctor in Madras. Has Rossignol come to find Xavier, or save him? Or both? The possibility that our identity is not single but plural arises more than once; in a later consultation with a seer (an *Ahrant*), the young disfigured woman is unable to 'read' him, and is apparently shaken, for she claims that he, Rossignol, is not there anymore; his mind is elsewhere and his 'karma cannot be read.'[12] Allusions to Shiva, the god of multiple identities, abound. However, Shiva is also the destroyer, the transformer. As the film ends, the spectator realizes that Xavier and Rossignol are the same person, yet the shadow of a doubt is cast over such an ending. If we are indeed made of multiple identities, are we to affirm seriously that he is the same one he was looking for while he was meeting people he (Xavier) had known? If this was the case, why did they go along and not recognize him? Was it all a device used for creative purposes since apparently Rossignol (Nightingale), the night bird is a writer? Does Rossignol pretend to convey some deeper metaphysical roots, as his encounter with a member of the Theosophical Society in Madras would have us believe?

Focused on seeing 'the real India' (321),[13] the Portuguese traveler featured in the short novel is equipped with *The Travel Survival Kit*, a Baedeker-type guide book on India. He demonstrates that he is the independent traveler-type, securely charting his own route, and as soon as he arrives arrogantly tells the taxi-driver that he is taking the wrong direction, and exits the cab.[14] It progressively becomes clear that before the end of the script (and novel), despite all these markers, the traveler is lost and the reputable guidebook inadequate.

Mon guide était un petit livre un peu bizarre, qui donnait des conseils parfaitement incongrus que je suivais à la lettre. En réalité mon voyage était lui aussi parfaitement incongru : ce livre était donc fait pour moi. Il ne traitait pas le voyageur comme un pillard, avide d'images stéréotypées, ... mais comme un individu vagabond et illogique, enclin à l'oisiveté et à l'erreur (321).[15] ('My guide was a thin book, a bit odd, that gave perfectly incongruous advice that I would follow to a t. In fact my trip was just as incongruous: this book was therefore made for me. It did not treat the traveler as a pillager, thirsty for stereotyped images ... but as a vagabond, illogical and bent toward idleness and error.')

Travel on Indian roads does not follow a Western-based notion of time and scheduling, rendering all advice futile and snobbish. *Nocturne Indien* shares elements with other travelogues, down to citing colonial narratives with similar hotels and as in 'the books of Conrad or Somerset Maugham, in the occasional American film based on the novels of Kipling or Bromfield: they seem familiar' (Tabucchi 62). Tabucchi cross-references all these writers. When stopped in the middle of the night on a bus from Madras to Mangalore (chapter seven of the novel), Rossignol wakes the sleeping driver to wonder why they stopped, for 'The stop wasn't indicated on the timetable on my ticket, but by now I had got used to this kind of Indian surprise' (Tabucchi 48).

The new Baedeker kind of tourist guidebook (1815) was designed for the unassisted solitary traveler, something totally unheard of at the time,

> Its principal object ... was to keep the traveller at as great a distance as possible from the unpleasant, and often wholly invisible, tutelage of hired servants and guides .... to render him independent, and to place him in a position from which he may receive his own impressions with clear eyes and lively heart (Mendelson).

While taking the spectator along on a suspenseful chase, the conclusion intimates that after the long quest for his friend, 'now that he has found me he no longer has any desire to find me' (Tabucchi 86), rendering the entire story even more debatable. The spectator is left entirely in the darkness of 'the nocturnal' part and extension of the title. We do not know if they are the same, or if there is an actual Xavier. The point is that after all this chasing, and based on Tabucchi, it does not matter, just like the story about the man who wanted to travel and lost interest in it altogether. The 'voyage' (or the chase) itself – the process of traveling – is what matters. Of course, traveling then can be done in full immobility or without necessarily leaving one's room, or one's country. This evokes the spirited novel by Xavier de Maistre, *Voyage autour de ma chambre/Voyage around my room* (1790) where the protagonist imagines in forced seclusion for six weeks an entire expedition in his room, describing its furniture, customs, as if he were in a foreign land; similarly, Karl Joris-Huysmans's *A rebours/Against Nature* (1884) is the perfect illustration of a stationary voyage that one can achieve through books and maps in one's library without leaving once. Des Esseintes, the eccentric, misanthropic main character 'retreats from ... modernity into a sealed-off apartment' (Schulman 36).

Other filmic narratives in the travel genre come to mind, particularly Michelangelo Antonioni's *Profession Reporter/Professione Reporter/The Passenger* (1975). David Locke (Jack Nicholson), a television reporter stationed in North Africa, assumes the identity of a dead man, while shooting a film on guerilla warfare in colonial Francophone Africa. Although he is not looking for anyone in particular, he switches identity when he encounters a dead man in his hotel room. In other words, he becomes the other person, and has to bear the consequences of the identity switch. As in Tabucchi/Corneau's narrative, the use of the camera and photography play an important narrative role.

Antonioni acknowledged that 'The greatest danger for those working in cinema is the extraordinary possibilities it offers for lying.'[16] Both films, while located in very different milieus, portray characters who are intrigued by others' identity, and want to lose themselves into another person's life for whatever reason. The person has a new lease of life, and it certainly adds mystery. Tabucchi sets his narrative in India and draws on the mystery of the country, what it represents for the French (and Western) traveler, as the birth of any 'spiritual' journey, inside and out. Its inspiration also lies in Portugal, and a feeling of nostalgia seeps through the narrative. It is clear that by the end of the film, the man has reintegrated his European body, speaks French again, and accordingly 'becomes what he never ceased to be: A tourist' (Pélegrin 53).

Rossignol is not a genuine tourist, nor is Xavier, who is/was apparently a businessman, especially if the markers of a touristic attraction consist of a sight, a marker, and a tourist (MacCannell quoted in Van den Abbeele 4). They have come to India but not to go sightseeing. Yet during their trip they do encounter some important sites, such as the island of Elephanta. The script takes the spectator on a visual and musical tour, integrating the musical art of the fugue. This is a term in psychiatry referring to when someone loses his/her memory in an altered state of consciousness, wandering away from home. The fugue state would last only a few hours. Returning to the title, a 'nocturne' implies an instrumental or vocal piece that has no imposed form, and must be played either at night or evoke nighttime (Larousse), all of which are at play in the narrative.

The premise of an individual getting lost in a country emerges in many filmic or non-filmic travelogues. Let us just mention a few that were adapted for the screen, starting with Paul Bowles's *The Sheltering Sky* (1949) as Bertolucci's eponymous film (1990); *Journey to Kafiristan* (Dubini brothers 2001) from Ella Maillart and Annemarie Schwarzenbach's travelogue; *Hideous Kinky* (1998), Gillies MacKinnon's adaptation of Esther Freud's autobiographical novel (1992); and *Transylvania* (Gatlif 2006). Travelers respond to the call for the elsewhere, for new horizons, even if this implies shedding their possessions and bearings. Some travel writers and characters for whom travel is also restrictive do not share the belief that travel is entirely liberating. For Bouvier, one is deprived of one's habits and familiar places, and made humbler,

> Le voyage fournit des occasions de s'ébrouer mais pas – comme on le croyait – la liberté. .... le voyageur se trouve ramené à de plus humbles proportions. Plus ouvert aussi à la curiosité, à l'intuition, au coup de foudre (80). ('Travel gives us the occasion to shake oneself, but not as one thought – of freedom ... the traveler finds himself brought back to very humble proportions. More open to curiosity as well, to intuition, to love at first sight.')

The temptation to ditch it all is there. At the same time, fears of the elsewhere arise, as the fear of losing oneself and being physically and psychically absorbed by the country. One has to shed all belongings and travel light, close to an anchorite condition, as the next film *Un si beau voyage* suggests.

The Sacred: Un si beau voyage

> I sit here all by myself, looking at the grey expanse of murmuring sea ... I am utterly alone on earth, and always will be in this Universe so full of lures and disappointments ... alone, turning my back on a world of dead hopes and memories. (Isabelle Eberhardt)[17]

Voyage and exile at the core of *Un si beau voyage/Such a beautiful Journey* (Khaled Ghorbal 2008) entails two parts: Paris or its suburbia, and Tunisia, with the return to one's native country as a final note. Its entire effort tends toward the épure, a purification process. The male protagonist's position is ambivalent since as the one who returns, he is no longer from the country, or no longer welcome at least, even if generously feted by the cousin and uncle's family when he returns; he is in the position of a double exile, in France and Tunisia, possibly, two places where he is not truly accepted. The mood sustained by the tracking shots by the Seine, and the soft jazzy scores underline his nostalgia for Paris before he leaves; he feels integrated in the country where he has lived for so long that he has not gone 'home' in fifteen years. Unlike other returns there is no longing for the original birth country.

The journey is shaped as a personal voyage towards death: the immigrant suffers from a terminal cancer and is rejected from his French suburban housing residence. Back in the country of his birth where he is forced to return to, he is socially excluded as one who had not formed a family with wife and children and had 'forgotten' his relatives.

Mohamed (Farid Chopel) is a retired Tunisian immigrant who lives in a small room in a workers' residence in a Paris suburb.[18] The first sequence establishes the communal nature of his living arrangements, as he washes a shirt in a collective bathroom sink. His gestures are careful and measured; he hangs his shirt on a line in his room, and unfolds it meticulously. All his gestures will be dignified until the end. He spends his leisure time in Paris on the banks of the Seine, watching the water flow; cool jazz accompanies his trajectory from Paris to the suburbs, and later back to Tunisia, his homeland. He sketches on a pad but the spectator does not get to see the drawings. He cooks for his friends at the residence hall and celebrates by making his 'special paella'. Preparing for this Spanish culinary treat, he shops at a busy indoor food market (St. Denis) where he buys seafood, saffron, and chorizo, a sensual gourmet trip in itself. Mohamed's walk is slow. Very early on, he is struggling with abdominal pains, but remains stoical about it. A retired single worker, he helps his younger friend plaster and paint the walls of the apartment the latter secured for his family, who are scheduled to join him from Tunisia. This interaction points to the future: this family will settle down, as his wife and children are coming to France, an opposite trajectory to the one affecting the main protagonist. Mohamed's training as a former house painter comes in handy as he advises him on the job and in so doing 'trains' him.

The visit at the Hospital *Avicenne* (or Franco-Muslim hospital) in St-Denis ushers in sombre news. The female doctor prescribes new medication, but mostly painkillers. Mohamed's illness has evolved faster than anticipated. They exchange few words. The gaze between the different protagonists and Momo is the central foundation of the story. Preoccupied by his condition, the doctor gently advises a trip back to the country, 'for some sun.' Mohamed, a gentle man, never complains and overlooks the doctor's insensitive suggestion. He is a passenger of the tramway line, the same route that traverses Guiguet's film *Les Passagers* and stops at the Bobigny-Pablo Picasso stop. The route here signifies his life path.

The director of the workers' residence summons Mohamed and explains that he has kept him despite the rules (no retired worker is allowed to live in the residence) and that he has to vacate the place. He made an exception, but with upcoming renovation plans and stricter regulations he gives him a two-month notice of leave. Mohamed Boufassa pleads with him not to tell the others about the eviction; he demonstrates agency and pride: 'c'est moi qui décide de partir' ('I am the one who decides to leave'). A large map of France hangs behind the director's desk.

After withdrawing his entire life savings (15, 236 euros) at the bank, he treats his two close friends to a traditional French restaurant where, to their surprise, he has treated himself every month for the past seventeen years, since his separation from his Spanish girlfriend. It is only later that one understands why they separated. He orders a 'tête de veau' for all of them, and a good bottle of Bordeaux wine. At the end of the meal, he proudly announces his departure for Tunisia, flashing his airplane ticket. They are stunned by the news: 'Je rentre définitif au pays' ('I'm going home for good'). He leaves them all his belongings, in one of the first instances in which he starts clearing his objects. Before his departure, he calls the loved one, a Spanish woman: they separated because he was sterile, and she wanted to start a family. They still love each other. She meets him for a last good-bye at the airport, and although he does not tell her what lies behind his return, the gaze they exchange is poignant. He stands at the threshold – an intermediary space, in-between the boarding area and the walkway to the plane, behind the glass panel, visibly shaken.

The second part of the film shot in Tunisia traces the interior pilgrimage, and the dignity he demonstrates in the way he self-effaces, and leaves his relatives soon after meeting with them again, in order to retire in the desert and prepare for death.

Farid Chopel, an actor known for his comedic roles who was then sick in real life, sustains the incredible (and unbearable) role until the end, lending his body and gaze to add depth to the character and be at one with him. Ghorbal understandably selected this actor (Chopel was a comedian) due to his gaze, whereas he did not know him personally before making the film (Figure 2.1).[19]

> Ne jouant plus qu'avec la maigreur de son corps qui se découpe dans l'immensité des dunes, il évolue dans le cadre pendant près d'une heure avec la grâce des grands acteurs du muet.[20] ('Playing only with his thin body that is cut out in the immensity of the dunes he evolves in the frame for one hour with the grace of the great actors of the silent era.')

The welcome reception back at the village is rather mixed and anti-climactic. The common Western vision of Tunisia, a land of sun, palm trees, and desert, collides with a harsher one. Mohamed spends time at his cousin's place as a guest. His brother comes to insult him: 'Tu n'as rien construit. Tu es parti ... Nous, nous sommes restés' ('You built nothing. You left ... we stayed') and orders the 'selfish' Mohamed to return to France.

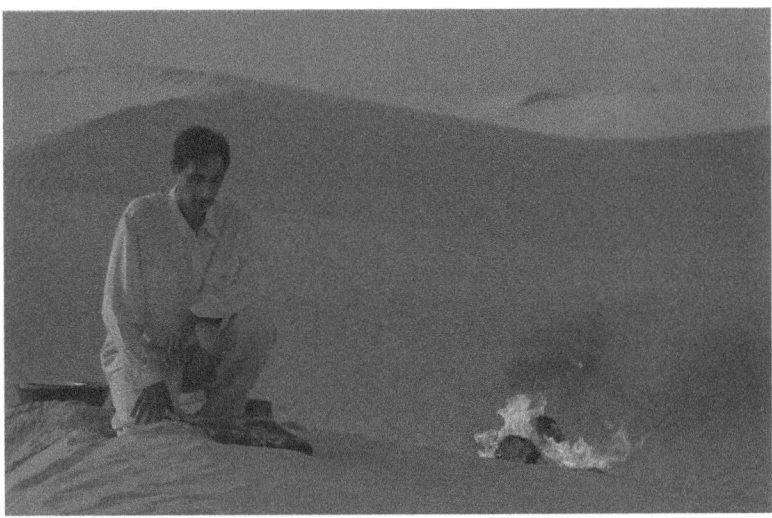

Figure 2.1   Khaled Ghorbal, *Un si beau voyage*
Note: 'The interior pilgrimage takes place in the Tunisian desert when Mohamed Boufassa decides to return home.'
Source: Emmanuel Rioufol.

Later on, that same evening, Mohamed confides in his host his reasons about his separation from Pilar (played by Spanish actress Assumpta Serna) years ago, 'Ici ou là-bas, je suis un exilé' ('Here or there, I'm an exile'). Circumstances pressed him to return: he could not have afforded rent in another place, now that he is retired with a small pension and sick. He goes home, to his original birthplace, fetches a camel and a tent, and leaves at dawn a few days later for the desert. His family owns camels, and the cousin serves as a guide for tourists during the season. Mohamed knows the proper gestures to make; this is his former habitus. He is familiar with the desert setting and lifestyle. The few remaining days of his life are spent in solitude, in the desert, meditating and slowly becoming one with the landscape.

He ditches his city shirt and jacket for a long-sleeve large blue shirt, and a 'cheche' to protect his head from the sand, sun, and wind. The return home is effected through a series of rides south from Tunis to Douz, the gateway to the Sahara, by collective taxi; then further south walking into the desert leading the camel carrying water, tent and other equipment. The more Mohamed walks, the more the place becomes desert-like, and white or pure; sand dunes appear, ever shifting, sand blowing away. The character reaches a state of purification as he slowly sheds every possession, like the cleansing process of a religious hermit in the desert. The filmic style follows. Mohamed observes the immensity of the desert as he did by the Seine, and absorbs the shifting terrain. After setting up camp, building a fire, and brewing some tea, the days pass, and temporality is cast aside. The lengthy panoramic shots of the horizon produce a feeling of plenitude (Figure 2.2). On the last day, he washes himself naked and puts on a pair of white pants and a white shirt. The camera is tilted at a low angle, while he stands, then sits, and lies down, sand softly blowing down his face and hair, covering him as he is, presumably dead. A soft jazz score accompanies his route, all the way until the end, when the voice of a female singer intervenes as a lament. The music follows the curves of the sand dunes, which are dance-like and more and more white before the final fade to black preceding the credit sequence. The exceptional cinematography by Jacques Besse, who worked on Abderrahmane Sissako's *Bamako* (2006) and *La Vie sur terre* (1998), contributes to the sacred dimension conferred to the film. The saxhorn player Médéric Collignon composed a score that mixes trumpet, and sometimes flute, with vocals.

Exilé en France, pays aimé, il se sent aussi exilé en Tunisie, pays de sa chair, qu'il a quitté depuis longtemps, et maintenant exilé dans

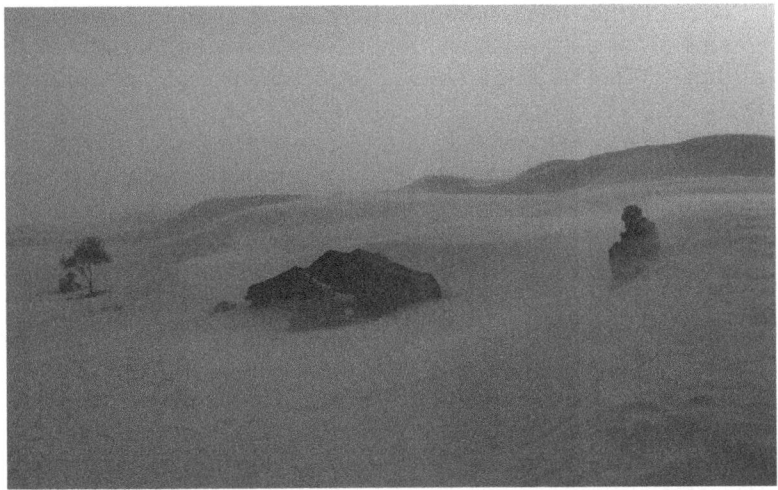

Figure 2.2   Khaled Ghorbal, *Un si beau voyage*
Note: 'The few remaining days of his life are spent in solitude, in the desert, meditating and slowly becoming one with the landscape.'
Source: Emmanuel Rioufol.

son propre corps, un corps usé, qui ne tient plus.[21] ('Exiled in France, beloved country, he also feels exiled in Tunisia, the land of his own flesh, that he left a long time ago, and now exiled in his own body, a worn out body, that is not holding.')

Mohamed is dignified in his ways; he is modest, and never lets any of his relatives or friends know the depth of his situation. Until the end, when he hands his cousin three envelopes with his savings ('I won't need this in the desert'), nobody suspects the reasons for his return, since this appears to be at odds with his rather urban personality. The story is not about a migrant worker and his plight in France and return home, nor is it about death; it is about exile and solitude, as well as the dispossession of one's material belongings before death. Thus it acquires a full spiritual dimension that speaks of the path one takes and the imprint one leaves:

C'est le chemin qu'on emprunte, c'est l'empreinte qu'on peut laisser dans la vie et ce sont aussi les chemins que peuvent laisser les empreintes sur nous, les circonstances, les gens que l'on croise, les événements que l'on subit ou que l'on provoque (Ghorbal 9).[22] ('It's the path one takes, it's the imprint one leaves in life, and also the paths that leave prints on us, the circumstances, the people one comes across, the events one lives or one provokes.')

The journey home is not a nostalgic one, but one which affirms that the protagonist has completed his life cycle, and has returned to the land of his ancestors, accomplishing ritual-like gestures and becoming one with the universe.

Tracking through dangerous landscapes

Emmanuel Finkiel's *Voyages/Tracks* (1999) maps out three destinations: Poland, France, and Israel. It is less about the distance and the countries visited than about the impressions that they create and that stay with us once the actual trip/film is over. The film establishes the gap between travelers and tourists as well as migrants. *Voyages* is shaped as an unlikely travel around the pilgrimage form. What is in Poland? What is there to see for a group of Jewish people of various countries of origins, some of whom belong to the generation of the Holocaust while others are the children or grandchildren of that generation? Can one become a tourist in such a place, and what is there to witness? Why is there a need to revisit such places of trauma? A distinction is established between tourist and travelers, two distinct philosophies. In his novel, *The Sheltering Sky*, Paul Bowles proposes that the difference between the traveler and the tourist is one of time. The tourist accepts his civilization without question but not the traveler (7).

Voyages/Tracks interrogates traces and memory, and explores places that testify to what 'has been.' The notion of a 'dangerous landscape' coined elsewhere by Nicolas Bouvier in *L'Usage du monde* is definitely at work for a third of the narrative. Bouvier, a crucial travel writer, originally from Switzerland, brings up the problematic issue of places that are too dangerous for the self, and that one should leave immediately; the danger is of course not necessarily physical but psychical,

Des paysages qui vous en veulent et qu'il faut quitter immédiatement sous peine de conséquences incalculables, il n'en existe pas beaucoup, mais il en existe. Il y en a a bien sur cette terre cinq ou six pour chacun de nous. (265) ('Landscapes that have something against you and that you must leave immediately for fear of countless consequences; there are not many of those, but they do exist. There are a least five or six of these for each one of us on this earth.')

Finkiel professes that the film is neither a documentary on Holocaust survivors and the Polish past, nor an interrogation of the memory of such a past, tasks that were taken up by Claude Lanzmann in *Shoah* (1985) or Georges Perec/Robert Bober in *Récits d'Ellis Island. Histoires d'errance et d'espoir* (1980). For Perec, going to Ellis Island was as much about the history of immigration attached to the island than the personal route that led him to write about it. Such a path exposed the absence of roots, and the loss of families. However, Finkiel casts his project as a present-day pilgrimage to Poland. It is aligned with a process that Georges Van den Abbeele considers the 'marking' and there is 'literally nothing to see except its markers' (4). The group of tourists in *Voyages* visits a Jewish cemetery as their main attraction and stops by a concentration camp.

In the subsequently released *Casting*, a fascinating documentary on the making of *Voyages*, Finkiel interviews most of the non-professional cast he recruited for his film through a small ad in Yiddish newspapers in Paris.[23] Some actors already appeared in his debut short fiction *Madame Jacques sur la croisette* (1996), a humoristic look at retired Jewish men and women located in Nice who meet daily on the famous boardwalk, La Croisette.[24] Shulamit Adar, Maurice Chevit, and others made their first appearance in the short film where Yiddish language is as present as it is in *Voyages*. Such characters include the father figure who returns from the East, and Mrs. Riwka Adler from *Voyages*.

Voyages features mostly non-actors, people of Jewish origins, former immigrants, some of them living in France, and others in Israel. Finkiel's casting call for Yiddish speakers and non-actors to perform in a film 'about the Franco-Jewish community' published in a Yiddish newspaper distributed in Paris was answered by many naturalized French Jews who migrated to France before World War II. The documentary is a touching sequel for anyone who watched the fiction film, as most of the older actors were Holocaust survivors nearing the end of their life.[25]

Several trajectories mesh, and through very little dialogue expose the implications of a trip East to Warsaw and Auschwitz for a group of Jews, some of whom are traveling to their ancestors' land, while others are traveling to the country to which they were deported, where they lost relatives, and which they left, never to return. The group is composed of retired citizens, with the exceptional presence of a few young adults, representing the new generation. They are taking their last trip, and they are the last generation of witnesses to what has been, and what will soon disappear entirely from the map and from oral history. Finkiel's documentary on the making of the film captures this rare moment. The survivors ended up in exile abroad, in France, North America, Israel, Russia, and for some in Poland. We do not know this directly through dialogue or explanations: we infer this from Finkiel's discrete and respectful approach.

Voyages stops first at the Warsaw Jewish cemetery. People are walking amidst tombs, in a wooded park. A middle-aged woman, Mrs. Adler (played by Israeli actress Shulamit Adar), visibly distracted and frazzled, stays behind, slowly contemplating headstones, trees, and sky. She ends up missing the ride back to town when the bus leaves without her.

Buses function extensively in the film, transporting the unwilling passengers back to town, and onward to their next stop: the concentration camp of Auschwitz. The interplay between travelers and tourists is invoked. The camera interestingly never leaves the bus once they arrive at the camp. It makes a point of staying inside, in a static pose, looking out through the windows, and panning to Mrs. Adler, who has refused to leave the bus and is still inside. Her eyes are shut, either asleep or in pain, or in a deep meditative pose. The spectator speculates on this state. Her husband, with whom she quarreled throughout the trip, stands outside, sadly looking in at her. She alludes to a future separation. The only images of the camp are relayed through an amateurish video film, made by one of the passengers, focusing on people's prayers and embraces situated in another camp (Birkenau).[26] Finkiel circumvents the voyeurism of a camera going into the camp. He left the actors free to express themselves and did not shoot the actual footage.

The trip within the trip

In the immense vastness of the countryside shot in wintertime, the bus breaks down on the way to the concentration camp. The passengers are immediately cornered and ghettoized in a place that they cannot leave. They patiently wait for hours inside the cold bus for the transfer bus. Some venture outdoors, such as Mrs. Adler, who contemplates the frozen landscape of her childhood. The son of a passenger sights abandoned railroad tracks while urinating on the snow. These are all key *moments* resonating with impressions that are unspoken and cannot be enunciated. These somewhat disturbing moments experienced collectively reinforce the link to an unspoken traumatic past and to other past ominous voyages, and modes of transportation. Once more, the work of the camera, its position inside and outside of the bus, looking in at the passengers from outside, or looking out from the inside, is configured in such a way that it affects the reading. The cold winter air fog up the windows making it harder to distinguish the passengers once the other bus, a mirror image of theirs, slowly passes by. The blurry vision could denote someone's tears rendering vision difficult. This uncanny image now complicates itself into a dreamlike bubble, originating from a traveler's psyche, and voyage within him/herself.

What Finkiel sees as a 'paranoid group' of Jews traveling inside Poland and 'not seeing the real Poland' reveals a group of willing survivors, bold enough to return to a place (or enticed to return to the place by the filmmaker) where there is nothing left to see.[27] The place has transformed into a museal commercialized culture. The shot of the passengers staring at the monument to the memory of the razed Warsaw ghetto, next to the modern high-rises stands as a gloomy mark of this erasure.

Nothing to see, nothing to say

Voyages reconsiders the vast bareness of a landscape, its dangers, the emptiness of pictures preciously kept as keepsake, as one's dearest belongings and inherent secrets. What is left of the people in the pictures? What is left to say as one arrives at a camp, a site that is probably on a list of preferred tourist destinations in Poland?[28] The film opts for silence then, and Mrs. Adler's gesture of shutting her eyes offers a much-needed symbolic closure.

Voyages depicts people's liveliness with the example of Vera's (Esther Gorintin) immigration from Russia to Israel at eighty-eight years old, when 'she has nothing to lose.' It does not wallow in the past. The shared past creates enough energy to transmute the impossibility of seeing (or that which constitutes the first part) into a film within the film – a documentary of their trip through Poland that they will screen at the (Jewish) Association back in Paris. The evening of the screening effects a smooth transition to Part two of *Voyages*.

Part 2. The Gefilte Fish Spirit[29]

After introducing the gentle and joyful atmosphere of the association in the second part, the camera enters the more intimate space of the apartment of Régine (Liliane Rovère), a middle-aged woman and member of the Association. Régine receives a telephone call that galvanizes her present life. She lost her parents and a sister to deportation, and unexpectedly is contacted by her father, whom she thought dead for the past fifty years. The arrival throws the story into a spin. Does Régine make up the return of the disappeared father, a ghost who has possibly haunted her for years? Or does it really happen? There are several ways to answer these questions, and two paths to take in order to interpret this pivotal moment. Opting for the second answer is easier for now, as in the next sequence Régine meets an old man carrying a suitcase at a train station. Close-ups of his gnarled hands throughout the segment indicate that this is a real man, in flesh. The old man comes from Vilnius (Lithuania) and is traveling one last time to France, a place where he had once migrated to and to which he does not bear ill feelings. Neither of them speak ill of France, which was necessarily an accomplice in and witness to their deportation. He talks to his daughter in Yiddish. His entire life resides in his suitcase, remnants of the past with old pictures, letters showing his patient detective work, trying to locate his daughter. Régine grows increasingly anxious as the film progresses with the unnerving possibility that he might be an impostor, someone impersonating her dad. As it turns out, the father does not share the same memories, and the small details add up, such as the number of the convoy departing for Auschwitz not matching. She spies on him in his sleep, looks into his wallet for traces of the past, for pictures of young children ... however, it is impossible to be sure that his face is not that of her aged father. The anguish of finding and recognizing a lost father is greater than the long mourning and acceptance of his/their death. She has grown accustomed to an ageless father, the young man in the picture who never grew old. No matter how much she touches and squeezes the old arm, what signs can she hold onto? We never quite know, as Finkiel omitted one scene from the final cut, leaving much to the spectator's interpretation and curiosity. Mr. Graneck is not her father; she does have the same name as his daughter, a Mrs. Adler who now lives in Tel Aviv. We never know if the two will meet, yet the spectator has been introduced to her in the first part, in the character of Riwka. The film leaves many doors open and foregoes a formal classical closure. Régine commits to helping him find his daughter, and in the meantime has adopted him as her true father. She gives her name to the doctor in order to get old Graneck some medical treatment under the French social security medical system. She temporarily gives her grandchildren a real grandfather to play with, and sing lullabies to, going along with this scenario of a return. She is happy and reconciled with her life, as dinner is served and everyone compliments her soup. The grandfather has easily filled the void that begged to be filled.

Their encounter happens too late in life, according to Finkiel.[30] This type of 'scenario' is common in Jewish history up until the 1970s when people tried to locate, identify, and communicate with long-lost relatives in the post-war years. It surfaces in Patrick Modiano's novels peopled with lost relatives, or friends and shady individuals carrying suitcases. It comes up in the many photo albums that his protagonists reconstitute, and the long itineraries and painstaking efforts he takes to rescue, or find some of these vanished individuals, the many abandoned rooms, the many telephones that ring endlessly in some empty room. Similarly, Modiano's protagonists play detectives in search of long lost relatives or friends.

Color schemes apply to the three parts of *Voyages*, acknowledging the influence of Krzysztof Kieślowski on Finkiel, who used to be Kieślowski's assistant. Shades of blue saturate the Polish part, shades of brown the Franco-Parisian part, and white light suffuses every shot of Vera's travel to Israel/Tel Aviv in the last part. The filmmaker picked Israel as the end of all destinations, the 'end of the road' for the film, as it is for Vera, as well as for many Russian immigrants who resettled in Israel at the end of the 20th century. The carefully edited transition is superimposed on Mr. Graneck singing to his grandchild in Paris, and fades into a passing bus from the outside, people looking out, and Israeli flags refracted on its windows. Mr. Graneck fades out of the picture.

The last segment is devoted to Vera walking through deserted Tel Aviv suburbs, taking public transportation into town to locate someone. It conveys one of the film's most interesting portrayals of energy, resilience, and creativity. Vera is an older woman, playing in a film for the first time. Esther Gorintin also performed the endearing Georgian grandmother in *Depuis qu'Otar est parti/Since Otar Left* (2003) directed by Finkiel's assistant, Julie Bertucelli. At the end of her first day in Tel Aviv, her path crosses Riwka's on the bus, while Vera is returning to the rented room she shares with her Russian roommates (a young couple and baby) in the suburbs. She loses parts of the pictures held in her wallet while suffering a slight malaise. A woman helps her pick up the pieces, and takes her to the correct bus stop. The woman is Riwka, the passenger on the Polish bus from the first part. She is transformed and luminous now, in her beautiful suburban home and garden. She rescues Vera, invites her to her home so that she can rest briefly, and offers her a cold beverage. They both speak Yiddish, a language that is disappearing and clearly a language in which Vera feels 'at home'. Vera complains of this and of the fact that Israel does not have 'Jewish people' anymore but 'Israelis'! None of these people could understand her as she was wandering and looking for her cousin. Yet, despite all this, Vera is ready for a new life: she 'has nothing to lose'. Again, it is not so much the place, and destination that matter, since deep down, the narrative presents a less than desirable picture of the location. It is more about the impressions and bond created between two women who are not blood related, yet instantly bond and nurture each other. Riwka, for the first time in the film as far as we can tell, comes out of her shell to help another person, for entirely selfless reasons. Vera is instrumental in the very short epilogue that takes place now that she has regained her seat by the bus stop. It is nighttime, and Vera is framed by Riwka's window, as Riwka is looking at her from the inside of her home. A telephone call interrupts her gaze while her husband returns at the same time. The sound of the call from Paris and her response to someone presumably asking (them) if she is Mrs. Adler born Graneck fills the soundtrack, with the parallel shot of Vera, a small hunched silhouette, waiting across the street.

The film concludes on the shot of the now deserted bus stop. Vera has disappeared from the frame, yet she was never depicted climbing onto the bus. One does not know if Riwka will ever be informed that her father is alive, looking for her, or that she might finally see him. She shrugs off the telephone call. There is no closure to the film. One can only suspect that Vera will adapt to her new land. Interestingly, the only one mentally young enough to emigrate from Russia is the older woman, Vera. All three women, Riwka, Régine, and Vera, have a shared immigrant past in France; they all speak French and all lived in France at one point until 1942 (a key date); only one stayed and survived deportation. Yiddish is the language that maintains the link with the old country, the ancestors, and the deceased relatives.

Sophie's adventures – No sex last night/Double Blind by Sophie Calle and Greg Shepard[31]

Most of the texts studied here cover geographic displacement, crossings, and sometimes transgression. Sophie Calle pushes the limits of the travel narrative genre in her photo textual projects. Taking her camera and following (male) strangers on the streets, one of them all the way to Venice (Italy), she records the man's movements and writes about his daily routine. This turns into a book of photos and texts, *Suite Vénitienne* (1979). Using several disguises in order to travel incognito, in the tradition of American photographer Cindy Sherman and her multiple costumes and subject positions, Calle develops several performances to track down the object of her quest. Jean Baudrillard, in his postface to *Suite Vénitienne* entitled *Follow me*, commented that Calle's trip is not about drifting, nor is it about encountering the other; instead the experience 'is entirely a process of seduction' (76). It is also not about voyeurism but about time. 'It simply says: Here, at that time, at that place, in that light, there was someone' (79). The contrary is also possible. Calle is interested in rituals, and performance.

In 1992, in *No sex last night*, also titled *Double Blind*, Calle switches to the video camera format. The film was released publicly in 1996. Calle records a journey that she took along with an American male companion across the United States. She reports candidly on her impressions of the country and culture. Calle's work is deeply grounded in the autobiographical genre, 'a quality it shares with the work of many other contemporary artists, such as Christian Boltanski, Annette Messager and Orlan' (Gratton 157). It is close to the diary format, and not unlike Beauvoir's 1947 journal of her American experience retraced in *America Day by Day*, her trip ends in California, at a college where she is scheduled to teach as a visiting professor.[32] Cultural differences between the country of origins and the toured country arise as strong focal points in these stories filled with personal impressions.

My interest in Calle's work goes back to 1990 and is grounded in a literary/filmic and cultural critic position.[33] I am removed from the art historians' and art critics' take on Calle's work, yet critics and curators have performed many analysis of her work for some time. I am foremost interested in her personal approach to travel narratives, which distinguishes her from her contemporaries. Her video film is identified as a road movie and certainly belongs to the genre, new in France, although this genre 'is perpetually caught in the process of becoming' as Altman suggests in his analysis and study of genres in Hollywood films (Altman 1999). The genre is 'given a new twist' and 'is the occasion for a self-reflexive investigation of the couple's relationship with each other' (Tarr/Rollet 230).

'Nous dédions cette histoire à l'écrivain Hervé Guibert qui est mort du sida à Paris le 27 décembre 1991 – 7 jours avant le début de ce voyage.' ('We dedicate this story to the writer Hervé Guibert who died of AIDS in Paris, 27 December 1991, seven days before the trip began'.) After this rather somber dedication to her friend, the film opens game-like to recount Sophie's meeting with a man in a New York City bar in December 1989. She knows nothing of him but crashes at his place. Sophie's voice is heard, sometimes over a black box/black screen at the beginning of the film.

She gives the man a date at the airport, a year later, on 20 January 1990, on which she calls him from France at 10am. However, he never 'arrived, he never called.' On 10 January 1991, a year later, she receives a call from a Paris airport. 'This man knew how to talk to me. That is how it all began.'

> A year later, I'm in New York again. This time to cross America with him and make a video along the way. The plan is to drive his old Cadillac car to California where I will teach for a semester. We were to leave 1 January – a few days after my arrival, but instead of meeting me at the airport, I found him asleep in his apartment he had not left for a week. Nothing had been done, the car was not ready, the camera not purchased (*No sex last night*).

Details fill in the gaps, and Sophie, the photographer and writer turned video filmmaker for the occasion, skillfully constructs and sustains a story. Chance encounters inhabit her narratives, such as the search for Henri B. in Venice (Italy), requiring that Sophie become a detective, hide her identity, and start following him, unbeknownst to him, for no reason, except for the chase and the thrill (*Suite Vénitienne*). Following people or being followed is one of Sophie's basic modus operandi. In this particular travel diary, constructed as a two-voice monologue and accompanied by two cameras, one wonders who follows whom, at least for the first leg of the trip.

Sophie's tone and personality are noticeably impatient and resolved. She is very protective of her artistic project once she has decided on her plan. This prompts her to cross the Atlantic to meet the man she is attracted to, Greg Shepard, an artist, and to convince him that they should both drive cross country. Once they leave, the narrative tells of their journey, laced with personal remarks recorded on each one's individual camera, and follows a diary format. Sophie uses French for her diary entries; English is the shared language, used by Greg for his entries.

Calle dedicates the trip to the memory of Hervé Guibert, a young writer, photographer, journalist, and friend who died in France, right before the trip. She enacts a ritual for him by the sea. 'Even if this is going to be a disaster, we'll go at least far enough to symbolically bury my friend Hervé by the sea. I did not want to wait for him to die in Paris.' The journey initially presents itself as a marker against death, and as a way to shun death,

> Leaving was my way in believing Hervé would live. He died while I was on the plane, Friday Dec. 27. I wasn't with him and won't be

with him next Friday for his funeral. If we cancel this trip, it would be a double failure. That's why we must go. (*No sex last night*)

This formal insertion initiates an uninterrupted dialogue with the friend, Guibert, present yet absent as objects and persons are in photography. Calle's motives are multiple; she is determined to stay on track with her initial plans. The amount of details placed in the narrative makes the trip palpable, hyper-real and intimate 'We left New York at 2 a.m. on Friday January 3, 1992 .... and without a word spoken, arrived at 5 a.m. at Smyrna, Delaware.' Greg stops the car and places his head on her lap in what corresponds to a fetal position. They stay like this for hours. At 9 a.m., she performs a 'symbolic burial' of Guibert, while his actual burial takes place on the Isle of Elba.

Still photography intersperses the moving images. This time, the pictograms display the sky and Sophie on the walkway wearing a black coat. She speaks to Guibert in French. 'Suis-je en retard? Est-ce qu'ils t'ont déjà enterré?' ('Am I late? Have they already buried you?'). The brief ritual is captured in a still, contrasted image of Calle dropping red roses in the blue sea. The trip starts under the dark auspices of death and mourning, intimating that Calle wants to preserve life and fights to accomplish this task. 'Leaving was my way in believing Hervé would live.' She even dials his phone, listens to his voice still playing on his answering machine, and leaves a message. The spectator listens to the voice(s). She shares with us a private moment she had with Guibert in Kyoto.[34]

Shepard participates from time to time in the voice-over narration of his own diary. However, Sophie's is the dominant voice. Greg kept his promise, and drove to the beach on schedule. The notion of time becomes crucial as they undertake the trip. When he tries to make conversation with Sophie, she is cynically surprised that he is speaking at all. Even though they are traveling together, the loneliness that she feels surfaces at different points; the monologic narration reinforces the notion that although a couple, they are separate lonely characters. Her speaking in French to the camera alienates the non-French speaking Greg. What the spectator ignores is that Sophie and Greg are already a couple that is disintegrating by the time of the filmmaking; this aspect remains private, and occluded in a film that otherwise exposes very intimate details. That information, absent from the script, reinforces the romantic and suspenseful journey, titled 'No sex last night', while leaving the spectator clueless. In retrospect, the pretext of the film is one way to (re)create and sustain a lasting image of an almost defunct relationship. Having little or no dialogue attests to the state of that relationship.

For two-thirds of the film, the video camera frames the road, sited at the front of the car, or in the rear of the car and registering the different spaces that they cross. The other third details shots of restaurants, motels, garages, car washes, and beds where they spend many hours of the trip. Most of the still photography captures exterior landscapes. The American road features as a major mythical attraction in most European mentalities and tour guides and is cast in several European made road movies, such as Wim Wenders's *Paris Texas* (1984), *Alice in the Cities* (1974), or Erick Zonca's *Julia* (2008), to name a few.

Motel nights

For the first night spent at a motel, Greg's voice-over fills the image. He thinks that Sophie probably asked for a room with only one bed. A snapshot of an unmade bed, in daylight time with her statement 'No sex last night' is supposed to testify to their night. Still shots of beds, many times empty and unmade, run through the film along with Sophie's deadpan voice stating the evidence of 'no sex last night.' These beds are reminders of her photographic work in hotels and in her own apartment, with *Les Dormeurs/Sleepers* (1979) and *L'Hôtel* (1981). In *The Sleepers*, Calle engaged in a forty-eight-hour marathon, inviting friends and complete strangers to come and sleep in her bed, day and night. She then photographed them and wrote about their journey.

Greg becomes Sophie's companion by day, driving with her across America, a country that in this way she is slowly discovering. It remains an introspective trip and does not open to another culture. Greg shares aspects of his personal life with the camera and talks about his job as an art dealer for ten years, his dropping out and his initial encounter with Sophie through her work. It predates her version of their meeting at a bar. 'I saw her exhibition in Boston and decided I wanted to follow her.' Through his point of view, we discern another version of the narrative. Sophie's work and ideas are contagious and have been referenced by writer Paul Auster in one of his novels, *Leviathan*, when he uses her as the character of Maria, the photographer (1992). Greg thinks out loud to the camera and introduces his version of meeting Sophie:

I knew that I wanted to reinvent myself like she had. A week later, I'm in New York and a woman walks by and introduces herself. She had found me first. I ignored her for a year. She violated my trust by looking through my papers. She didn't see it that way. Then I called her from an airport and she answered. Since then, it hasn't been that easy ... but it's the game that helps me keep my distance. I like driving. (*No sex last night*)

The car becomes a major object of contention between the two, yet Sophie shares her frustration with the camera, which becomes more or less a third person in the car. The diary style is confessional in this sense and the spectator her accomplice. She complains that Greg is more obsessed with his car than with her, and shoots the Cadillac much more than he does her. This leads to the beginning of a series of car problems that send them to mechanics along the way. In other words, the car requires some adjustments that for Calle, always prone to psychoanalytical explanations, are implicitly of a sexual nature. She mentions:

At 2:10 p.m., he said 'You got to promise me a car wash honey ... I wonder if they caress their women as much' ('Je me demande s'ils caressent autant leur femme.')[35]

Greg represents the stereotypical American man, Sophie's creation that she holds onto throughout the trip, as she is prone to generalizations.

Destinations. California via Connecticut, Florida, and New Orleans

Calle directs Shepard to drive to Florida, as she wants to meet his father, a man that he dislikes: 'I can't even be in a room with him!' Sophie forces Greg to 'resolve' personal issues that go back to childhood. As we will see, she too has personal problems to resolve and the journey is meant as partial therapy. Greg, reluctant to embark on this trip and to visit his father, apparently likes her bossy side. They drive down South before making it West and they meet ordinary people in bars along the way, an ethnoscape familiar to Wim Wenders or Jim Jarmusch's spectators. The road map does not carve a straight line, and even though a trip from New York to California involves a curve, this is more than a simple deviation. At rest stops, potentially dangerous situations could erupt and Calle is either conscious of them or imagines them.

Love letters

Greg's parallel activity when not driving is letter writing or telephone calling. There is the distant possibility of another woman, called Kate, for whom he records his impressions in love letters. Sophie reminisces on her own unlucky experiences with love letters. 'I have never received a love letter.' She once paid a public scribe to write one for the equivalent of one hundred francs for eight pages. She recalls that the letter had the following line: 'Without moving from my chair, I was everywhere with you.'

Even though the two companions share the road and travel experiences, intimacy is non-existent. A constant underlying sense of humor and irony is present with Calle, yet is not shared by Shepard, who does not appreciate any of it and wishes that he 'were more in love with her'. Despite her joy, a deep sadness prevails throughout the trip that has to do with mourning and the inability to let go of one's personal problems. 'Basically, when we travel, we still take ourselves as our baggage, and psychological demands control who we are wherever we are and sometimes our capacity to enjoy ourselves' (Botton 24).

Greg is battling some form of depression; Sophie grows increasingly frustrated with him. She reminisces about a quasi-Freudian childhood episode when her father sent her to see an analyst because she 'had bad breath', alluding to the fact that the trip has healing properties that are affecting her as well. Mounting mechanical problems continue to plague their progression. Intimacy is avoided, and static shots of their separate naked body do not precipitate any sexual act. Yet, their bodies are exposed to the lens. We witness a shot of a naked Greg and Sophie's bare bottom and leg on a bed.

They are both unsatisfied with each other. Language plays its part in the drama, and Greg cannot stand listening 'to her (speaking) French to her camera.' Could this explain the next cue 'no sex last night' – a line that immediately follows his previous critique? Sex becomes an issue between them, with the conventionally expected sex from Greg, who guiltily confesses his lack of desire.

Resistance

Maybe when the car is finally checked by several mechanics with a large invoice he will be ready for sex? This is one of Sophie's constant wishes during the trip. Greg has a rich inner life and dream-life, and slips away from the more pragmatic controlling Sophie. Where does she fit when he announces that he 'has slept with three different women last night' or 'dreamt of three different women'? She is excluded from his world, and instead caught in the contingency of his car/sexual problems as the two are obviously paired in her mind. He escapes her unwillingly, yet her camera catches snippets of his intimacy. However, as in photography, the subject resists capture. Sometimes, the signal of 'no sex last night' is reduced, or condensed to an abbreviated version of 'no'. The spectator understands the cue and becomes an accomplice. For instance, in Taos (New Mexico): 'No.'

Exasperated with the trip, Calle feels 'contaminated' by Shepard's lack of desire. The fact that Calle is footing the bill for the entire trip, inclusive of food and the many repair shops, kills any desire. In the desert, she finally brings up Las Vegas and the question of marriage. She confronts him with conventional marriage vows as just one more ritual to observe along the way. She does not think that he can refuse this plea, guessing that the kitsch aura surrounding Vegas will attract him. Greg finally agrees to a trial wedding that will be performed in a Las Vegas drive-in chapel and witnessed on-screen. The camera positioned at the back of the car looks at them voyeuristically. After the ceremony is performed, Calle feels different: 'she is someone else now' and can 'no longer be called an old maid.' Their wedding night is spent chastely in the car parked in the desert. In front of the sublime sunrise, Calle voyeuristically and surreptitiously films Greg Shepard's penis in a close-up, probably the first time that she does so, while he is urinating. When they finally reach Los Angeles, a shot of a bed and an affirmative note 'Yes' indicates that they have consummated the marriage (off-camera). Calle questions the fact that marriage authenticates sex. Greg apparently was aroused by the marriage vows and by Sophie. She sarcastically comments on this turn of events: the 'first thing that marriage brought to me: an erection!' The fairytale-like ending is compromised by Greg's infidelity. Almost following the plot of a soap opera, Calle exposes Greg's deception. After the couple has been legally sanctioned by marriage, Calle discloses its demise. It has been suggested elsewhere that Calle's narratives feed on unhappy stories, and mostly her unhappy love relations. This trait is not necessarily typical of Calle, but of many literary texts, classical or modern.

Once they reach their destination in the San Francisco bay, at Mills College, he carries her into the cottage 'and that's how it all began', or rather how it ended. They stayed together for three months. During that time, she spotted a love letter addressed to H. They went back to France and simulated a wedding ceremony for her relatives, with a photo as proof. While she returned to California to finish the video they had made of their trip, she found a bag full of love letters that Greg wrote to H., including one in which he said to his correspondent 'I'll be free in October.' Sophie finally concedes that 'all this year, we had been three.' Greg's voice interrupts and claims that 'the movie kept them together.' However, the predicament was that he loved Sophie but was writing love letters to another woman.

The credits roll on a final dedication to Chris Marker and *La Jetée* (1962), a film entirely made of still photographs (except for a half-second eye movement), which is the Urtext of travel narratives, and attempted departure, complete with time travel and space travel. Calle undertakes several trips in her film.[36] The trip that she offers readers/spectators with her public and sometimes hilarious exhibition of private life and intimacy, and the more reserved trip offered by Shepard and the trip that was the pretext for this faux road movie. The latter is untold, and unravels the myth of the couple and its demise, while hiding beneath the surface of a typical American road trip film, perfect in its Las Vegas and California ending. Borrowing from an American genre, yet in a hybridized format with its French input, the formula is modern, if not postmodern and new. Calle's trip harks back to an earlier classical travel narrative that plunges into the demise of a couple, with a last minute reprieve. Roberto Rossellini's *Voyage to Italy* (1953). A British bourgeois couple, played by Ingrid Bergman and Paul Sanders, bickers throughout a road trip and stay in Southern Italy (Naples) to the point of contemplating divorce. The car in which they are forced to be both alone at the start of the film propels the realization that they are not suited for each other. They wonder if they can start over. Of course, in 1953, talk of sex was not openly expressed but understated. Their bedroom has two single beds. The husband looks for other romantic relations during his visit to Capri where Italians (and even a French woman) are stereotypically represented next to him. Meanwhile, the wife is lamenting her now dead former lover (fiancé) and reciting his poetry. *Voyage to Italy* is an early narrative where literally nothing 'happens' as Giuliana Bruno aptly remarks (369). Similarly in Calle/Shepard's road-trip, nothing in the conventional meaning of the word happens, except for the lure of a sexual act, which on its surface is the overall quest implied in its title. However, as in Italy, motion and the American scenery participate in Sophie's emotional evasions. It is a sentimental journey taken out onto the American landscape. The woman (Calle) is foreign and displaced; she does not quite fit as Katherine (Ingrid Bergman) and is somewhat out of place in the vastness of the land. Yet, for a French person, Florida and Alabama are exotic places, as is Route 66 (and its myth), but Calle does not dwell on these aspects. Her views are totally different in terms of sensitivity from Greg's. But unlike Katherine Joyce, who can only voice her headaches and relative frustration to herself, Sophie expresses her point of view and taste loudly, in front of Greg. The erotic components are integrated along with her frustrated desire. Calle travels in haptic pursuit but fails to reignite love.

Calle, as an artist and performer since the late 1970s, skillfully blurs the codes, building up the suspenseful 'sex' or 'no sex' moment which bids the reader/spectator to share and participate in the couple's intimacy as it would (albeit mildly) in a classical Hollywood narrative. However, ironic remarks about the partner and the open lack of desire further confuse the reader's possible expectations, while toying with them. The individual mythology at work helps fabricate and maintain the biography of the artist, rendered public elsewhere in her autobiographical works such as *Journaux Intimes* (1978–1992), which relates the story of her meeting with Greg Shepard in handwritten format: 'I met him in a bar in December 1989. I was in N.Y. for 2 days on my way from Mexico to Paris. He offered me a place to stay' (Calle 2003). It corresponds to the beginning of *No sex last night*. Similarly, *Histoires Vraies* and *Histoires Vraies + dix* inserts the story of the husband in ten episodes, opening with the 1989 encounter at the New York bar (Calle 1994, 2002).

Calle can easily pass for a traveler in many of her texts. Travel is a recurrent trope and stands out clearly as a section in her exhibition of over twenty-four years of her works at the Pompidou center (*'M'as-tu vue'* 2004). Chases are displacements through the streets of Paris or any other town, like New York. *No sex last night* is a travel-chase that follows a precise geographical line with a departure point: New York, Shepard's living quarters, to reach Mills College, next to San Francisco, where Calle is due to teach. Trying to convince Shepard that he must accompany her becomes one of her reasons to make the trip, which could have been made alone: 'Au départ, ce n'était pas un film, mais un piège d'amour.' ('Initially, it was not a film but a love trap') (Mérigeau). Calle rarely initiates single rituals; they mostly involve a partner or partners. For both of them, the form was new, and they tinkered with the camera, using it for the first time. For Greg, the desire to finally make a movie (and change his career orientation) is what attracted him to participate in the travelogue. Ultimately, Sophie views travel as cathartic and as a goal in and out of itself, thereby inscribing the process into a healing ritual.[37]

3
Vagabondages

Vagabondage: from Latin vagabundus (vagari wander)

vagabond n. & v.i. 1. Having no fixed habitation, wandering etc. 2. Wanderer, vagrant, esp. idle & worthless one; (colloq.) scamp, rascal. 3. v.i. (now colloq.). Wander about, play the vagabond. Hence (vagabond)age (2, 3), -ism (2), -ish, a. -ize (2) v.i. (Oxford Dictionary of Current English 1435)[1]

The first part of Chapter 3 observes the figure of the nomad or vagabond, the quintessential traveler. Several cultural philosophers and writers such as Walter Benjamin, Georges Steiner, Michel Maffesoli, and Joseph Roth inform my reading of nomadic traveling that occurs in the following films: Sarah Petit's (now Sarah Léonor) *L'Arpenteur/The Land Surveyor* (2003) and *Le Lac et la rivière/The Lake and the river* (2002), Ermanno Olmi's *La Légende du Saint-Buveur/The Legend of the Holy Drinker* (1988), Siegried's *Sansa* (2003), and Tony Gatlif's *Transylvania* (2006). These French productions venture into the world, introducing the figure of a global traveler not geographically bound by borders and nations. In the second part, Jean-Claude Guiguet's testament film *Les Passagers/The Passengers* (1999) relies on the metaphor of the train or tramway for the meaning of life. Located at the periphery of Paris, Guiguet conveyed a poetic incantation on life and death, and the state of our world at the end of the 20th century. I focus on the form of the tramway, and the various lines that crisscross the film.

The quintessential traveler, whose main attribute is that of leaving, and not being sedentary, unable to settle down with any fixed ties or 'moorings' – a figure of modernity – is very much present in filmic narratives. The vagabond or wanderer has throughout history been perceived as a mysterious and potentially dangerous individual because of his itinerant nature. He is a transient being passing through town. Culled from a vast body of legends, George Steiner conjures up Walter Benjamin's 'enigmatic prophecy' of the beggar who comes knocking at doors and is suspect of being an agent of the devil or of god (Steiner 30). He is the uncanny messenger sometimes, threatening the moral order of the city or village. Although probably over-borrowed recently in theoretical arguments, the term 'nomadic' stands out in direct opposition to the 'sedentary' person at the junction of the two modes of being that have existed for millennia: the shepherd and the farmer (Onfray 10). Tension between both exists for the sedentary man envies the nomad's existence (Adorno in Maffesoli 72).[2]

In Greece, the nomad led the sheep to pastures (*nomos* is the name for pastures). In various countries of the world, nomadic herders form a large part of the population, which under all its types (hunter-gatherers, pastoral, and peripatetic) numbers 30–40 million worldwide.[3] Departing largely from the etymological root of the term, none of the filmic characters under discussion are cattle herders, yet the term has been adapted to theories related to migration and travel.

French authorities in 1912 assigned the word 'nomad' to a new category of population – although one 'not clearly defined, which meant Gypsies' – in an attempt to avoid racial bias under the cover of trying to regulate their movement and facilitate their sedentariness.[4] Special encampment areas or *'Emplacement réservé aux nomades'* ('a space reserved to nomads'), legally sanctioned and mandatory in each French village, are situated at the outskirts of towns or villages. Such areas are now designated by the more neutral expression *'gens du voyage'* – or traveling people. Often, the camp is in close proximity to the village dump.[5] The characteristic of this 'bird of passage' that is preferably welcome outside of town and is underlined in Maffesoli's *Le Voyage* (2003) reminds us of laws promulgated about foreigners. The case of Gypsies occupies a large portion of this project and is best illustrated in Gatlif's films, as previously examined in Chapter 1. Their nomadic status is at the heart of his work. Silvia Tuozzi and Carolina Angrisoni's volume *Tony Gatlif: Un cinéma nomade* (Lindau 2003) is the first study (originally published in Italian) to integrate the direction of his work (Figure 3.1).

The status of Gypsies rings familiar in view of the treatment of Jews in France, especially during the Occupation. During World War II, nomads were no longer 'permitted' to circulate freely. Under the Vichy government in 1940, a new law was passed limiting the movement of nomads, who were required to settle down under police surveillance (Fogg 91).

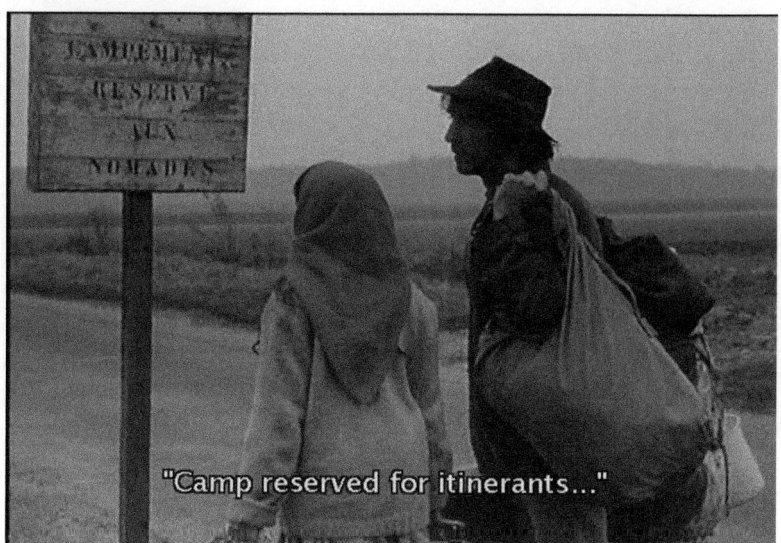

Figure 3.1 Tony Gatlif, *Les Princes*
Note: 'Zorka reads the sign imposing their nomadic condition to Nara.'

Because he/she does not have any baggage and moorings, the vaga-bond – a peripatetic character – is someone from the outside, a foreigner who usually passes through a place, and whose function is transient. Some cultures make space for him/her, welcoming him/her with respect. Others, on the contrary, attempt to get rid of or detain him/her, and designate geographic areas where he/she will be assigned. Walter Benjamin in his essay on the historical nature of storytelling praised the historical association between the two archaic types (or tribes): that of the resident and the traveler, or in his words the 'resident tiller of the soil' and the 'trading seaman.' Both produced storytelling and were sometimes in unison, not at odds: 'The resident master craftsman and the traveling journeyman worked together in the same room; and every master had been a traveling journeyman before he settled down in his home town or somewhere else' (Benjamin).

In the 19th century, the Napoleonic code turned vagabonds into criminals who could be fined and imprisoned in order to preserve the public order (Cailler 198). There is a crime called *un délit de vagabond-age*, thus transforming wandering poets/writers like Arthur Rimbaud or Isabelle Eberhardt into criminals. The nomadic figure is dominant at the beginning of the 21st century when economic contingencies force people to leave their home, country, or continent and flee elsewhere in search of employment and a new life, although the name attributed to such persons is that of *migrants* or refugees. Differences exist between nomads, exiles, and diaspora. 'For the nomad, home is always mobile' (Peters 21). A resurgence of laws condemns them and defines new 'zones' where they can be safely relocated, 'removed', or placed in transit.

Dreams of a sedentary life

C'est ça l'arpenteur, un cinéaste, quelqu'un qui arpente, pas seulement avec un mètre. Pour filmer sur cette planète, il faut être un peu géographe. Gé c'est la terre en grec, graphe ça veut dire écrire. (Straub)[6] ('The land surveyor, a cineaste, someone who surveys, not only with a measuring rod. In order to film on this planet, one must be a bit of a geographer. Ge, meaning "earth" in Greek, graph, meaning to write.')

A filmmaker is someone who walks the land with a camera, akin to a geographer who traces roads and paths between people and links them. The *arpenteur* (a land-surveyor) applies to Pierre, a man from nowhere, who emerges in the middle of an Alsatian rural space, only to disappear one day for an unknown destination. Sarah Petit visually engages the concept of borders and border crossing in the opening sequence of *Le Lac et la rivière*. The Armenian landscape in *L'Arpenteur* is the main character whereas in *Le Lac et la rivière*, it is a décor.[7] Alsace is a region that has been at the center of wars and conflicts over its borders, situated at the eastern tip of France/ Germany, a region where Petit and Klein originate. As we can infer, landscapes in European cinema are not empty of meaning: they are 'a nationally charged space' (Galt 27).

Some texts launch an invitation to travel and to dream imaginary roads. Written and directed by Sarah Petit, both *Le lac et la rivière* and *L'Arpenteur*, interweave different paths, leading to wandering, walking, exile, and a return to one's origins.[8] The two medium-length films released in 2003, programmed to be screened back to back, search into one's identity and one's place in the world, against the backdrop of Armenia and Alsace, two eastern regions.[9] While shot in a realist mode, and displaying many breathtaking vistas of the Armenian and Alsatian countryside, they seem to be timeless. They stay away from an exoticizing gaze and orientalist discourse. They enter an unknown area, surrounded by a mysterious, if not mythical tone that leaves the narrative open to a metaphysical interpretation. They draw their strength from a feeling of the uncanny that accompanies some travelers, the traveler typically cast in most cultures as the outsider, or the foreigner. Accordingly, the traveler may or not be welcome. This principle still operates on many levels globally. Maffesoli draws from Plato in order to describe the traveler's uncanny aspect in his study on *Voyages*:

> Quel que soit son objet : commerce, voyage d'initiation, simple vagabondage, il n'est qu' 'un oiseau de passage', et comme tel devra être accueilli, certes, 'mais en dehors de la ville.'(16).
>
> (Whatever his object is: trade, initiation travel, simple wandering, he is nothing but a 'passing bird,' and as such shall definitely be welcome, but 'outside of the cities.')

Le lac et la rivière/The Lake and the River opens with a shot of a man's back, standing on a boat, looking at a river. The opening segment situates the film in a no-man's land, thereby producing a disorienting effect. Where is the spectator? Once he 'lands' on the shore, he walks away from the river, with his back to the camera. In retrospect, the arrival illustrates the meaning of the term *voyage* with an emphasis placed on the 'arrival' or entry point. '*Arriver*' literally means to come to the shore (the '*rive*'). Road markers clearly differentiate between French and Alsatian territory, along with a French flag, verifying that the man is indeed in France. Europe is a walkable *lieu de mémoire* 'a place of memory' – here the history of Alsace and its partitioning along national identity lines comes to mind. The pace of the walk reinforces the European spatial peculiarity of a history made up of long walks (Steiner 30).

The character strolls along country roads and across fields until he arrives at a hotel at nightfall. The next day, he finds work in an Alsatian farm run by a woman. The film does not rely much on dialogue to communicate, but on facial expressions and gazes. Pierre, the traveler, gets hired to work in the vineyards and protects a young woman from a farmer who beats her for stealing cherries. The young woman is from Armenia, a country he has visited. Many of the inhabitants have either traveled from outside of France to migrate or settle down, as is the case for the Armenians. Even Anne, the boss, has returned 'home' to Alsace after years spent away in an African colony.

'I am someone who travels'

Pierre's co-worker friend is Italian. He has lived in France for many years, and speaks of his 'fusion with the landscape', suggesting that nobody would believe that he is Italian and further suggesting that national identity is no longer relevant. Pierre addresses the young Armenian woman as an Oriental woman. She is amazed that he speaks Armenian, Bulgarian, and Russian, and wonders who he really is. He answers: 'I have wandered on this earth since 1800, and have seen all the miseries of the world.' He resembles a weary traveler.[10] Pierre dreamed of a house where she lives, surrounded by rising water. She mentions that she had the same dream in which both of them were unafraid. He describes himself as 'someone who travels'. According to him, she is his soul mate. He wishes to go to Italy, as he cannot stay too long in one place. She is afraid that he will never stop traveling. She wants to be sedentary and settle down somewhere, refusing to follow him.

In a subsequent sequence, he discovers that she is married and pregnant, and that her husband is about to be return any day. Though upset by the news, Pierre tells her that he loves her. Another time, she applies an Armenian proverb onto the situation: 'Man is a river, and woman is a lake.' The day after hearing of her pregnancy, he leaves. The narration picks up through the voiceover of the Italian worker, who narrates the story in Pierre's absence. According to him, Pierre left for Italy. His brother (back in Italy) has told him that he did see a man pass by and work in the marble quarries, but that that man had already left. He also remembers that when he was young, he saw the same man before, passing through their village and looking for work. According to the Italian immigrant, his brother likes stories or fables and he dismisses the possible implications of such a story, were it true.

After the man's leaving, things changed magically. The people of the farm and village all became a big family, a reconstituted 'tribe.' In fact, one of the last shots of the film presents a convivial setting: the female boss, a few Armenians, including the young woman and her baby, are sitting and eating together outdoors – an idyllic image of a pietà and harmonic family. The itinerant work hand subtly contributed to the strengthening of the community. His fleeting episode connected everyone. However, no one ever knew precisely who he was, and he remains as enigmatic as when he arrived. He was a foreigner, a man of passage, able to speak many languages yet unable to settle down and become sedentary.

Tracing roads

With the type of narrative described in the previous paragraphs, we enter a world of *fabula* and the fantastic. The films *L'Arpenteur/The Land Surveyor* and *Le Lac et la Rivière* feed from each other and arguably are best seen as a diptych. They communicate with each other.

In *L'Arpenteur*, a young man returns to Armenia, the land of his ancestors, as an escape from France. Avedis left France, and took refuge at the land surveyor's place in Armenia; his boss is a French friend of the family, now working in Armenia and overseeing the blueprints for a new road. The pattern from the previous film centering on Armenian immigrants in France is inverted. Avedis works with him on the tracing of a road that will link two villages in the Southern part of the country. The producer Michel Klein argues that *Le Lac et la rivière*, while being shot in Alsace, is clearly about Armenia. Both border films are paired and belong to a new genre of films that go east, an 'Eastern' in opposition to a Western, a genre Klein proposes.[11]

The films' narratives contain fairytale or fantastic elements yet practice an economy of shots. Slow pace and long takes characterize them. They contain no special effects and hardly any dialogue. The core concepts of each film are traveling, the role of the traveler, or the need to travel at a certain pace while its mirror image or counterparts found in sedentary living are refracted at the traveler as a possible lure. *L'Arpenteur* defines the employment of the male character in the second film *Le Lac et la rivière*, enabling a free flowing exchange between them and echoing each other. The young Franco-Armenian man is interested in the ruins of the past, and his family background. He successfully locates a relative in the city at the end of the story.

Petit, now Sarah Léonor, made a second Alsatian-based feature length film, *Au voleur* (2009). One of the last films featuring Guillaume Depardieu, it unravels as a long ballad into the countryside with an outlaw – a thief, and his new companion, a woman teacher. It is heavily marked by the frontier-culture of Alsace, the director's region. (Levieux 2009).

The filmmaker as landsurveyor

The landscapes are shot but not framed in a picturesque way. Both *L'Arpenteur* and *Le Lac et la rivière* are about a deeper voyage. One must pause on the notion of filmmaker as the *arpenteur* – a land surveyor, as someone who walks a certain path. Incidentally, the French term encompasses much more than just land surveying. An *arpenteur* is thus someone who walks the land, not just to measure it – an *arpent* being an old measure of land (the equivalent of 58.47 meters). *Arpenter* refers to a specific type of walk and pace. A filmmaker is someone who walks through space with his/her camera, not the usual land-surveying instrument, and writes with light.

The itinerant land-surveyor cannot stop still in one place for too long. As a surveyor of land, he helps trace and spin invisible threads between people, and connects them without their knowledge. Contrary to the Biblical apostle Peter (the term for a rock), he does not build houses, or churches; yet, as Peter, he leaves everything to be on the road and cannot remain sedentary.

New terms should emerge in view of the 'off-the beaten path' films or 'walking movies' that are contrary to Westerns and formulate a new genre of the 'Eastern'. River navigation is used in Léonor's films with the boat arrival or the run on a canoe. Tight schedules are tossed out. Slow speed is the new way to measure man versus time, as examined in the next chapter with *Mr. Ibrahim ou les fleurs du Coran* (Dupeyron) as well as *Le Grand Voyage* (Ferroukhi), and further in Chapter 7 with Rozier's or Tati's films.

The vagabond permits new ways of seeing. He points the way. The gaze is what matters, besides the actual path. Along the way, the nomad casts a new look on people and things, and grows from it as they grow from his presence. The freedom to take off, and break with all known moorings is not easy; for some, it is an urgency, based on geo-political conditions (wars, economic warfare, lack of resources); for others it may be a call from some unknown source; for others, it is a religious call, a call to practice a form of travel that I will call here a pilgrimage, a return to one's roots. It can be a domestic situation that some have to attend to, independent of the above examples. In what follows I will continue my exploration of the trope of the wanderer.

In my examination of travel films, I come across wandering movies where the protagonist(s) is drifting.

> Not to find one's way in a city may well be uninteresting and banal. It requires ignorance – nothing more. But to lose oneself in a city – as one loses oneself in a forest – that calls for a quite different schooling. Then, signboard and street names, passers-by, roofs, kiosks, or bars must speak to the wanderer like a cracking twig under his feet in the forest. Walter Benjamin.[12]

Olmi's feature film *La Légende du saint-buveur/La Leggenda del Santo Bevitore/The Legend of the Holy Drinker* (1988) based on Joseph Roth's short novel is such a narrative, in which the main protagonist is a homeless man in 1934 Paris. One day, in a bizarre encounter, he is entrusted with a donation to be deposited for Saint-Thérèse de Lisieux at the Holy Mary Church of Batignolles (17th arrondissement). He strives to honor the request. Yet as in a bad dream, everything concurs to delay the moment where he will physically make it to the neighborhood and set foot inside the church.[13] Written in 1939, a few weeks before Roth's death, the tale of Andréas, a sort of celestial bum[14] spins miracles in front of our eyes, thanks to his devotion to Saint-Thérèse and her intercession. The experience forces an interior trip, a descent into oneself that culminates in a final illumination. The tale of a drunk is common in literature, yet the 61-page novella, Roth's haunting poetic legacy combined with the unforgettable oneiric film and performance by Dutch actor Rutger Hauer, compels a re-reading. Roth, a Jewish Austrian writer living in exile in France at the time, a self-proclaimed *apatride* (stateless person) and wanderer, is even more gripping since he witnessed the storm over Europe and drank himself to death right before World War II was declared. A former theology student, he is according to Michael Hofmann 'a walking paradox', attracted to Catholicism while being Jewish. (18)

Andréas the drinker is an exile Polish coal miner who comes to Paris looking for work and to escape justice; he ends up in abject misery in 1930s Paris. Yet he is given a chance to redeem himself. Olmi, the Italian director, shoots the city with the gaze of a foreigner, inspired by Roth's vision, 'a veritable Guide Michelin de Paris' (Heymann 1989). The itinerary throughout the city is mapped out with such areas as Bercy, le Quai de la Gare, and most importantly the locus (focal point) of Andréas' constantly deferred final destination to return the money he was lent, the church of Holy Mary of Batignolles (Figure 3.2). The association with two charismatic feminine religious figures is hard to miss. Just as it is true that some landscapes stay with us after travel is concluded, some films do; and we (spectators) travel with them through the film.

Sansa (Siegfried 2003) the name of the protagonist (Roshdy Zem) is the quintessential nomad and wanderer.[15] The entire film revolves around his peregrinations over the world and as such the world belongs to him and is open to him.[16] He does not have a specific goal or destination in mind, nor a care. The restless nomad is 'emptied of all interiority, their strong presence on screen comes from the void of consciousness, a void perfectly assumed with heroism, since it leads to death or absolute solitude' (Goldmann 19–21). Unlike what has been discussed, Goldmann interprets the wanderer as a person who is not open to Others. Jacqueline Dutton draws a stylistically close parallel between *Sansa* and Chris Marker's travel narrative in Japan and Africa in *Sans Soleil* (1983).[17] Sansa is full of humanity, seeking contact and dialogue wherever he goes. He is no hermit or recluse. An outsider in the different societies and cultures he crosses, he is a mere spectator.

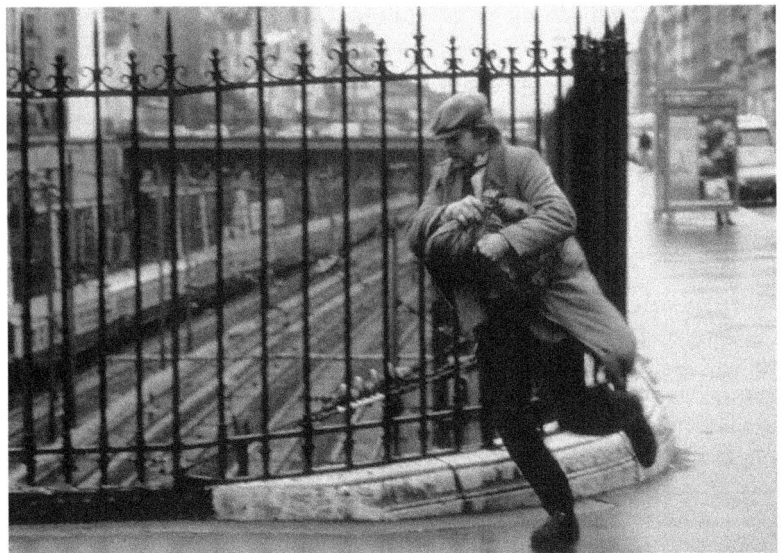

Figure 3.2   Ermanno Olmi, *La Légende du Saint-Buveur*
Note: 'Andréas (Rutger Hauer) is hastening to the Church of Sainte Marie des Batignolles, a constantly deferred destination.'
Source: The Kobal Collection at Art Resource, NY.

He is a free spirit and self-proclaimed world-citizen, yet in spite of open borders and free circulation zones in Europe, he is constantly harangued for identity verification. He is first and foremost suspicious and can be imprisoned for vagabondage in flagrante delicto. Wherever he goes, be it France, where the film starts at a train station with 'a little routine police check up', or Spain, Hungary or Russia, he is subject to verification or hunts.

He forges his way East, by riding trains, or walking relentlessly. The camera trails him all over the world, wherever he materializes. There are gaps, and hiatuses in the progression. For instance, the transition between India and Tokyo is left out despite the fact that he had to 'walk' all the way there. He takes a plane on the way back from Tokyo. His route appears seamless despite ellipsis. As an embodiment of nomadism, there is no longer any consideration of fabricated borders, the world is ours and Sansa is at home everywhere,

Le dynamisme et la spontanéité du nomadisme étant, justement, de faire fi des frontières: nationales, civilisationnelles, idéologiques,

religieuses, et de vivre concrètement, quelque chose d'universel, ...
les valeurs humanistes (Maffesoli 32). ('The dynamics and spontaneity of nomadism being, rightly so, to do away with borders: national,
civilizational, religious, and to concretely live something universal ...
humanist values.')

Sansa, an enigmatic film and character, conveys an ingenuous portrait of a restless man, haunted by music, with a mix of slow motion
or fast motion sequences, shot in guerrilla warfare style. As a wanderer
and world citizen, he is under constant threat, yet because of his good-
humored nature he is able to extricate himself of complex situations.
One of them is the rather tragi-comic episode when he, like Voltaire's
Candide, runs into guerilla warfare in a former Soviet bloc country. He
is saved from ransom, and his life is spared because he is an artist. His
name (Sansa) is never clarified, yet opens up playful interpretations
(*Sans* meaning 'without', therefore 'without an A' could be one logical
meaning). He has no family, no bearings, no 'home' (*Sans Abri/sansA*,
without an A literally meaning without a shelter, or homeless). He is an
artist and sketches people's portraits, or paints them wherever he goes;
he carries his sketchbook for sole baggage along with a beat-up passport.
He is dressed in the same outfit for the entire film, only sporting a winter hat while in Russia and then doing away with his signature beret,
which can be interpreted either as a French iconic sign or a revolutionary one, or both. Wherever he is, the authorities are never satisfied with
the worn-out identification papers he presents them.

The Chase

The film sticks to the mode of the chase, a mode that recurs in the
scripts observed. Two positions best characterize him: that of the run-
ner, someone who is pursued by police, security forces, or revolutionar-
ies, or that of someone who stands still amidst the crowd of passers-by
and just gazes at people, in a caring way.

The choreographed pace follows the fast rhythm of the director's own
musical score as Siegfried, the film director is a musician and *Sansa* is
his second film after *Louise (Take 2)* (1998). It is composed as a fugue
and a chase. The electro-jazz soundtrack agrees with the material. In
his adventures, he befriends Mr. Click, an older Jewish music conductor whom he casually meets at different stopovers, in Lisbon, Milan, St.
Petersburg, and Tokyo. The then 81-year-old Israeli violinist Ivry Gitlis,
who is a world-famous musician-traveler, plays Click. He is like a brother

or his double and they get along well, especially in their joint taste for freedom and women. The narrative is a happy one, because of Sansa's carefree, street-smart and good-humored nature. His Bohemian ways are endearing to all. His traveler's gaze is friendly, well intentioned, and people return the gaze in kind, to the camera as it dances around them.

Nomadic filmmaking-Transylvania

> Rouler, c'est faire défiler le paysage, comme dans le panorama mobile ... symboliquement le film prend feu et se détruit sous nos yeux: la route brûle, elle consume celui qui la parcourt (Aumont 222). ('To drive is to make the landscape scroll down, as in a mobile panorama ... symbolically the film catches fire and self-destroys in front of our eyes: the road burns, it consumes the one who takes it.')

Jacques Aumont perceives the developing 'asphalt' trope back in the 1960s, entailing the omnipresence of roads, replacing railroad tracks in filmic representations. One of his key examples sticks to Bertrand Blier's road movie *Les Valseuses/Going Places* (1974) where the main character physically and symbolically enters the road (222). Gatlif's *Transylvania* (2006) springs from the same source as *Gadjo Dilo* (1998), *Vengo* (2000), *Exils* (2004), *Swing* (2002), and *Je suis né d'une cigogne/Children of a stork* (1999). Travel, wandering, and music reign supreme at the heart of most of Gatlif's work. Besides, it is the first time that he has directed and written a female-centered road-movie, led masterfully by actress and adopted nomad Asia Argento. Gatlif revisits post-Ceaucescu's Romania, a place he cherishes in at least two of his films.

Female wandering is depicted as magical, fragile, painful, and violent. Gatlif pushes the limits of the genre (road-movie) in his portrait of a woman on the road. Along the way, his female character, called the Zingarina, undergoes a transformation, and gradually relinquishes all moorings, be they Parisian, Italian, or European (Western European that is) in order to adopt a nomadic habitus. An atmosphere of fantastic is released. In the rather masculine enclave reserved to traditional road-movies, the film does not propose a traveling female role model, but it stands unique in the director's work, and within French cinema at large through its anchoring. I plan to analyze the feminization of the genre as Gatlif orchestrates it.

At its start, the road scrolls fast in front of us as a large ribbon, and by moments, in the dazzling of near freeze-frames, the camera stands still for a quarter of a second, capturing the face of a man, or a woman, all peasants, by the roadside, somewhere ... in Transylvania. It is through these unique moments that the film touches on the *punctum*, endearing the spectator to the Romanian country and its people: Affect and emotion are at the basis of Gatlif's films. They are never about psychology and narration. The scrolling (*defilement*) starts again, immediately. It could be material for an ethnographic reportage at the heart of Romania. The car stops, and the camera pulls away to reveal its position behind a car transporting three young women.

The three women travelled from France to a non-descript village in which they disembark at dawn in search of Milan Agustin. Zingarina has come to follow or chase after her lover – a Romanian Gypsy musician who returned home.[18] Her expectations are immediately deflated. The lover rejects her in the seconds that follow their 'meeting' leaving her alone and desperate, walking across a crowd of revelers celebrating a Pagan holiday.

The film is musical through and through. Gatlif composed its score, in parallel with the script he wrote. The music irrigates – a term Gatlif uses, which curiously film musicologist Michel Chion has used elsewhere in another context – about fifty of the 103 minutes of film.

Devoid of many actions and without practically any dialogue – the mark of Gatlif, the film spans a specific duration: seven months elapse between the pregnant Zingarina's arrival and the birth of the child in the middle of a snowed-in backdrop, in the closeness and feverish worry of her new-found travel companion, Tchangalo.

The firing of the script[19]

The road belongs to Zingarina, a young woman from nowhere, designating a 'Gypsy' in Italian. I can speculate that she is from France, of Italian origins, as she at first speaks of going home. In a flash decision, she unpacks all her material possessions, abandons them, and leaves her past to err on the roads. Instead of going back to France with her friends, she flees unexpectedly and ends up meeting a man of passage along the way. Tchangalo is an itinerant salesman, an antiques dealer – a trader who buys and sells people's goods (such as gold). His ties are specific: he is close to Gypsies, and can converse equally in Romani and German. He might be German-Turkish since he trades with Hamburg. Zingarina intrigues Tchangalo as soon as he meets her at the village café. Accented English becomes their *lingua franca*. The casting of Asia Argento (of Italian nationality, daughter of filmmaker Dario Argento) and Birol Unel (Turkish German) affects my reading of the characters and most likely Gatlif's casting after he had seen Fatih Akin's *Head-On* (2004) and lead actor Unel.

Gatlif is not interested in the past or origins of his itinerant characters. Only space and present time matter for their deambulations. Tchangalo is familiar with Gypsy rituals; he is a traveler and shares their dislike for being trapped inside a house. The road trip is performed outdoors, in the cold, mud, and rain, in frugal circumstances, devoid of any romanticism. Interiors are rare if not inexistent besides cafes. He drives a dilapidated car, and sometimes Zingarina takes over at the wheel.[20] The first time they meet, he is puzzled: 'what makes a girl like you come to Transylvania?' Indeed the terrain is not auspicious to tourism, especially in the middle of winter, along frozen roads and rivers. She answers that she is looking for love. She reciprocates by asking him 'What makes a man like you go out on the road?' In fact, Gatlif states that one goes to Transylvania in order to lose oneself, not for a vacation (Rebichon 135). The location signals the end of the world. The first track of the musical score called *Libre Zingarina* gives the film its lyrical as well as liberating mood:

> Je l'aime plus que ma vie, mon coeur est malheureux,
> Je regarde avec envie ceux qui ont de la chance
> Ceux qui sont heureux de vivre
> Donnez-nous un brin de paille pour mettre le feu au monde
> ('I love her more than my life, my heart is unhappy,
> I look with envy at those who are lucky
> Who are happy to be alive
> Give us a wisp of straw to set the world on fire').[21]

The unlikely romance is rooted in the road, despite the demons that besiege the young woman. Incidentally, female characters (in Gatlif) are typically plagued by their past, which returns to haunt them, yet the past remains untold; they must ritually cleanse themselves in order to 'survive.' This is illustrated in the trance sequence (*Exils*) and the Christian orthodox ceremony (*Transylvania*). Tchangalo organizes a ritual with an orthodox priest to exorcise her demons. She dresses in a long white transparent dress, bare-foot, while the priest chants and pours milk on her head, giving her a new baptism and birth.

Zingarina makes a clean break with her ties (past, national, and cultural). If the trip stops for her female French companions (one of them, a Romanian, translated for them), she subsequently hits the road, and fuses with the surroundings. Glimpses of the post-Ceaucescu grey urban scenery revert visually to Gatlif's earlier films such as *Les Princes* (1982) with similar looking deserted factories, unfinished buildings, and misery that one finds globally, and not specifically in Romania. The woman stays despite all logic, and far from the comfort of the modern world. Initially displaced (and out of place), as shown in the unique scene where she is walking in pain against the crowd on the street of a village, she embraces the road.

Layer by layer she progressively 'gypsifies' herself, adopting female Gypsy wear or our Western notions of it. Coco Chanel is credited for introducing the Gypsy skirt to modern fashion and most spectators are familiar with large broom skirts; Zingarina sometimes makes gestures that no woman – Gypsy or not – would make. One of the forbidden acts (in Gypsy customs) is to drive while pregnant, as it is remarked upon by an older man, or boxing her companion, in order to let steam off, and riding a bicycle. The sexy tight-fitting black dress she was initially wearing in the village café, complete with black boots and stockings, gradually vanish. It is replaced at first by a black and white broom skirt, followed by several colorful skirts and 'gypsy' slips and headscarf. She stops exhibiting her 'real' tattoos on her stomach.[22] She destabilizes people she meets, who take her for a Gypsy (a 'nomad' would probably be the most appropriate term to qualify the character); Tchangalo's business sales are reportedly down due to her outrageous outfits and wild behavior. Gatlif slips rings on all her fingers and forces her to deviate from her initial trajectory – that of a sedentary (*gadje*) woman. Either way, she does not disavow people who question her ethnicity and is untouched by their comments.

Given a second chance at life, after the ceremony, she lives again, and her features are more and more akin to those of the virgin (Mary), at least as in iconography. Gatlif is not religious in the strict meaning of adhering to a church. Yet Gypsies have a long cultural tradition of worshipping the Virgin Mary. When she delivers the child in the snowed-in car, assisted by older female villagers, the final image harks back to that of a nativity scene: the virgin and child, together, on a bed, waiting for Tchangalo's returns from his celebration.

The two finales

A disconcerting structure provides two possible endings in turn. It is up to us to choose. Thus the two finales: in the first one, Tchangalo is visibly overwhelmed by the birth of the child, and in an outpouring of emotions, goes to town to hire Gypsy musicians, and asks them to play (for him) on the way back. They perform in the lonely countryside while he dances, drinks, and breaks bottles on his head and face. This pure *Kara Sevda* ritual harks back to a long tradition in Balkan and Turkish cinema, which relates to a state of life and an emotional numbness involved with self-inflicted wounds at a key moment of crisis. Inebriated, he loses track of time, and returns some time (possibly days) later, in the somewhat elastic temporality. In the first version, she left and is said to have followed a camp of Gypsies with the baby; the frame opens on an empty camp. Tchangalo finds two old women, laughing and playing the bass on the bed, instead of Zingarina.

In the second more idyllic version, which follows the first one, closest to the sacred 'icon', he returns and finds her, smiling in the comfort of the hollow bed, with the child asleep at her breast. The softness of the image, a nativity scene, contrasts with the rigor and violence of the road traveled until now. In fact, the spectator realizes that not once did she see the couple in the intimacy of a bedroom. The child signals the anchoring, the end of the road, and maybe the end of nomadism. The image of the idealized woman and child, as a Pietà, has cropped up once before, in a scene that was like a vision of her friend Marie (Amira Casar) whose stomach and large coat sheltered and united several children in a manner close to magical realism.

Transylvania thwarts the masculine road-movie and its celebration of male brotherhood and virile friendship that functions in the absence of women and within a system of masculine friendship, allotting considerable importance to the car (Corrigan 144).

This no longer applies to the film, where the car is used in a strictly utilitarian fashion, as it was for the earlier *Gadjo Dilo*. Solidarity and feelings between these two (of opposite sexes) happen on the road. The first man Zingarina was chasing all the way from France to Transylvania and who rejected her (Milan) is erased and replaced by the other one, the one she never expected. The film possesses unique religious accents (at least in Gatlif's film world). Its iconography is lyrical and baroque. The child born out of this 'bastard' union will be Gypsy, born on the road, and his arrival is feted by Gypsy music. Tchangalo, not the biological father, becomes the de facto father of the child. Gatlif wanted a 'free woman', distancing himself from his earlier masculine-inflected travel narratives; he is inspired by a woman he knows and respects: La Caita.[23] Nevertheless, vagabond or nomadic women or 'girls' are rare cinematographically-speaking. Thus, consideration of Agnès Varda's example of *Sans toit, ni loi/Vagabond* (1985) is tempting, and I discuss this film in Chapter 6 on strong women in films.[24] However, such a comparison falls short. These films are at two different poles from each other. Mona signifies social exclusion and a programmed death (*Sans Toit, ni loi*). It is a measure of the depressive climate found in 1980s' French cinema treated at length in Phil Powrie's work (1997). For Gatlif (and la Zingarina), the road equals freedom and *jouissance* (pleasure) as well as life in the present on unknown paths. The woman is a rebel, and throws herself into adventure, body and soul. She flourishes. She is possessed by the soul of the place, dance, and trance (Jean-Luc Douin).[25]

Interior voyage: *Les Passagers*

One of the first films ever made in France at the beginning of cinema was the Lumière brothers' *Arrivée d'un train à la Ciotat* (Auguste and Louis Lumière 1896), a document on the arrival of a train in the small southern town of la Ciotat. Connections have been made between riding the metro/or train and conducting one's life, especially by Marc Augé,

Car les lignes de métro, comme celles de la main se croisent; non seulement sur le plan où se déploie et s'ordonne l'entrelacs de leurs parcours multicolores, mais dans la vie et la tête de chacun (Augé 11–12). ('For metro lines, like the lines of one's hand, crisscross each other; not only on the map do they deploy and orchestrate the interlacing of their multicolor trajectory, but in one's life and one's head.')

The metaphor of the tramway or for that matter the train or the metro for one's life is strongly anchored in narratives; the tramway in *Les Passagers* is the central character and runs through it like in *Un si beau voyage*. The machine (implying modern technology of the tramway and cinema) drives the narrative and reminds one of the forces at work in society, and one's life in general. It cements Guiguet's film and borrows different lines, some of which are imaginary, echoing Augé's similar thoughts vis-à-vis the metro.[26]

Le tramway est une machine éminemment cinématographique : il ne fait pas de bruit, il traverse la ville, et la ville le traverse, via ses passagers. C'est surtout une métaphore de la destinée humaine, de l'incroyable éphémère de nos vies (Guiguet).[27] ('The tramway is an eminently cinematographic machine: it makes no noise, it crosses town, and the town crosses it, through its passengers. It's above all a metaphor of the human destiny, the incredible ephemeral of our lives.')

The tramway/train metaphor registers elsewhere in Alain Tanner's film *La Salamandre*, Claire Denis's last film *35 Rhums* (2009), and Khaled Ghorbal's *Un si beau voyage* (2008), as well as the earlier and now classical film *Un soir, un train* (1968) by Belgian filmmaker André Delvaux, not to mention *Europa* (1991), a Danish film by Lars Von Trier. Jean-Claude Guiguet's *Les Passagers/The Passengers* (1999) works as a choral film. The genre mixes multiple stories and different people that cross each other, yet few of them meet; they are bound by the same movement (here, the tramway line) or different locations in our global world. In choral films, the collective is more important than the personal. Sometimes characters meet, and are found at the same place (and time); often they never meet. Jacques Mandelbaum penned a working definition of the choral film,

> Etymologiquement, c'est un genre qui emprunte sa définition à la forme musicale du chœur. Cinématographiquement, c'est une œuvre qui se distingue par deux caractéristiques majeures : la transformation de la plupart des protagonistes en personnages principaux, la nécessité de faire se croiser leurs destins selon un plan préétabli (Mandelbaum).[28] ('By definition, the genre borrows from the musical form of the chorus. Cinematographically speaking, it is a work that is distinguished by two major forms: the transformation of most of its protagonists into main characters, the necessity to intersect their destinies according to a pre-established plan.')

Examples of choral films include Robert Altman's *Short Cuts* (1993), Alejandro González Iñárritu's *21 Grams* (2003), and Cédric Klapisch's *L'Auberge espagnole* (2003) and *Paris* (2008).

The vector of the tramway is the perfect place for encounters between multiple characters and their inner thoughts on their way to their work place, their apartment, or their favorite haunts. Guiguet's community of passengers shares the newly built tramway route, which circulates in the suburbs north of Paris around St-Denis and Bobigny and connects people to their jobs or to possible intimate encounters. Its cartography maps out figures on the metro plan and is tied to real places and people. Much of the film can be read from the view of cinema and the city, and the way people embrace the everyday. The trip is located in a *non-lieu* (a non-place), an interstitial location in between towns, or on their margins, here somewhere near Paris and its suburbs.

The film is born of Guiguet's desire for *vagabondage* in view of his other preoccupations (Guiguet).[29] Guiguet took the tramway several times to scout for locations, and observed the different topographies traversed by high rises, fields of ruins, churches, and cemeteries, suggesting that 'the script was born of this trip'.[30] Resorting occasionally to cinema-vérité techniques, yet amidst the crowd of passengers, several actors stand out who have made a name in the film world: Bruno Putzulu, Fabienne Babe, Véronique Silver, and Stéphane Rideau.[31]

Les Passagers screams about life and death, work, and social structures, as well as communication and the lack of it. A female narrator's voiceover and physical presence (Véronique Silver) run through the film; she comments on the state of things and on people whose lives she imagines. The woman whom Guiguet designates as a spectator and guide[32] (played by Silver) is one of the passengers; she looks at the camera, in a direct (forbidden) gaze,[33]

Je ne suis pas une cliente ... je ne suis qu'une voyageuse et j'entends le rester le plus longtemps possible. ('I'm not a customer ... I'm just a traveler, and I intend to remain one for as long as possible.')

Many times the poetic converges on the 'politique' (Liandrat-Guigues 161). The traveling narrator is in charge of a hospital. In the automatic tramway, the camera often slips into the position of the absent train conductor, enabling the spectator to directly absorb the urban landscape passing by. Tracks and road lines are embedded in the opening panorama shots as the electric tram moves silently along its route. Each tram stop is announced by a recorded voice on a loudspeaker. On top of the tramway circulation, a flow of desire circulates en route. Susanne Liandrat-Guigues observes a double movement at play between the female character's trajectory and that of the tramway and its passengers (155). The drama plays out once the passengers have stepped out and are on the ground. A young man (Stéphane Rideau) follows a man he spotted on board (Bruno Putzulu) to his place; they become lovers. Another young male passenger connects with a young female nurse and they fall in love with one another, against the urban setting, which they contemplate from the bay window, naked. Another passenger takes a stand against homosexuality and vents his discontent at sexual labeling, only to be discovered as a homosexual. Another one avows his desire to find and marry a woman who has perfect feet.

The film waxes lyrical at different intervals and closes with the narrator's salute to the dead, an homage to Arthur Rimbaud's poem *Le dormeur du val*, now lying at peace in the dark cemetery that opens and closes the film: 'bonsoir mes dormeurs' ('goodnight sleepers'). The cemetery is a central motif and location; the script inserts a segment of a man dying of AIDS at the hospital, visited by his lover. Guiguet openly addresses the issue of AIDS: 'le système pulmonaire de la planète est malade' ('The pulmonary system of the planet is sick'). The resting grounds are found bordering the tramway line, a stone's throw away from the tracks.

Death or mortality haunts the narrative, yet Guiguet presses on to other topics and issues intersecting the lives of people, all of whom are rather eclectic yet ordinary. The script combines the circulation between the dead and the living, between those who are present and no longer are, with the understanding that the dead are very much present whereas the living are very much dead.[34] Yet these issues surface at the end of the last millennium and start of the one just beginning: anxieties condemn rising unemployment, layoffs, the spectre of an environmentally sick planet, decaying urban spaces, and the absence of communication or contact between people in a world that Guiguet perceives as 'dead'. 'People no longer look at each other' (Guiguet), imprisoned by their Walkman, cell phones, or other technology, now replaced by iPods and iPhones. The core concern touches on the collective since all lives are affected by the communication crisis and draws on individual fears: a woman speaks to her dead husband by his tomb alongside to the young man who visits his now buried lover. Many of the passengers voice their intimate thoughts.

The film blends the various threads that tie these ordinary people's circumstances. Desire and love are the glue that holds them together. The people who will be 'saved' according to Guiguet's vision are those who can still touch each other, look at each other, listen to each other, or help each other – possibly grounding the emphasis on nurses (healers) and hospital administrators throughout the film and the permanence of desire as a guiding thread.

The musical choices add to the lyrical and popular dimension of the narrative. The song of unity *'Y'a tant d'amour sur toute la terre'* ('There's so much love on earth') interpreted by Patachou is diegetically inscribed en route when two youths take up the song in unison. The classical music concert attended by the newly formed couple invokes a hymn to the dead. Other pieces include Bach's Cantata no. 170, or Couperin's *Troisième leçon de ténèbres* (Tenebrae Readings for Holiday Wednesdays 1714), a Baroque piece written for Holy Week that combines a choir of two voices and a harpsichord and best evokes the conflicted sentiments of agony and ecstasy at once.[35]

Many cinematographic references punctuate the film; the most eloquent one pays homage to Jean Vigo's *L'Atalante* (1934). When the math teacher (Putzulu) bicycles along a canal with a friend, after a brief discussion and scathing critique of *Les nuits fauves* (Cyril Collard 1992), he reminds his friend that they are bicycling in the natural setting of *L'Atalante*: 'tu reconnais le décor de *l'Atalante*' ('You recognize the set of *L'Atalante*'). The sequence appropriately closes with an unexpected aerial view of the river and town, poignantly shot over Léo Ferré's rendition of a Baudelaire poem *Spleen*. One effectively recalls Vigo's *L'Atalante* and its last aerial sequence of the glistening barge moving on the river. That shot is a poignant reminder of the final stages of Vigo, unable to finish the film as he was dying of tuberculosis, and which instead, was shot by his editor Louis Chavance.[36] This echo resonates in view of what was to be Guiguet's final film.

The eclectic soundtrack ranges from popular to poetic music, including Patachou and Léo Ferré, and then moves up to higher spheres with sacred and classical music by Ludwig van Beethoven (9th symphony), Haydn (93rd symphony), Tchaikovsky (*Swan Lake*) and the Baroque-era composer Couperin. The credit sequence and opening segment juxtapose at least three or four of the dominant musical themes of the film. In the last segment, voices and people stage litanies in dramatic fashion discussing society's ailments. Léo Ferré's voice closes with Baudelaire's lament *Spleen,*

> Quand le ciel bas et lourd pèse comme un couvercle
> Sur l'esprit gémissant en proie aux longs ennuis,
> Et que de l'horizon embrassant tout le cercle
> Il nous verse un jour noir plus triste que les nuits
> Quand la terre est changée en un cachot humide,
> Où l'Espérance, comme une chauve-souris,
> S'en va battant les murs de son aile timide
> Et se cognant la tête à des plafonds pourris;
> Quand la pluie étalant ses immenses traînées
> D'une vaste prison imite les barreaux,
> Et qu'un peuple muet d'infâmes araignées
> Vient tendre ses filets au fond de nos cerveaux...
> (When the low, heavy sky weighs like a lid
> On the groaning spirit, victim of long ennui,
> And from the all-encircling horizon
> Spreads over us a day gloomier than the night;
> When the earth is changed into a humid dungeon,
> In which Hope like a bat
> Goes beating the walls with her timid wings
> And knocking her head against the rotten ceiling;

> When the rain stretching out its endess train
> Imitates the bars of a vast prison
> And a silent horde of loathsome spiders
> Comes to spin their webs in the depths of our brains ...)
> (Baudelaire)[37]

These incantatory lines play as the camera ascends along a snow-covered mountain slope, echoing Vigo's aerial closing shot of *L'Atalante*. The tramway symbolically flies away and takes off with a cable-car view of the mountain performing an ascending (and aerial) movement, before returning to a nighttime view of the dark cemetery, revisited one last time by the tram's passage before fading to black, marking the end of the line, or the film, or life.

4
The Return or the Nostoï

'The Return or the Nostoï' addresses going home – or a return to the country – in contemporary French films that focus on the Maghreb and near East regions; however the term can apply to other locations. The term *'nostoï'* draws from *Ulysses* and Vladimir Jankélévich's reflections on nostalgia. In negotiating a return home, films tackle the situation of exile, the location and meaning of 'home', and displacement. In so doing, history and identity are reexamined along North-South lines. Rabah Ameur-Zaïmeche, Ismaël Ferroukhi, Tony Gatlif, and François Dupeyron adopt this figure in their respective films: *Bled Number One* (2006), *Le Grand Voyage* (2004), *Exils* (2004), and *Mr. Ibrahim* (2003). All four films, which stem from different perspectives, share the return motif, configuring a North-South trajectory and a masculine outlook on homecoming.

The majority of the films discussed belong to what Hamid Naficy defines as 'accented cinema', whose subject matter involves journeying, displacement, and identity (4). Each director imparts an auteurist approach to the subject of displacement and identity, proposing his own version of a North-South migration script that unravels memories of a colonial past, the war, and independence, as well as immigration and diaspora. They negotiate a cathartic approach in which the young male (rarely female) protagonist learns after an unusually painful trajectory and is ultimately reconciled with the past and therefore the present.

Each inverts the classical South-North migration movement for the North-South return to the home country. Their open-ended scenarios lead to a critical reinterpretation. While this chapter explores some of the personal traits, it teases out the shared elements in the narratives. Many of them, scripted by male filmmakers (and scriptwriters) involve an all-male scenario grounded in the experience of a young man, the child of immigrants who finds himself displaced and forsakes his familiar grounds for uncharted territories. The developments of these stories run parallel with each other and echo the preoccupations of the protagonists. Many conclude on an open and hopeful note even if their protagonist undergoes a series of trials. Plots situated mostly in the present engage the colonial past and memory related to the time of the parents' migration north and reconcile past and present. If the South-North migration route is visually and physically absent from these scripts, it haunts the protagonists in their southward journey. While the path traveled resembles that taken by a tourist, it goes one step further to include the figure of a traveler-pilgrim whose ultimate destination and return home is pivotal. Traces of the past, remembrances, memories, and scars all combine to create a cathartic experience. The colonial heritage lies at the juncture of such postcolonial return scenarios. The Southern routes suggest multiple sensory experiences to the spectator and critic. The spectator turned traveler negotiates unfamiliar landscapes and borders through space and time.

Homecoming implies leaving France, 'the center' in a reverse movement of the classical migration pattern that tends to show a northbound movement. 'Self-discovery through a complex and sometimes arduous search for an Absolute Other is a basic theme of our civilization, a theme supposing an enormous literature' (MacCannell 5). Unlike a classical travel narrative where the traveler is bound to discover the other and seeks an elsewhere, the script rooted in the socio-economic constraints of migration reverses its structure and privileges the return 'home', like Ulysses in Homer's epic travel poem. An analysis of four films that best exemplify this movement follows: *Bled Number One* (Rabah Ameur-Zaïmeche 2006), *Monsieur Ibrahim et les fleurs du Coran/Monsieur Ibrahim* (François Dupeyron 2003), *Le Grand voyage* (Ismaël Ferroukhi 2004), and *Exils/Exiles* (Tony Gatlif 2004). I leave out *La Fille de Keltoum/Keltoum's Daughter* (Mehdi Charef 2001), which I include in Chapter 6.

Some film critics view the films as very apolitical, mostly preoccupied with aesthetic qualities, yet other readings contradict this assertion. In fact, many of the films 'reflect part of the socio-political reality of France: racism, unemployment, drugs, the distressing conditions of the HLMs and suburbs of Arab inhabitants' (Hayward 288). They reproduce a male-dominated world and are spearheaded by male filmmakers and focus on a diversity of themes and genres. Among them are the topic of the journey; interracial relationships; the exploration of one's sexual identity, as was done with the transvestite character in *Miss Mona* (Mehdi Charef 1987), or the character of Felix played by

Sami Bouajila in *Drôle de Félix/The Adventures of Felix* (Olivier Ducastel and Jacques Martineau 2001); science fiction; comedies; and historical films, to name a few. Escaping stereotypes and labels has become an arduous road; Zaïda Ghorab-Volta's difficult trajectory (examined in Chapter 6) steps outside of the mold. 'Majority' filmmakers conversely appropriate some of these concerns for the colonial and postcolonial past and present and integrate them in their scripts, such as for instance Austrian-born director Michael Haneke's *Caché/Hidden* (Haneke 2005). The film blends middle-class French white guilt over the Algerian colonial conflict along with revenge and voyeurism. *Chaos* (Coline Serreau 2001) is a key example of a critique of everyday racism and sexism in France. The earlier narrative *Chocolat/Chocolate* (Claire Denis 1988) moves between the 'worlds of the colonized and colonizer' (Hottell 220) and reassesses the weight of the colonial past in its gaze back to a former French colony in West Africa. In *L'autre côté de la mer/The Other Shore* (1997) Dominique Cabrera imparts a double movement to her narrative, involving a French *pied-noir*, Georges Montero (Pierre Brasseur), the owner of an olive oil company, who stayed in Algeria and returns to France for medical reasons. Montero opts to return 'home' at a moment when 'a civil war' starts. He befriends his surgeon, a young '*beur*' Tarek (Roshdy Zem) who has cut off all ties to his Algerian roots. The term '*beur*' 'signifies Algerians and North Africans of Arab origin that were born or bred in France and has been widely adopted in criticism for the past thirty years'. The two shores of the Mediterranean Sea epitomize the strong emotional links maintained by pied-noirs and Algerians abroad with the mother country. As Catherine Portuges relates in her article on transnational cinema and women directors, 'the other shore of the title can, of course, depending on one's perspective, be either Algeria or France' (56). Montero suffers from 'blurred vision' and represents the colonial past (57).

The transnational films under focus traverse European borders, crossing over the sea for the Maghreb or the Near East (Turkey). If northbound movements are implied they are never shown. For instance, *Le Thé au Harem d'Archimède/Tea in the Harem* (Mehdi Charef 1985) adapted from his novel and *Le Gone du Chaâba/The Kid from Chaâba* (Christophe Ruggia 1998) based on Azouz Begag's 1986 autobiographical and eponymous novel do not explicitly illustrate the migration trip north yet build on the condition of immigrants once they arrive and settle in France. Charef's *La Fille de Keltoum* (2001) is a quest for one's mother that reverses male-oriented fictions and pursues the North South passage. *Depuis qu'Otar est parti/Since Otar left* (Julie Bertucelli 2003) displays an East-West migration from Tbilisi (Georgia) to Paris, imagined from the point of view of those left behind in Tbilisi, a family of three generations of women. The focus is on the three women who stayed behind and who eventually decide to visit France, viewed as the promise land for work opportunities and hope. The only male member of the family, the son, has moved abroad for illegal work in building construction. The family remains in touch with him through an epistolary relation. He is absent yet virtually present throughout the film and the family lives suspended in expectation of his letters.

In order to concentrate on the North-South paradigm, I leave out eastbound fictions although they gesture a parallel displacement to and from the home country as evoked by Pierre Rissient's *Cinq et la Peau/ Five and the Skin* (1982), a sensual trip in Manila (Philippines), or Lam Lê for a transposed Vietnam (through Java) in *20 nuits et un jour de pluie* (Lê 2006), or Rithy Panh for Cambodia in some of his fiction as well as documentary films. *Un Barrage contre le Pacifique/The Seawall* (Panh 2008), a new adaptation of Marguerite Duras's 1950 novel, sets out a good example of a geographical return eastward to colonial times. These constitute a larger pool of films such as *La Fille de Keltoum/The Daughter of Keltoum* (Charef 2001) or *Drôle de Félix* (Ducastel & Martineau 2001). In *Le Grand voyage* (Ferroukhi 2004), instead of returning home, supposing that they are recent immigrants, the protagonists, a father and son of French-Moroccan origins, take a voyage to Mecca,[1] the locus of a desired return for Muslims as about two million of them make the trip every year.

In their respective returns, which involve an implied departure, the directors and/or scriptwriters bring to the fore issues of colonialism, post colonialism, integration, deterritorialization, and illegality. Characters are uprooted in search of a new way of life. With one exception, *Monsieur Ibrahim* (Dupeyron 2003), the films examined here bear the label of '*beur* cinema', as established by Carrie Tarr and/or Hamid Naficy. Created in the 1980s under a literary genre identified at first by Alec Hargreaves and Michel Laronde, *beur* cinema as a category has been debatable and is 'neither stable nor universally accepted' (Rosello in Naficy 99). However, it is perceived as a realist, narrative, commercial, and popular cinema in France as well as a fundamentally male cinema (Naficy 98). The expression 'second generation' filmmakers is also used.

Three tropes operate in these films: 1) the trope of the traveler as economic migrant, 2) the trope of the tourist–traveler, and 3) the trope of traveler as pilgrim bound toward some form of enlightenment and healing of past wounds: past wounds are tied to the personal, the historical, the past and the present. Only two of these tropes will matter here as none of the films fits in the category of the traveler as tourist. (If Gatlif intermittently relies on the traveler-tourist, the figure soon transforms into a pilgrim as I explain further.) The more pressing issue of forced displacement and forced returns emerges recently with deportation of persons to the land of their parents. *Bled Number One/Back Home* (Ameur-Zaïmeche 2006) is such a narrative.

Filming the Bled. Nostalgia for the country in Diasporic cinema

Rabah Ameur-Zaïmeche was born in Algeria in 1966, and moved to France when he was two years old; he is self-taught, acts the central role in his films (or plays himself, as he says) while casting his entire family as active participants in all his ventures. *Bled Number One* (2006), his second feature-length film, chronicles Kamel's forced expatriation from France back to his country of origin, Algeria, after a stay in a French prison. The film is part of a trilogy that includes his earlier *banlieue* film *Wesh Wesh, qu'est-ce qui se passe?* (2001) and closes with *Dernier Maquis* (2008), a chronicle of migrant workers in a factory on the outskirts of Paris. In *Wesh Wesh, qu'est-ce qui se passe?* a young man clandestinely returns home to the cité (a housing project) of Montfermeil, in the sub- urbs of Paris, after spending time in jail. In retrospect, *Bled Number One* happens chronologically prior to *Wesh Wesh*. The second film moves away from the suburbs and crosses over to Algeria. A transformation occurs in *Bled Number One* alongside the exiled (male) character (Ameur- Zaïmeche), a female protagonist, Louisa (Meriem Serbah), a singer, who is also going home to her parents with her child, escaping her husband. *Bled Number One* refers to the country of origin whose 'ground is vital'.[2] *Bled*, a familiar term in French language, comes from the Arabic *bilad* signifying the 'terrain', country, or homeland. We come across the term in Jean Renoir's 1929 colonial film *Le Bled*, an early silent film, located in Algeria.

Bled Number One exposes the 'disarray' (Ameur-Zaïmeche's term) of Algerian people in the Diaspora, where men and women are torn between their parents' home, (Algeria), and their adopted home (France, or the *cité*), although the location should be perceived as timeless:

We wanted to depict the Algeria of 10,000 years ago and of today without being stuck in the present. My ambition was to return to ancient times. At the same time, I paid much attention to what I could say about Algeria because it is a country that – to tell the truth – I know very little about and that I don't want to judge (Ameur-Zaïmeche).[3]

Bled Number One builds a compelling nostalgic feeling for the country, and at times, borrows from documentary filmmaking techniques to reveal an unusual facet of contemporary Algerian society in a predominantly rural area, in the northeast corner of Algeria. On that level, it is an accomplished and luminous film. Although it is not a recognized genre, it fits in the category of the 'forced' return film or coming home narrative. Carrie Tarr sees this kind of film as being made possible after the end of the Algerian civil war (Tarr 292).[4] It belongs to wandering and exilic films, or espouses Naficy's call for an accented cinema, 'a cinema of displacement made by people from the diasporic community, of and about displaced subjects, somewhat distinct from third cinema in its less oppositional stance' (30).[5]

My study of *Bled Number One* is attentive to the way the exilic filmmaker problematizes the notion of 'place', and plays out the relationship with the 'homeland' while laterally exploring the bonds between Algeria and its diasporic communities inclusive of women. It is a voyage through time and space, in which time is suspended (Frodon). It ultimately questions the place of independent women within Algerian society. Both the protagonists Kamel and Louisa are located in an in-between place, an interstice where they physically and psychically do not belong. The script emphasizes that impossible location.

'My style borders on ethnographic filmmaking.'[6] The cinematography deploys characteristic extreme long shots, sequences cut by fades to black and some slow fades-to-black at crucial moments of tension and despair; such devices are normally used to establish a temporal division between two narrative sequences. In addition to long shots, the cinematographer uses the zoom: both techniques remove the spectator from the story, and according to Will Higbee force the spectator to observe the *bled* from a position of detachment 'through a distancing technique.'[7]

Algeria and most specifically the *bled* and its surroundings are shot like a Western.[8] Home has a location: the *bled*, a small area, here the rather small town of Loulouj. The 'Western' components are reinforced in part by the use of an electric solo guitar by Rodolphe Burger, over the uncanny inclusion of a William Blake poem: 'The Little Vagabond' – a poem that refers to church (organized religion) and the ale-house (café), two opposites, expanding the nomadic aspect. Several factions compose the town: the villagers, called the 'patriots', take it upon themselves to defend their village against the arrival of young Islamic outsiders/insiders who pretend to establish the law and threaten and humiliate the village's inhabitants. The credits refer to the group as the 'desperados'. The script inserts not so slightly veiled references to terrorists and Islamists. The opening of the film begins with a traveling shot, from the potential perspective of a passenger on board of a taxi, presumably Kamel. However, for the first few shots, the point of view is elevated, on what may be a truck, and has a rather dominant perspective of the streets and inhabitants as they casually go about their business.

Women

A French expatriate of Algerian descent, Kamel drifts between two worlds, Algeria of his roots, and France or the notion of freedom and equality for women, which is never verbalized, but is captured in each frame, at two different instances.

First, the ceremony of the Zerda reconstructs an ancestral tradition of sacrificing a bull in the fields to honor God before harvest. The blessed meat is distributed among the male villagers who gather to collect their share. The ceremony is entirely male, including male children. Kamel steps away in order to join the women's procession as they arrive with food and utensils in another frame and space; from a left angle, at first off camera, women enter the field carrying heavy platters on their head, escorted by young girls. Kamel bridges the worlds separating genders; women who live in the *bled* are absent from the streets and cafes, which is visibly determined as a men's world. They are found on rooftops, or in the kitchens once the camera makes its way inside the walls.

Second, Louisa, Kamel's cousin, arrives at about the same time back in town. She finds refuge at her mother's and brother's place. They do not know the reasons for her return. Once they do, the brother becomes physically and verbally abusive, and locks her up. She escapes the 'dungeon' where she is imprisoned and walks out once on the streets at night; the streets are peopled by young men, who mock her as 'crazy'. The spatial configuration places women in an '*hors-champ*' (off-screen). This pattern runs in other recent Franco-Maghrebian films; an example is found in *Française*, directed by Moroccan director Souad El-Bouhati (2008), where the main protagonist, a young woman born in France, returns 'home' to Morocco with her parents and subsequently escapes her dorm and walks at night in the dangerous streets of a city.

Around the time of the Zerda performed in real time, a message is handed to Kamel to stay with the men, and not eat with the women: 'Tu ne peux pas toujours manger avec les femmes, tu manges avec les hommes' ('You cannot always eat with the women. You eat with the men'). From that point on, his name change to *Kamel la France* splits him from the rest of the inhabitants and marks him as different. As the film progresses, Kamel clashes with the villagers who are trying to impose a lifestyle onto him. He sides with Louisa, against the patriarchal order. Incidentally, the tensions between Kamel and his relatives explode when the villagers organize themselves and take control of their village endangered by the group of Islamists after a series of humiliating episodes.

The place

A cineaste whose origins are in the migration from Algeria to France (or *'cinéaste issu de l'immigration'*), a 'migration director' as French critics commonly designate such directors, returns to Algeria, to his native Eastern province and the village of Loulouj. Quite paradoxically, the director claims that the film opts to film Algeria and his roots in order to discuss the urban condition of Algerians in the diaspora.

Si, dans *Bled number one,* nous retournons dans le pays d'origine, c'est quand même pour évoquer le désarroi d'une grande partie de la diaspora algérienne dans les grands ensembles urbains (Ameur-Zaimèche).[9] ('If in *Bled number one*, we return to the country of origin, it is to evoke the disarray of a large part of the Algerian diaspora in urban housing estates.')

Kamel endures 'a double-penalty' which results in prison and expulsion from France. He does not have the choice to return to France, nor the required papers to travel. Panoramic shots of the hills, the adjacent slopes, and the river help situate the (rural) place. When the guitar solo accompanies Kamel's spleen, the camera in a characteristic long shot faces a panoramic view of a river and lake-like formation, with the sight of hills/mountains in an extreme depth of field. The camera is (dis) placed outside of the village on different occasions, hinting at a possible escape or get-away route. The guitar intrudes twice in the narrative, and each time at a moment of extreme tension experienced by Kamel or Louisa. Each sequence foregrounding Kamel, with the musician and his sound equipment inserted in the shot, functions as a reminder of the filmic apparatus, a distancing act for the spectator.

The film leaves the *bled* on different separate occasions, which I will detail next, but inevitably returns to it, and when not in the *bled* the film is situated in an asylum. At first, Louisa leaves with Ahmed, her husband – and her son – to return home, to the city. However, her husband abandons her by the roadside in the middle of the countryside; she walks back at night to her parents' village, where she is unwelcome.

Louisa, in her second departure, heads back towards her husband's house in Constantine by taxi, only to be kicked out once more and told to leave by an unseen woman. This signals her repudiation, although it is never verbalized. Desperate, she attempts to commit suicide on the bridge and is subsequently rescued and sent to the psychiatric ward.

The third instance – a trip to the coast at Cap Bougaroun – is part of the healing process she has to undergo in order not to become sick. The village healer, the Taleb, prescribes this treatment. Kamel accompanies Louisa along with two other women (Figure 4.1). The camera captures two half-sunk rusty ferryboats, denoting earlier (colonial) displacements and sea voyages between France and Algeria, or between North and South. The image of the boat is featured on the film poster.

The film concludes in the psychiatric hospital of Constantine, one of Algeria's largest cities after Oran and Algiers, 80 km away from the

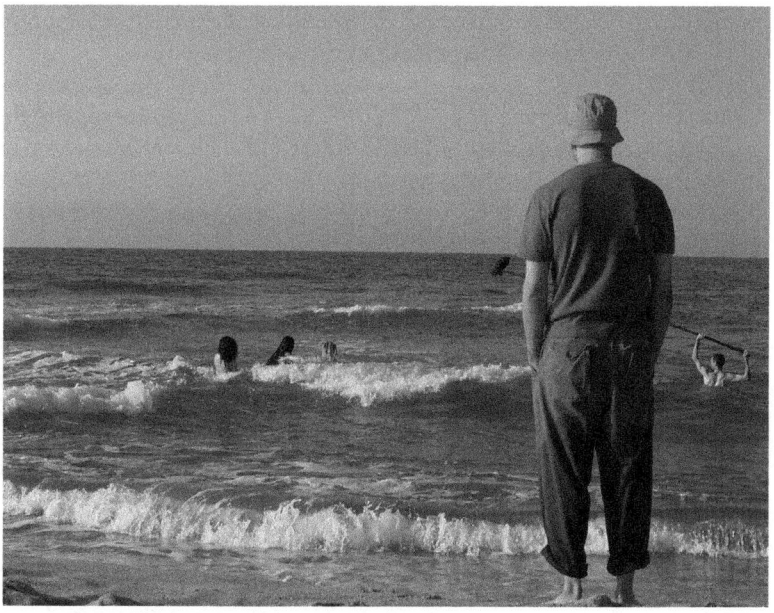

Figure 4.1   Rabah Ameur-Zaïmeche. *Bled Number One*
Note: 'The trip to the coast is part of the healing process.'
Source: Sarrazink Productions.

coast. The city is situated on a plateau with a deep ravine; it is somewhat picturesque, especially with the viaduct crossing the ravine. It is on this same viaduct that Louisa tries to end her life. The city was demolished by the French – almost 500,000 people were killed during the colonization; it was the capital of Numidia, a Berber empire that emerged in the 3rd century BC. The area has been the site of many invasions and occupations by foreign nations. Paradoxically, it is within the psychiatric asylum that Louisa finds a refuge and protection from the outside world, and is able to share her vision and desire to sing with the main female psychiatrist, played by a Constantine doctor herself.

In the last part, parallel to Louisa's incarceration, Kamel, unwelcome, powerless and sickened by the villagers' attitude, considers leaving for Tunisia stating that he will become insane if he stays any longer. The distance to Tunisia (360 km away) implies illegal border crossing since he has no passport or visa.

Outside/inside

The remainder of the film stays within the confines of the village, in the fields, mosque, and cemetery, where villagers practice the Zerda, a pre-Islamic ritual (the killing of a bull) discussed previously, and attend to their fields. Roadblocks are set up in order to organize against the 'terrorists'. The patriots come together to evict any undesirable elements from within and without and to defend their village. However, in their zeal, and growing anger against the 'desperados', they make the collective patriotic decision to dispose of Kamel since he resists their treatment of Louisa. Suddenly he has become on par with one of the Islamic outside elements, a 'bandit' from France, a thug threatening the village order. Once the villagers are back in control of their village, the bandits disappear and Kamel becomes a perfect target for the renewed local policing efforts. His past in France (jail time) suddenly threatens the internal order: 'il faut défendre le pays' ('one must defend the country') is the excuse given prior to organizing road blocks. Bouzid (the cousin) decides to handle Louisa, his sister; he beats her up because she has humiliated the entire family when she left her husband, who then repudiates her and takes the child away. The question of control is raised: who decides how to rule the village? Control is displaced at the cost of getting rid of the other, the brother/cousin/sister and their collective decision shapes itself around the expulsion of foreign diasporic bodies (Louisa/Kamel). Louisa, although not part of the diaspora, is an outsider since she lives in the city, and as a modern woman is treated as a pariah, next to Kamel, a returned child of the second generation.

Danger zones

A sense of impending doom and violence runs through the film despite its carefully arranged landscape shots, and bucolic imagery. The *bled* is a place where sheep can walk freely onto the streets of the village, but it is also the place where a bull can be ritually sacrificed, and a man almost killed like a bull with his throat slit (this happens to Bouzid). Humiliation is displaced from Bouzid, whose masculinity is threatened by 'terrorists' and beaten, onto Louisa, who is twice victimized and who, instead of finding protection with her family, finds yet another humiliation at the hands of her brother. The male villagers can only detect a pathology in Louisa's (marital) problems; the Taleb (medicine man) prescribes a cure that consists in going to the seaside and bathing in seawater, and running several times around the rural mosque. Louisa obediently complies each time; however, the end cure is internment, away from the village.

Music and time

Time is rather elastic. Intercut by several fades, it is easy to identify night and day, yet clear temporal markers are avoided. Several days elapse between two separate significant moments: the arrival of Kamel, then Louisa's and their expulsion. But how many days do elapse? Rodolphe Burger's blues solo (considered by some to be the French equivalent of Lou Reed) comes out like an improvised performance within the film.[10] Ameur-Zaïmeche uses him in a mode that breaks with the temporal film cycle, and constitutes a pause within the film and its mood.

Several musical moments include the last sequence at the psychiatric hospital in a party organized by the patients, where Louisa is finally able to show case her talent and perform a Billie Holliday song in English: 'Hush now, don't explain.' The mostly female patients who are playing themselves are quietly crying during the performance. Music works in synchronicity with the main character's melancholia; Kamel's feelings of estrangement, displacement, and growing frustration with the overall *bled* yet love for his native country are paired with Louisa's inability to lead a normal life that would combine raising her son and singing. Music erupts, especially in the finale when emotions culminate: her inability to get her son back, her unfulfilled desire to become a singer, and Kamel's ostracization, not to mention the unspoken love between the two pariahs. The sequences are edited in parallel montage with each other in order to establish the link between both characters constructed

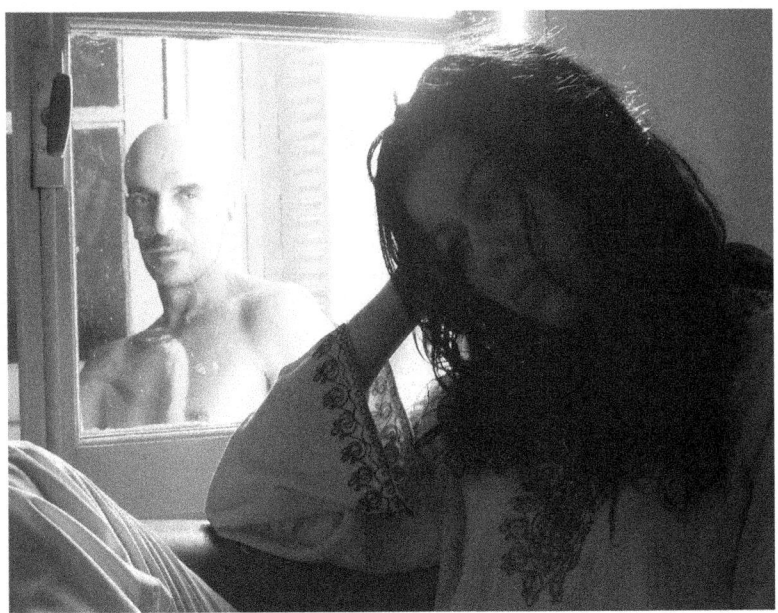

Figure 4.2 Rabah Ameur-Zaïmeche, *Bled Number One*
Note: '*Bled Number One* is an impossible love story.'
Source: Sarrazink Productions.

as an impossible couple (of outsiders). In many ways, *Bled Number One* is an impossible love-story (Figure 4.2).

Outsiders-the threshold

Kamel is constantly shot outdoors: on the road, in the fields, at the beach, and at the Zerda. Never once do we see him inside his room with his relatives, or within the café. He is distinctly outside, on a terrace, on doorways, or thresholds, bridging both worlds of men and women. The villagers plan to 'reeducate' him immediately after the argument he has with his cousin Bouzid. He is powerless to intervene on Louisa's behalf. Louisa, on the other hand, is only allowed to perform at the psychiatric hospital, her refuge from society. The final scene strongly states that madness reigns outside of their walls, in Algeria: 'les fous sont dehors' ('The mad ones are outside').

The director does not explain, but suggests visually and aurally. The structure placing the last segment in a real asylum peopled with mostly women argues in favor of this group, for some have been victimized and abused. The two outsiders cross paths; their feelings for each other are not permitted. They are chased away from the village in two opposite directions. Their paths never cross within the *bled*, but outside of it. In conclusion, madness would occur for Kamel had he decided to stay within the village, just as it presumably does for Louisa. They are both evicted from the place of origin where they are no longer welcome.

The films selected in this chapter illustrate the state of French society in the late 1990s and at the beginning of the 21st century, not so much in terms of what they document as much as in terms of the magnifying lens they apply to France's policies of exclusion, expulsion of illegal immigrants and sometimes its national citizens, its avowed new claims of a *'politique de l'immigration choisie'* ('the policies of selective immigration'), and its use of quotas.

Travel narratives work at reconciling different cultures and histories as well as generations. Linguistic barriers are commonplace and the protagonist struggles to understand a language from which he/she has been estranged, such as the language of the parents or ancestors. The films rely on music, a mode of communication that is non-verbal, as a major healing component within the narrative. Traveling encompasses the cathartic experience and redefines the location of home and identity. It follows the way travelers negotiate the process of displacement in the 21st century, going against the notion of speed that has been brandished in the 20th century, especially after the advent of the industrial age in the 19th century. These narratives reflect on the identity of the filmmakers, although identity is not fixed. Gatlif, whose films constitute a personal trajectory of a return to Algeria and his Berbero-Gypsy Algerian roots, exemplifies an identity in flux over several decades of filmmaking.

The return exemplified in these films reenacts the *nostoï*, a long poem telling of the return of heroes after the Trojan War in ancient Greek mythology. In the films examined, the protagonists belong to the postmodern and postcolonial global world and are not heroic; instead their characters are questionable and the return painful and joyless. Many of these films venture into the colonial past and its repercussions onto the present, constituting a breach in Franco-French fiction cinema that reluctantly opened itself to the colonial past as well as to migratory movements in the 1970s. In 2006, a (fiction) film tackled the neglected history of North-African soldiers enlisted in the French army in World War II and fighting alongside Allied forces with *Indigènes/Days of Glory* (Rachid Bouchareb 2006). Much earlier, Sembène Ousmane explored the fate of West-African soldiers at the hands of the French army at the outcome of World War II, interned in a Senegalese camp in *Camp de Thiaroye/The Camp at Thiaroye* (Sembène Ousmane 1987). Because of its controversial nature, the French government/institutions banned it from any public release for the next twenty years.

The past may be situated elsewhere or within the hexagon, in what constitutes 'the contact zone', which according to Dinah Sherzer 'is now in France itself and immigration, the presence of the Other on French soil, has polarized the country' (8). Sherzer dates the opening back to the 70s:

> Immediately and for several years after decolonization (1962–1975), a reluctance set in that prevented directors from looking outside French borders. Only since the mid-1970s has France dared to examine its colonial past (2–3).

At about the same time, directors of the majority population and of the Diaspora were willing to venture outside the French borders and investigate countries of origin as well as countries of migration.

Monsieur Ibrahim and the journey

Monsieur Ibrahim (2003) traces the fate of Turkish immigrants in a Western country in a move back to the country of origins. Dupeyron adapts Eric-Emmanuel Schmitt's play *Monsieur Ibrahim et les fleurs du Coran/Monsieur Ibrahim and the Flowers of the Koran* (1999). The play is shaped as a monologue recited by someone who remembers. [11]

The film results from an encounter between Schmitt and Dupeyron, who directed widely different films such as *La Chambre des officiers/Officers' Ward* (2001), *Inguélézi* (2004; studied in Chapter 5), and more recently *Mon âme par toi guérie* (2014). Momo recounts his sexual initiation at a precocious age, around the same time that he meets the wise man next door, the Arab grocer, Mr. Ibrahim. 'For Monsieur Ibrahim was considered a wise man. Maybe because for forty years he had been the Arab of the Jewish street' (Schmitt 11–12).[12] The plot centers on the relationship in 1960s Paris between an Arab grocer, a generic label given indiscriminately in France (just as it is given indiscriminately to the 'Chinese' for any Asian restaurant), to grocers of Arab origins and/or Muslim faith and a thirteen-year-old Jewish boy, Moïse (Moishe), renamed Momo. Momo is phonetically close to Mohammed, as the character Momo developed in Emile Ajar, the pseudonym for Romain Gary's novel *La vie devant soi/The life before us* (1975). Schmitt's style is loosely reminiscent of Ajar's that relates the love-story of Momo, a young abandoned Arab boy who is adopted by Madame Rosa, an older Jewish woman (and former prostitute) in charge of fostered children. She raises them in her safe Parisian Belleville apartment. *La vie devant soi* was adapted into a movie with Simone Signoret, *Madame Rosa* (Moshé Misrahi 1977). Much like *La Vie devant soi*, *Monsieur Ibrahim* alludes to a post-Holocaust trauma.[13] In Ajar's narrative, Mme Rosa attempts to protect Momo from his father, by forcing him to pass for a Jewish boy in an epic scene when he finally encounters his biological father.

Ibrahim exposes the position and meaning of 'Arab' in the context of French society in the 1960s: 'Arab, Momo, this means open from 8am until midnight, even on Sundays, in the grocery business' (Schmitt 14).[14] Fending for himself in a motherless household where the father is increasingly absent and later dies, the child is responsible for purchasing (sometimes stealing) and cooking his own food. Moïse's depressive father (Gilbert Melki) lives in the (fictive) memory of an older son, Popol, Momo's putative brother, who disappeared along with the mother who abandoned Moïse at birth. The father eventually commits suicide.

Ibrahim, the Muslim Turk storekeeper, spontaneously adopts Momo as his son and takes him to visit Le Croissant d'Or – his native Anatolia (Turkey). Turkish immigrants accounted for 8.6 per cent of migrants living in Europe in 1996, with the largest portion residing in Germany.[15] The grocer teaches his son how to enjoy life fully. His philosophy belongs to a larger Sufi dimension that suggests traveling as a mode of understanding and a mode of life. The scenario is the second installment of a trilogy titled *'De l'invisible'*, which Schmitt presents as a 'fable, a lesson of life, an initiatory voyage'.[16]

The trip itself

The Parisian neighborhood that Moïse never left is one where various immigration waves have taken place over time, in the popular neighborhood of the Faubourg Poissonnière tucked between the 10th and 9th arrondissements of Paris. The trip to Turkey opens Momo's senses and enables him to open up to and embrace cultural, religious, and racial others:

> In addition, on the drive to Turkey, it is what is smelled and heard that are crucial. Istanbul itself is met through its sounds and smells and tastes. Ibrahim blindfolds Moses when he enters places of worship in that city – Greek Orthodox, Catholic, and Muslim – so he smells them first, through the incense, the candles, and the shoes (Ruf).

Europe is constructed as a feminine entity in the original text. The film simulates the same sensory feelings and crosses different countries through a strangely borderless and free European cartography. Frontal shots of the road and of the arid and mountainous landscape of Anatolia abound in the very last part after Ibrahim has acquired his driver's license and hastily lowered the iron curtain of his store to leave Paris. From Paris to Istanbul and beyond, they avoid the more modernized highway system despised by Ibrahim. In the play, Momo, although under-age, drives in order to assist his father, but in the film, actor Omar Sharif plays a confident Ibrahim capable of driving his newly purchased American convertible car for the entire journey.[17] While Momo drives focused on the road, Ibrahim describes the landscapes they are traversing, rendering the journey less visual than auditory, sensory, and poetic: 'Europe, I did not see it – I heard it' (Schmitt 54).[18] Yet despite the distance traveled, the narrative does not feed on any exoticism that it otherwise contains intrinsically. It de-dramatizes the notion of geographic borders that are invisible to the spectator's eyes yet must have been omnipresent in the 1960s.

The seamless drive south on country roads parallels *Le Grand voyage* (2004) Ferroukhi's first feature-length film, with father and son heading toward the middle-east; the son Reda (Nicolas Cazalé) is enlisted to drive his ageing father (Mohamed Madj) intent on a pilgrimage to Mecca, after the older son is sent to jail for a minor offense. They cross Europe, starting off in Marseille and passing through Italy, former Yugoslavia, Bulgaria, Turkey, Syria, and Saudi Arabia. Borders and mileposts are present throughout. An old refurbished Peugeot miraculously makes the 3,000-mile journey. Reda, a high school student preparing for the Baccalaureate, is required to drive his older father on a once in a lifetime pilgrimage to Mecca. Tensions abound during the trip, where the two communicate in their own language; the father tosses his son's cellphone in a garbage can near Milan. He imposes his own rhythm and wants to take side roads, away from the interstate. 'Why drive so fast? Those who hurry are already dead' is his answer to Reda's question. They bypass some of the tourist markers that Reda longs to visit: Milan and Venice. He brought along a camera, and will take some pictures in Istanbul, at the Mosque. Ironically, the length of the trip lessens the distance between father and son, which partially results from a linguistic barrier, as the son is unable to understand classical Arabic; linguistics distances separating generations are also based on two different modes of thinking and lifestyle.

In many ways, the perception of speed, fast travel and constrained time is tested in what may seem as a provocation especially at the turn of the 21st century or in the diegetic film world of the 1960s dominated by the increase of car production and traffic. As projected in Tati's *Trafic* (see Chapter 7, Part 2), the traveler must release some of the restraints imposed by time (speed) in order to fully appreciate space and others. A new wisdom formulated by several philosophers at the end of the 20th century (Pierre Sansot for instance) applies to the films presented in this project. Cinema adopted what Gilles Deleuze has termed 'the ballad-form' in the second part of the 20th century, doing away more and more with action and speed for a deeper exploration of time and optical sensations as can be found in narratives by Wim Wenders, Michelangelo Antonioni, Chris Marker, Alain Resnais, and Yasujirō Ozu. By this, any references to popular Hollywood action-packed cinema and its imitations in other national cinemas are overlooked for a more artsy auteurist film-form. Deleuze interprets what he sees as the advent of new signs in this type of film and a cinema of '*voyant*' replacing action (Deleuze 18). The narratives under scrutiny are far from being avant-garde, yet they do not represent mainstream commercial French cinema either.

While driving east to Afghanistan in 1953–1954, the Swiss travel-writer Bouvier acknowledged the distinction and luxury offered by time; leaving Serbia for Macedonia, he commented in *L'Usage du monde/ The Way of the World:* 'We refuse ourselves all the luxuries except for the most precious one: slowness' (56).[19] Later on in his travelogue, Bouvier remarks on the different notions of Time he detects in Asia: 'Time in Asia flows larger than ours' (381).[20] The dialogue between father and son in *Le Grand voyage* echoes the relative importance of time, when Reda, the son, asks his father why he did not want to fly to Mecca:

– The son (Reda):	Why didn't you fly to Mecca? It's a lot simpler.
– The Father:	When the waters of the ocean rise to the heavens, they lose their bitterness to become pure again
– Reda:	What?
– The Father:	The ocean waters evaporate as they rise to the clouds. And as they evaporate they become fresh. That's why it's better to go on your pilgrimage on foot than on horseback, better on horseback than by car, better by car than by boat, better by boat than by plane.

The traveler that one becomes in these fictions (film, novels, plays) as spectator or reader, is invited to get a sense of the geography and the path traveled along the transformation of the self: 'Slowness ... is the secret for Happiness' (Schmitt 55).[21] Large panoramic shots and aerial views give a sense of the dimensions of the journey undertaken to Mecca, as well as the architecture of the places. Transformation occurs for Reda and the father en route: they both admit that they 'learned a lot' during the trip. The son starts to listen to his father, becomes more patient and asks him about the importance of Mecca for him.

Mid-way into the trip, on their way to Belgrade, they encounter an old woman dressed in black who rides forcefully with them, pointing to the road 'dilichi' ahead of her, for direction. However, she vanishes to reappear, and is like a premonition of death. Reda experiences several dreams – one in Saudi Arabia, vision-like of his father dressed as a sheep-herder walking away with his flock of sheep in the desert-landscape, whereas Reda sinks into a sand-hole. Upon arriving in Mecca, with a community of other Muslim pilgrim-travelers warmly greeting them, the father dresses in a Ihram, a white garment, and vanishes into the sacred space. A day later, Reda goes looking for his father amidst a crowd, only to find him at the morgue. *Le Grand voyage* concludes on Reda's selling of the car, ready to return to France.

Upon arriving in Turkey (*Mr. Ibrahim*) Ibrahim initiates Momo into Sufi dances and the latter release his anger and frustrations; 'it was incredible. My hatred was melting' (Schmitt 58).[22] The father peppers the story with Sufi aphorisms that teach Momo about life. There was a sense of urgency to pass the driver's test and acquire the car, and in a premonitory way Ibrahim did not want to wait for the required fifteen days: 'In fifteen days, I will be dead.'[23] Effectively, in film time, based on the sequential order and chronology, Ibrahim is deceased. His fatal car accident upon arriving home near his village marks the end of the trip; he returns to the sea of his birth and the notion of the whole as he informs Momo that 'the trip ends here' (Schmitt 61). In a fairly condensed and fast-paced conclusion, spectators and readers discover that Momo hitchhiked back to Paris and took over Ibrahim's shop, fully accepting to become now the Arab grocer in what probably used to be a Jewish neighborhood (rue Bleue). Both characters exchanged their identity and destiny through their displacement to Turkey. Ibrahim's legacy survives through Momo.

The last segment that places Momo and Ibrahim in Anatolia con-curs with locating the film in the travel film mode despite its rather static first part. Such a mode supports a fertile and holistic ground for exploring, among other issues, economics, sexuality, gender, class, and multiple (personal or physical) geographies. The character of the Arab grocer and migrant worker in France, a static persona in his store and seen as a permanent fixture in his neighborhood, elects to go home, possibly to reunite with his native land and people in order to die peacefully. The natural evocative and poetic image of a tree is conjured up for Monsieur Ibrahim – 'never moved, as a branch grafted onto his stool' (Schmitt 12).[24] It is accurate to remark that 'although the subject of the road movie is the journey represented by the road, it remains nonetheless a genre "obsessed with home"' (Wendy Everett citing Robertson 21). In Ibrahim's situation, home is the birthplace and not Paris, or the grocery store in which he spent 40 years at work in exile.

The decision to leave France and travel south imparts a circular movement and converges back to a point of departure known by the protagonist, a point remote from Momo's background. The main protagonist as implied in the title is Ibrahim himself and not Momo, although the camera devotes more time to the teenager and his sexual awakening. Ibrahim's legacy highlights the meaning of adoption and certifies that Momo is the one who chose him for his father, of his own free will – a decision that gives him agency. Interestingly, the father figures – not only Ibrahim but also Moïse's biological father, who survived the Holocaust and deportation of his Jewish parents, yet killed himself years later unable to face life – share the element of displacement, as Ibrahim explains,

> Your father had no example in front of him. He had lost his young parents who were arrested by Nazis and died in camps. Your father was unable to cope with all this. Maybe he was feeling guilty to be alive (Schmitt 43–44).

Monsieur Ibrahim and Exils

The past road north to exile and migration is never reenacted, leaving out the very moment when each protagonist (or their parents) left home for France and his reasons for doing so in *Monsieur Ibrahim* and *Exils*; for example, the way Ibrahim left Anatolia forty years before is overlooked, or the way both protagonists' parents left Algeria (*Exils*). The circular movement remains on the level of the imaginary and the spectator has no visual marker or trace of the arrival north; the films avoid any flashback. However, in using two young characters from different backgrounds, one *beur*, one *pied-noir*, Gatlif reactivates the colonial past and the memory of exile that accompanies each generation through its parents. By combining these two distinct groups that can be viewed as second generation immigrants, the child of *pied-noirs* and the child of Arab immigrants (all of them new immigrants once they arrived in France), the narrative invokes what Benjamin Stora called 'memory that became nomadic'. The accent is placed on the return to the country as opposed to departure, for example, for Ibrahim (Dupeyron/Schmitt) the birth country, for Zano and Naïma (Gatlif), the country of their parents. Naficy's exploration of *beur* cinema perceives return journeys as a perennial theme. One film showing a full itinerary complete with departure time and place is Yamina Benguigui's *Inch' Allah Dimanche/ Inch' Allah Sunday* (2001). The opening segment is shot in Algeria, and frames women boarding a boat with children, leaving their tearful relatives behind. Zouina and her three children leave Algeria in order to join their father who works in France. The painful departure closes in on the last panoramic view of Algiers, shot in sepia tones before the abrupt arrival in St-Quentin (Northern France).

In each case, the return consists of finding the land of one's parents and making peace with the past. In *Exils*, the past is dual: it is that of the French colonizers-settlers who eventually fled home during the Algerian war of independence as well as the migration of Algerians to France that took place in order to join the workforce and/or for other political reasons, as in the case of *Harkis*, a group of Algerian volunteers who worked for the French army. The focus is on the present time and return home. However, the pain associated with the past surfaces in the way it is processed in the present of the film. In his 1995 analysis of migrant literature, Alec Hargreaves concluded that,

> Very few of their works describe the act of migration from Algeria to France. Granted that most of these authors were born in France, and that much of what they have written is heavily autobiographical, this absence is hardly surprising (92).

Reception and distribution stories

Gatlif, Schmitt, and Ferroukhi are of different origins. Gatlif's Algerian Roma and Berber origins influence most of his films, whereas Schmitt the author is Jewish while Dupeyron the scriptwriter is not. Ferroukhi is Moroccan. Schmitt was largely inspired by his personal childhood experience with his grandfather Abraham on *rue Bleue*, as well as by the experiences of Abraham-Kremer (a Franco-Jewish actor) and his encounter with Sufism during his travel in Turkey. A simple humanist fable, promoting friendships and connections across religious and racial lines, *Monsieur Ibrahim* made the short list of the relatively few French films exported yearly to the United States where it curiously fared better than it did on the domestic front, as is the fate of a few French films abroad. Distributed in the USA by Sony pictures since December 2003, it jumped from six copies in February 2004 to 71 circulating copies in March 2004, grossing $1.2 million by 1 April 2004 (Unifrance statistics).[25] Unlike *Monsieur Ibrahim*, *Le Grand voyage*, Ferroukhi's first film produced by Humbert Balsan, was not distributed commercially in the USA, but rather through the festival circuit.[26]

Healing narratives

At the end of both *Le Grand voyage* and *Monsieur Ibrahim*, sons have become orphans though enriched as well as healed. The characters transcend the traumatic events that took place on their journey for a more uplifting and open-ended closure. Momo's anxieties were cleansed through Sufi dances, for instance. Reda gained wisdom through observation of his father's last actions as giving alms to a widowed mother, or explaining his faith. The fathers reached a sense of completion and bliss in their lifetime when they died, one in Mecca, and the other in Anatolia. If their death is abrupt, knowledge and spirituality are transmitted to their sons.

Exils/Exiles (Gatlif 2003) departs for Algeria, the country of origin for both protagonists, Zano and Naïma, a young couple. Their identity and origins are crucial in the latter part of the film. One is a *pied-noir* and the other is *beur* or second-generation French-Arab. The first part opens in a Parisian suburban apartment overlooking a giant network of interstate roads with Zano's spontaneous proposal made as he looks out onto traffic from the window: 'Let's go to Algeria.' This marks the single shot of France along with the shot of a brick wall where Zano buries his violin before their departure. The journey subsequently goes south, traverses Spain, accidentally passes through Morocco, and finally enters Algeria illegally in a dream-like view when the two protagonists walk against the tide of immigrants crossing a desert-like landscape projected through a crane shot. Likewise, Gatlif's crew entered the Algerian territory illegally as well, reproducing the pattern of his protagonists.

Healing dances occur at the closure of *Exils*, as the couple come to grips with their uprootedness; Zano joins his feminine counterpart Naïma. Filmed in a single long take and in real time, this extended part casts the bodies as recipients of the sacred and the *mystère* found in trances, a phenomenon that Albert Memmi once discussed in his autobiographical novel *La Statue de Sel/Pillar of Salt* (Memmi 171). Memmi devotes a chapter to a trance-dancing ceremony which he witnessed as a child with women in his family and neighborhood and which he utterly disliked and feared.

The entire ceremony is spiritual and therapeutic; according to Gatlif, trance is a spectacular ritual where 'individuals can escape from themselves. They gain enough strength to overcome their inhibitions, fears and frustrations' (Gatlif 2004b: n.p.). This indicates the transgressive role of actors, who from mere actor-performers cross a threshold and become real-life participants. Naïma and Zano, 'two children of the Diaspora', reclaim their identity at the end of the journey (Gatlif 2004b: n.p.).

The filmmaker returns to his native country for the first time after a forty-three-year absence, turning the experience into a personal reconciliatory act and a cleansing of personal wounds. If Gatlif did not always speak freely about his own Gypsy perspective throughout his career, he now strongly advocates his Gypsiness. Discussing *La terre au ventre* (Gatlif 1978), his first feature-length film about the last years of a French family of farmers in Algeria before its independence, Gatlif recognizes that it was not about Algeria and Algerians, but about Gypsies, yet he could not articulate it as such at the time of its production:

> *La terre au ventre* was not a film on Algeria, Algerians said: this is not about us; it was a film about Gypsies, and I did not want to claim it at the time because I was not interested in revealing my origins; now I can say it. I say it all. For years, I hid my identity. I used to tell that I was French, that I had studied in Art School ... I now say that I am neither French nor Arab. I have no more restraint (Gervais 31).[27]

Different from the rest of the migrant seasonal workers or immigrants that Zano and Naïma pass along the Andalusian roads or in the Algerian-Moroccan desert, the French couple in their southward progression keep running into their double, a brother and a sister, on their northward path to France. The couple is composed of two seasonal migrant workers from Algeria heading north to an industrialized Europe, roughly the reversed trajectory of Naïma and Zano. The French couple in turn acts as transmitters by giving a letter to the Algerian mother, who has stayed back at home. The subsequent Spanish police raid is a reminder of the plight of migrant workers and the repression they endure across borders.

The pair do not enter the classification of traveler-tourist or traveler-migrant proposed earlier as they engage a third way: that of the traveler-tourist turned pilgrim. Zano and Naïma expose a modern nomadic version of the couple previously formed in the *Gadjo Dilo/The Crazy Foreigner* (Gatlif 1997) where the main protagonist (Romain Duris) crosses paths with Romanian Gypsies as he roams along wintery Central European roads in search of the voice his musicologist father recorded. The character fled the center, generally designated as Paris, heading for the margins, here Central Europe and Gypsy villages. Each time a Gatlif protagonist sheds his/her past and belongings, he/she opens to another culture and in turn becomes 'gypsified.'

Gatlif's films resist any tendency for classification. His actors are in constant mobility and transformation, as evidenced in their drifting. Silvia Angrisani and Carolina Tuozzi's first auteur study of Gatlif confirms the importance of the travel motif in most of his films; indeed this is found in *Gadjo Dilo* (1997), *Transylvania* (2006), and *Mondo* (1995):

> The spectator is forced to travel on a journey where the place of arrival immediately becomes the place of a new departure; the representation of a given world produced by the film is immediately put into question in the next film, Gatlif invites one to discover the possibilities of transit. (Angrisani, Tuozzi 5).[28]

Their liberating passage through space (and time) allows them to make peace with the past and the present, viewed as a burden on their shoulders.

Travel narratives seen in this chapter under the figure of the 'Return' demonstrate a search for one's origins and the location of a home, away from the designated home country of France (or Europe), the place of exile for some. Such quests problematize the relationship with the parents' generation that did not speak out. Such a *problématique* (issue) revives the colonial memory, to reflect an economic, political, and psychological crisis at the core of the migratory path. Displacement and travel serve the narrative in its pursuit, which in turn takes a path back to the home country. The North-South movement inadvertently reflects on the figure of the absent other (father and/or mother), the absent northward migration path and the vanishing of time (or a suspension of time) while going south. The absent northward migration, as referenced all along in the chapter, states that the representation of the initial migration is suspended for various reasons by filmmakers (and writers) although it haunts the characters. While the figure of the parent(s) is perceptibly absent or disappears in media res, reconciliation across time and geographical borders ensues and initiates a new dialogue. There is a move towards auteurism implying that each director attempts to present his personal vision in each work and scripts, rewriting an initial traumatic displacement of a collective and historical nature and negotiating a more positive return to the home country. In adopting this route and such scenarios of a return, the ethnic and diasporic identity of the filmmakers meshes with their film. Most directors discussed in these pages are reworking some of the colonial past which they excavate (both corresponding to the war, their economic migration north) in light of contemporary (postcolonial) events taking place in France and the native country (Algeria/Turkey); they all point to the future. Their films are open-ended and move beyond what have been read elsewhere as traumatic endings.

5
Transit

The end of the 20th century has witnessed an influx of displacements with refugee population transiting through different European countries and continents in search of a better life, complete with regulatory papers and permits. With the fall of borders and walls, a result of the Schengen agreement (1985), and the fall of the Berlin wall (1989), the circulation of refugees has increased, although as anticipated 'nationalism, ethnic absolutism, religious bigotry and economic backwardness threaten to descend' (Hall 46). This issue is a part of national and European electoral platforms and politicized debates. Stuart Hall denounces the way Western Europeans perceive Eastern Europeans 'in the same language they used to reserve for North Africans, Arabs and Turks. No sooner have the barriers collapsed but Europe is busy constructing a new set of margins for itself' (Hall 46). A new 'ethnoscape' has risen, which involves the diverse groups discussed in the project, from tourists to immigrants, and workers. Arjun Appadurai's terminology fits this particular scenario as 'the landscape of persons who constitute the shifting world in which we live: tourists, immigrants, refugees, exiles, guestworkers, and other moving groups and persons' (Appadurai 295).

The rise of such narratives of displacements at the beginning of the new millennium is factoring a new 'genre' or a new type of hero. Several cultural critics have remarked on the phenomenon, such as Carrie Tarr, Mireille Rosello, and Lydie Moudileno. The recent trend is 'a swell of interest in undocumented migrants, a category once largely absent from mainstream films' (Tarr in Gott 147). The displacements correspond to economic factors and internal conflicts within one's nation as well as the opening of borders. Max Silverman draws a synthesis of this problematic situation in French contemporary culture:

The de-industrialization of the West ... the globalization of economies and communications, and the migration of peoples in the post-colonial era have certainly shattered the two major forms of identification of the modern period, those of class and nation (50).

One can indeed question whether films have unwillingly ushered a new type of character and hero despite himself/herself as proposed by Anne Laffeter's article *'Le sans-papier. Nouveau héros de cinéma.'*[1] The character of the migrant, in between two countries, was always present. Chris Marker refers to migrant travelers as 'Vertical people' in his meditation on memory and travel encapsulated in *Sans Soleil*, following the intrepid peregrinations from Africa to Asia, France, and Iceland of traveler Sandor Krasna, via his letters (Marker 1983).

I plan to illustrate the way such displacements factor into some key films; however, the intention is not to write a nomenclature of such films. The area is vast, and ever expanding with the release and distribution of each new film. It is not limited to recent history nor is it limited to one nation as recent events demonstrate with the influx of immigrants on European shores described as one of the worst crisis in history since World War II. Yet for the sake of our argument, the analysis covers *Nulle part, terre promise* (Emmanuel Finkiel 2009), *Inguélézi* (François Dupeyron 2005), *Welcome* (Philippe Lioret 2009), *Le Havre* (Aki Kaurismäki 2011), and *Little Senegal* (Rachid Bouchareb 2001). I will point to other films and suggest further readings. Some of the traits relevant to these narratives surfaced in earlier chapters and are not new, particularly in light of the status of Gypsies as Europe's others (Eng 29), most of which are verified by Gatlif's films, in the steps of Matéo Maximoff's narratives (fictional and autobiographical), the migrant worker in Ghorbal's *Un si beau voyage*, and in Ameur-Zaïmeche's *Bled Number One*.[2]

The predicament of the clandestine (*sans papiers*) individual testifies to a state of emergency experienced by individuals who are on the run, without legal documents enabling them to establish 'legal residency' in France; as such they are chased by the police, coast guards, border patrols, and local authorities. Their situation is at the core of (post) modernity. They are targets of xenophobic sentiments that run rampant in wealthy countries (Debray 77).[3] France used to be a haven for refugees and defender of human rights yet lost its status as a hospitable nation a while ago. The definition of hospitality begs revision. Mireille Rosello, revisiting this notion in *Postcolonial Hospitality* (2001), approaches hospitality as a 'gift' – as 'practices that transform two individuals or two communities into, respectively, the host and the guest' (viii).

The film spectator witnesses and takes part in this situation, which suddenly has a new face that otherwise remains occulted or reduced to a simple headline in newspapers or televised newsfeeds. Additionally, the scripts include members of the French population who decide to commit themselves to the cause of immigrants, as they can no longer remain silent bystanders or witnesses in light of new laws condemning participation, therefore placing themselves at risk. The native (French) characters sometimes take center-stage as they step into caring for a refugee, clearly a breach of article 622-1 of the *Code de l'entrée et du séjour des étrangers et du droit d'asile*.[4] This law is still valid as of August 2014. People assisting and sheltering refugees can be fined 30, 000 euros and incur a five-year jail sentence.

These 'cross border films' awaken different reactions within spectators. Yosefa Loshitzky in her study of migration in contemporary European cinema specifically addresses the position of the spectator, 'the spectator of the refugee's journey film is transformed into the reflective/analytical spectator in the Bretchian tradition' (Loshitzky 29). Each director's involvement is perceived differently but usually incites various reactions, either in the audience or the government. The directors remain affected by the story and can (loosely) be construed as dissident voices. For instance, Dupeyron declares about *Inguélézi* 'J'ai commencé ce film comme cinéaste, je l'ai fini comme citoyen' ('I started the film as a cineaste, and finished it as a citizen').[5] Still, *Inguélézi* opens with an odd if not cautious claim: 'This film is a fiction. The reality of transporters is another one'.[6] Lioret was attacked by the right for making *Welcome* and denounced by Eric Besson, minister of immigration, integration, and national identity under François Fillon's UMP government. Emmanuel Finkiel states that his intentions (*Nulle part, terre promise*) are 'not to deliver a political message, but rather to take up writing about things as they unravel in the present.[7] Each film on the topic is by essence polemical, and infiltrates a larger debate about our modern western societies, and their ability to host immigrants or reject them. The issue of immigration 'has been politicized for more than three decades' (Rosello 23).[8] It goes beyond political affiliations; in fact governments on both sides have successfully been responsible for tighter policies and deportations. The specter of sending refugees 'home' haunts the debate; statistics and figures are brandished yearly in view of the policies and their adoptions. Aki Kaurismäki, indignant about the refugee situation in Europe, confronts it head on in *Le Havre* (2011):

Le cinéma européen ne traite pas beaucoup de l'aggravation continue de la crise économique, politique et surtout morale causée par la

question non résolue des réfugiés. Le sort réservé aux extracommu-
nautaires qui tentent d'entrer dans l'Union Européenne est variable
et souvent indigne. Je n'ai pas de réponse à ce problème, mais il m'a
paru important d'aborder ce sujet dans un film qui, à tous égards, est
irréaliste (Kaurismäki).[9] ('European cinema does not deal much with
the continued strain of the economic, political, and above all moral
crisis provoked by the unresolved question of refugees. The fate of
the non-residents who try to enter the European Union fluctuates,
and often outrages people. I have no response to the problem, however it seemed important to broach the topic in a film, which is, in
all aspects, unrealistic.')

Because of the nature of immigration throughout Europe, and the nature
of cinema in Europe at large, the scripts covered in this chapter are not
limited to a single nation; they plunge directly into the larger European
crisis that is linked to unemployment, restrictions on immigration, and
the ensuing new laws. This crisis is not solely European-based but is
grafted onto a global crisis. Most of the scripts involve foreigners who
attempt to cross over and settle down in a country, fleeing theirs. The
way they are perceived in the growing world of uncertainty is best conveyed by Zigmunt Bauman's description,

> in our world of massive migration, in the world increasingly popu-
> lated by voluntary tourists and involuntary vagabonds, it is difficult
> not to notice the stubborn and vexing presence of foreigners, aliens
> or strangers. Or rather the already anxious and sensitive eye is more
> likely than not to frame the unfamiliar workmates, neighbours and
> passerby, into the generic figure of the alien, ill-willed and threaten-
> ing stranger (8).

Nulle part, terre promise

Nulle part, terre promise (Finkiel 2009) weaves three different perspectives
on the notion of travel,[10] all of them being at the antipodes of each
other.[11] It features a young female student (Elsa Amiel) who is a tourist
in Eastern Europe and goes from Berlin to Hungary, documenting what
she sees with a small DV camera. She travels by train. As she crosses
Eastern Europe, she has the ability to capture large spatial expenses, and
vistas of cities; thanks to her camera, she records what she sees but it is
arguable whether she actually sees what she records. By only checking
what she registers through the viewfinder, she is limited by the frame.

As a critical observer (the Hungarian friend's boyfriend in Budapest) remarks, she essentially captures shots of poor people. Most of her images zoom in on vagrants, or homeless people, as well as youths and workers marching and protesting their government from Berlin to Budapest. These transnational protest marches incidentally occur in every city she visits, an obvious sign of a growing global crisis and massive unrest. Two worlds collide as well as two forms of travels: the world of tourism and illegal immigrants, the world of refugee workers and the general population.

The other crossing of Europe is transmitted through the narrow scope of Kurdish refugees on board a truck for a portion of the film, and through their attempt to cross the channel to England, the 'promised' land of their destination. Each time, their perspective is defined by a narrow frame that intends to show that each point of view on the world is prescribed by the viewer's physical/geographical and economical location. Most importantly, the film is made in the aftermath of the collapse of the Berlin wall in 1989, and points to an 'Eastward extension' (Gott).[12] On board the confined trucks, a wide peripheral vision is practically non-existent, and instead a narrow vision of the outside is filtered through a crack, or an interstice through which one is barely able to see one's surroundings. Two of the truck's occupants attempt to map out their trips on a European map while in semi-obscurity.

The third trajectory follows a young French white-collar worker (Nicolas Wanczycki), who witnesses and attends to the dismantling of his factory in France and its delocalization to Hungary. He oversees the transition and accompanies the move. The film has sparse dialogue. Each character is very much alone and seemingly in disarray with his surroundings. The engineer travels for his job, visibly alienated from the rest of the world; he communicates with people through his cellphone and leaves messages many times in their absence. He appears like a small cog in the middle of the vast emptiness of the warehouse, and its implicit heavy bureaucracy – a recurrent image. Pieces of the puzzle that makes up *Nulle part, terre promise* are to be assembled by the spectator herself, just as parts are transported and travel from one country to another, to be reassembled elsewhere. If we piece these together, we may reconcile them with the fact that the *Waberer's* trucks transport refrigerator parts. Amidst the many transportation modes observed in the film, the predominance of the yellow and blue vehicles stands out. They convey parts from the factory that was dismantled despite French workers' protests in favor of its new European future site in Hungary.

The young female traveler bonds with a Hungarian female worker at the new site, the only close human interaction she has in the movie, besides her cellphone connection and its multiple shallow messages. In a sense, these cellphone connections are evidence of a highly connected contemporary global world, yet one with relayed communication through messages (vocal or text). As established in Chantal Akerman's film *Les Rendez-vous d'Anna* (1978), discussed further in Chapter 6 – a travelogue film containing multiple telephone messages left on answering machines prior to cellular phone communications – physical contacts are non-existent or failing and characters are very lonely, a recurrent sign of postmodernity. These films are geo-politically situated; Akerman's film preceded the fall of the Berlin wall by eleven years, a watershed moment in European history, whereas Finkiel's happened twenty years after. Both directors take Berlin as a central historical nexus. These two moments are meaningful for the world and the opening of formerly closed Eastern European borders, a moment ripe with enthusiasm and possibilities.

The dominant temporalities are nightfalls, sunsets, or dawns in a wintery landscape. The Kurdish refugees who are locked into a truck cargo container are able to free themselves when abandoned in the middle of nowhere by cutting the rooftop open. However, such an image is a dark visual reminder of other containers loaded with people who are locked up and who, unable to free themselves, and without air meet their death as recorded in the fictionalized docu-drama by Michael Winterbottom, *In this World* (2003).[13] The audience is aware of such images that circulate in films and other media. As I examine later in this chapter, a similar sequence with trucks and hidden Iraqi Kurds crops up in *Welcome* (Lioret), and resonates when they immediately get caught in Calais before embarking on the ferry. The following markers run through these films: multiple security checkpoints, border zones (with the examples of ports and boats), police controls, violence, traffickers, surveillance cameras, barbed wires, and barking dogs; they convey an aura of doom, security, and hopelessness. These are spotted in other border films such as Akerman's *De l'autre côté* (2002), Costa Gavras *Eden à l'Ouest/Eden is West* (2009), Xavier Koller's *Journey of Hope* (1990), and Gatlif's films. However, if the refugees successfully reach Calais, *Nulle part, terre promise* closes on them being escorted by the police out of the tunnel seen from the female student's perspective aboard the Eurostar train. Whereas she will comfortably reach her destination (London), their future is uncertain, or rather, they will most likely be deported back to their country for whatever fate awaits them. The woman (*Nulle part, terre promise*) meets the migrants' gaze this time, not unlike the female character in Krzysztof Kieslowski's *La Double vie de Véronique* (1991) who runs into her double in Warsaw – one is on the bus, the other standing on the plaza, in a speechless exchange.[14] In each film, there is a moment of quasi-recognition.

Finkiel traces lines that belong to geographic movements across Europe. The Kurdish refugees cross Europe diagonally from the southeast to the northwest. The female tourist goes east before returning west to the safety and affluence of London. The male 'cadre' (white collar worker) involved in the delocalization of the factory goes east before returning west – possibly to London as well. Their zigzag motions seem of a provisional nature. Following this topographical reading, *Inguélézi* weaves a direct straight line. Its movement is singular: it is a straight ride north and west to London. The Western European characters have a place (home) to return to, like Akerman's Anna (*Les Rendez-vous d'Anna*). Finkiel is indebted to European directives that promote flexibility, movement, and exchanges. The film was commissioned among a series of films on Europe. Not every participant sees the world similarly. Amidst the comfort and confidence afforded by a plane ride, a fast train, a luxury hotel, and/or a DV camera, most characters suffer from a deep sense of solitude and alienation from the rest of the world. The only ones who form a collective, the Turkish Kurds, are together, but prisoners of a cargo '*container*'. Once freed, they must go separate ways, in order not to be spotted as a group.

The female traveler is unable to have any human interactions except through her digital camera. We never know what she is exactly looking for while she is filming, which touches on issues of voyeurism. Criticized once for filming poverty, she reacts negatively and objects to such a proposition. She is separated from the world by her digital camera, which she uses indiscriminately on homeless persons, vagrants, and passing '*sans papiers*'. It protects her yet gives her (and us, spectators) a filtered view. Once the camera is stolen, she is lost and devastated; she secures a 'new' replacement camera at the end of the movie, as she crosses the Chunnel. The '*cadre*' repeatedly asks his Hungarian interpreter to join him for a drink, an offer she repeatedly turns down. His only 'contact' at the close of his trip will be with a young homeless woman, who joins him in his hotel room for sex and what may be construed as a desperate attempt at intimacy. Yet, at that moment, the narrative elliptically eludes the physical encounter between two human beings.

Inguélézi

Most of these films gather different agendas and gather lines traced by trucks, cars, and refugees across invisible borders, an invisible grid of people who pass each other on their way to their destinations. Kurdish (or Afghan) refugees present recurrent figures and models amidst these fictions, as in the example of *Inguélézi* (Dupeyron 2003). They prompt the characters of civic helpers amidst the French population, a figure from the recent past that shares significant resemblances with another historical situation that dates back to World War II. Therefore, such fictions are historically and politically charged and elicited stern comments from different politicians or historians as they raised specters culled from our traumatic national past.

Inguélézi grabs the spectator and pulls him/her on a frantic road movie with mobile shots provided by a light DV camera. It confronts the situation of the Kurdish migrant Kader (Eric Caravaca), who is temporarily stranded in France after the truck transporting him and his companions crashed. While most of the passengers tragically burned to death, he escaped and found refuge in the trunk of a car driven by a recently widowed woman, Geneviève Mertens (Marie Payen) who lives in a rural house, near Carcassonne, in Southern France. After initially rescuing him from the scene of the accident and sheltering him in her trunk and at her house, Geneviève without explanation decides to drive Kader to Calais and London. Despite the initial unlikeliness of the story, the hand-held camera closes in on faces and witnesses raw emotions; it is shot in a rush, like a Dogme film, building a suspenseful story. The two characters whose paths cross in Southern France drive the narrative. Dupeyron mixes the two tragedies and breathes in a new life that transcends personal loss and mourning. Geneviève braves the law in order to transport Kader, initially in her trunk, through France and then into Great Britain. By defying the legislation restricting all movements and hospitality granted to travelers/migrants, she becomes a delinquent, and could be accused of a '*délit de solidarité*' (an offense) with an immigrant.[15] The film does not dwell on her psychological condition, an introspection that Dupeyron's subsequently published novel conveys through the use of first person narration. The film is shot in the immediacy and urgency of a live situation. Geneviève will help Kader. Images of cops abound, raiding the area, in the southwestern landscape and later the port city of Calais; they paint the alternate reality that refugees face. The story is a travel narrative, and Geneviève is constantly at the wheel, from day one for the burial of her deceased husband, which she cannot make, until the end when she returns to her 'home' and child after successfully dropping Kader off in London. The film tackles two individuals' tragic paths and their wandering, away from any psychological pathos, following a topographic movement. It opens itself to the 'cold' reality of clandestine migration, and the lack of cooperation from the general population.

Dupeyron est parvenu à rendre cette rencontre et ce trajet en une forme quasi topographique, de mise en scène: les mouvements valent des mots, les expressions font les sentiments, et les paysages qui changent, dans la lumière crue de l'hiver, sont comme une peinture mentale des personnages et de leurs évolutions progressives (Antoine de Baeque).[16] ('Dupeyron managed to turn this encounter and trajectory into a quasi-topographical form, of mise-en-scène; movements are worth words, expressions create the feelings, and landscapes are changing, in the raw winter light, as a mental painting of the characters and their progressive evolution').

Inguélézi differs from Dupeyron's other films in the way it is shot. His films have a more classical signature (*La chambre des officiers, Mr. Ibrahim*).The cinematography of Yves Angelo, a director who often works with him, enhances the story.[17] It is rooted in a news event Dupeyron overheard on the radio. Dupeyron fine-tuned his skills as a writer for this 'story' yet refused a romanticized version of the event, as he rejected making what he called 'a Sangatte film.'[18]

Borders

Ten years after *Voyages* (1999), examined in Chapter 2, Finkiel chose a semi-documentary form, or a choral film mode, in which three groups of individuals whose trajectories are interlaced at some point crisscross space. *Nulle part, terre promise* makes a cold statement on the condition of Europe, and offers no solace. It does not embrace the border-free Europe that many celebrate. Instead, it adheres to Balibar's notion of 'vacillating borders', or borders that are not located at the periphery of a country, but sometimes within its centers (Balibar). Borders have been reshaped on the new European map, after World War II, and after the collapse of the Eastern bloc. Glimpsed through a filter each time as in *Voyages* (1999) during the bus sequences, Europe seems to be nondescript, or uniform, without any specificity, encapsulating *non-lieux* such as highways, open fields near airports, unnamed hotel rooms, underground passages, countless trucks, and containers. It resolutely stays away from identifiable tourist markers except for the Potsdamer platz in Berlin.

On ne peut déceler ni identité, ni repères. L'Europe traversée n'est pas définie. C'est un no man's land, en construction ou en désolation. Un non-lieu, façon de revisiter le 'nulle part' du titre du film. (Finkiel)[19] ('One cannot detect any identity or bearings. The Europe they cross is non-defined. It's a no man's land in construction or desolate. A non-place, as a way to revisit the 'nowhere' part of the title.')

Welcome

The clandestine in *Inguélézi, Nulle part, terre Promise,* and *Welcome* is invisible. He/she must remain hidden in the shadows. Most of them are unseen, concealed in trucks, cars, camps, containers or underground passages, and ferries. If a film reveals their face, it is to make visible that they are at risk, unprotected, and out to secure a safe passage across the channel for a better future. The fiction films I explore in this chapter document such characteristics borrowed from real situations, in a 'documentary' format. Documentary 'Sangatte' films have been made, many of them produced in the United Kingdom, or Switzerland, including the short *Border* (Laura Waddington 2004), *After Sangatte* (Oscar Beard 2008), *Calais, the last border* (Marc Isaacs 2003), the documentary-style fiction film *In this World* (Winterbottom 2003), and Xavier Koller's *Journey of Hope* (1990).

The Ministry of Immigration, Integration, National Identity and Solidarity Development, instituted under François Fillon's government (2007) and minister Eric Besson, denounced the myth-making position of *Welcome*.[20] In his open letter to Besson,[21] Philippe Lioret asserts that he is exposing repressive mechanisms towards migrant men and women in Calais through his film. A swimming coach (Vincent Lindon) is drawn into helping a young Kurdish Iraqi refugee (Firat Ayverdi) swim across the channel, and be reunited with his fiancée in London. Lioret does not want to create a parallel with the Occupation or 'la traque des juifs et la Shoah, avec les persécutions dont sont victimes les migrants du Calaisis et les bénévoles qui tentent de leur venir en aide' ('the hunt for Jews and the Shoah, persecutions whose victims are the migrants from Calais and their helpers').[22] The filmmaker reminds the minister that the film stays within the fictional mode, and therefore is not a documentary on the condition of migrants, but a script based on thoroughly documented facts. This intervention, not unique in its type, is a reminder of the reaction films provoke as they reflect upon contemporary events. Furthermore, allusions to World War II, and its round-ups, deportations, and detentions are highly polemical in France. The irony of the title escapes no one.

Lindon joue bien et c'est un très bon film, ce que je regrette, c'est l'avant-vente ou l'après-vente du film, il y a eu un dérapage qui est lourd, grave et inacceptable de Lioret [...] Le vocabulaire qui est issu de la Seconde Guerre Mondiale, traque, rafle, assimilation aux juifs en 43, est un vocabulaire que, selon moi, on ne devrait jamais utiliser dans le débat politique. ('Lindon acts well, and it is a very good film, but I regret that in the pre-sale, or post-sale of the film – there has been a grave and inacceptable slippage by Lioret ... Vocabulary stemming from World War II, hunt, roundup, assimilation to Jews, is a vocabulary, that in my opinion, should never be used in a political debate.') (André)[23]

In the film's pre-production stage, Lioret traveled to Calais and spent time with refugees and volunteers, enough to form an opinion on the 'réalité indigne'.[24] The overall critical response applauded a 'politically-committed film' that was courageous enough to dive into reality.[25] Yet many disliked the allusions to Jewish history. Historian Henry Rousso, an established scholar in the field, was critical of Lioret's comparison of the refugees to the Jews in World War II, which for him was a provocation made by intellectuals in general since 1945. In other words, the comparison between the Jewish Holocaust and present day events is too facile for some. The fate of refugees cannot be compared to that of Jews who were in a similar situation in 1943 yet had to face deportation and death once rounded-up (Rousso).[26] Similarly, the critical reaction distinguishes two attitudes typifying the refugee situation in its filmic representations: one is a journalistic tendency to report on the phenomenon, and the other an aesthetically 'unabashed' romantic vision, the latter applying to *Welcome* (Ahmed).[27]

Visions of port cities and invisibility

Bilal, a 17-year-old Kurdish asylum seeker, finds temporary refuge in the local swimming pool in Calais, but he is barred from bringing his compatriots to the only place where they could shower, reinforcing the repressive risks they incur if made visible; the pool showers and the supermarket are off limits to them. He decides to swim across the channel to avoid the perilous ride in a locked truck container. Kader (*Inguélézi*) finds refuge in the trunk of a car, and cannot ride as a 'normal' passenger.

The location of the port city is a crucial backdrop. It is where the entire film takes place for *Welcome* and *Le Havre* and is the crucial point of passage for *Inguélézi*. The port and the coast become the last remaining border on European soil, construed as 'the European fortress' (Loshitzky) that must be crossed. Away from Paris, French provinces have become the new loci for migration patterns in France as Lydie Moudileno argues in her article 'The Postcolonial Provinces' (66).

Five main locations run through the film to set out the city of Calais: the detention camp, the municipal swimming pool, the apartment of swimming coach Simon Calmat (Vincent Lindon), the police station, and the seaside. Four of these spaces are porous, and under constant surveillance. The asylum seekers are cordoned off; they 'have found themselves "welcomed"' (Thomas 178) in the detention camp. The camp is located in a nondescript zone near the harbor. Bilal (*Welcome*) is determined to join his fiancée in London, despite the odds against him (her family does not want anything to do with him despite the fact that he has clandestinely trekked from Kurdistan to France over three months and they have arranged a marriage with a cousin for the daughter). Unable to make the journey on board a truck, he decides, based on his athletic prowess in football, to take swimming lessons and train to cross the channel. The rather surly swimming coach commits to him, after initially delivering a sober yet realistic assessment of such a crossing. Bilal becomes like a son to the man who thus presents a more caring side to his ex-wife, who is actively involved in the local soup kitchen for refugees. However, Bilal's fate is tragic. For his second crossing attempt, the British navy – who spot him 800 meters away from the coast – return Bilal to Simon in a body bag. It is not clear that Bilal did not die because he did not want to get caught and imprisoned. The elusive borders of the 'promised land' (England) and the Dover hills are visibly within reach before Bilal disappears and drowns. At the tragic outcome of the crossing attempt, Simon buries Bilal in the local French cemetery, and despite strict police surveillance shows up in London in order to break the sad news to Bilal's girlfriend, who is about to be married off to a relative.

Allusions to war-time situations surface especially when each immigrant is stamped on their hand with a number, when they are rejected from a store, and when Calmat's neighbors zealously denounce him to the police for housing refugees. The police search his home in the middle of the night without a warrant. These allusions helped fuel some of Besson's and Rousso's objections to the film; they further point to the origins of the title – a simple word (either a verb or a noun) 'Welcome' written on the neighbor's doormat, which under these circumstances is suspect. The same neighbor denounced Calmat for housing refugees, and furthermore intimated possible homosexual bonds between him and Bilal to build a case against him. The film's dark mood mirrors the impotence of people in the face of such a situation, as well as the general apathy and seemingly indifference toward migrants. Lioret decodes the desperation vis-a-vis immigration and the way some residents take the law into their own hands.

The Port City

The situation of clandestinity is exposed in *Le Havre* (Kaurismäki 2011) when the character of the young African child, Idrissa, (Miguel Blondin) successfully escapes the cargo container and police thanks to the complicity of the head police officer Inspector Monet (Jean-Pierre Darroussin), and Marx, the shoeshine (André Wilms). Idrissa is the future, and as such is compelled to flee: his grandfather instructs him to do so when they are arrested. Kaurismäki, a Finnish director, scouted different European towns and selected Le Havre for its maritime light. He offers an uncompromising vision of Europe, which according to him is in shambles, 'je parle d'une humanité en miettes. Je parle de l'Europe. De l'immigration en Europe. D'un monde qui est détruit. D'une humanité en miettes.'[28] ('I am speaking of a humanity in shambles. I'm speaking of Europe. Of immigration in Europe. Of a world that is destroyed. A humanity in shambles.')

Dans peu de temps, le "choc" que l'on peut connaitre pour avoir vécu dans un port de mer ne sera plus qu'un souvenir, peut-être maintenu en permanence par des livres et la photographie, ou encore la télévision qui devrait se hâter d'en garder les images dans ses collections de films. L'aéroport apportera pour quelque temps son pittoresque agrémenté de bruits qui se calmeront dans un unique décor à tendance hygiénique (Mac Orlan 28). ('Not too long from now, the shock that one knows for having lived in a port city will only be a memory, maybe permanently maintained by books and photographs, or yet by television, which should hasten to keep its pictures in its film collections. The airport will bring for a while its picturesqueness, enlivened by noises that will quiet down in a unique décor, and hygienic tendencies.')

Port cities run through such fictions; they harbor refugees as well as active police forces, whose surveillance is deployed in order to catch any suspect. At its origin, Le Havre (literally meaning harbor) was initially named *Hable de Grace* under King François I. The port cities are shown as a microcosm of France or any western affluent society, yet Kaurismäki leaves the struggle to working class individuals who must work together in order to rescue some of these passengers from their fate. They do their part. Le Havre, Calais, or Marseille are such destinations. So are Helsinki, Nantes, New York, Tangiers, Trieste, Malta, Gibraltar, and Lampedusa. The first installment in the new Kaurismäki Harbor Town trilogy at first harks back to Marcel Carné's *Quai des brumes*, and displays a *rétro* aesthetic anchored in the 1940s and 1950s.[29] Most of his films revive the nostalgia of earlier times, fitted with all the collectibles he can find. This applies to his film sets starting with Finland, or France.

My soul could not tolerate the kind of rough realism necessary to depict the modern city of Helsinki – I am as if forced against the stonewall. I am as well forced to redesign all the towns behind several decades. I can't show a modern car, as they are so ugly and impersonal. I managed to photograph London and Paris without showing one single car, and in spite of that my films were in modern times. I'm for a camera that gets identified with the sets of the epoch it is depicting – and represents that epoch in all its savagery (Kaurismäki).[30]

The film summons Pierre Mac Orlan's poetic prose about different ports, such as Le Havre, London, Brest, or Hamburg. Jacques Prévert adapted MacOrlan's novel *Quai des Brumes*, situated in Montmartre, and transposed it to Le Havre for Carné's film (Sadoul 204).[31] The city of Le Havre recalls the scathing depiction of the fictitious city of Bouville and its bourgeois inhabitants in Jean-Paul Sartre's *La Nausée* (1938). Kaurismäki chose the port for its emblematic appearance as a border zone. Although his style is removed from any attempt at realism, he brings in the poetry of the past, paired with the loss and dignity of the working-class in a refined language, lifestyle, and commitment. In Kaurismäki's film world, characters desire to get out of their country, to escape, and flee, not unlike 1930s French poetic realist characters or

1980s depressive films. Kaurismäki, who is known for his love of the past and its traces, was proud to discover an area of the city that dates back to the 1930s before it was slated for demolition, not far from the port: 'j'ai découvert une petite zone derrière les docks, ouvrière, des petits pavillons des années 30 qu'on allait détruire' (Kaurismäki)[32] ('I discovered a small working-class zone behind the docks, small villas from the 1930s' that was slated for demolition'). Le Havre was destroyed during the Second World War, under heavy Allied bombings. It was rebuilt from 1945 to 1964 under the supervision of architect Auguste Perret into a 'modern' reconstruction that gained a UNESCO World Heritage label in 2005. This mix of retro is puzzling, but not unusual for Kaurismäki.

The imagery of the elsewhere (what lies within and beyond the port) is inscribed visually but is also part of the soundtrack with the inclusion of popular songs, blues, and tango, or distant boat sirens. Many of the musical numbers disrupt the pace, and allow for nostalgic tunes to air. If the character is temporarily 'caught' in the frame, he/she dreams of displacement and 'elsewhere'. In her essay on melancholy in cinema, Gisèle Breteau-Skira acknowledges the importance of the port city: 'C'est le départ, la fuite, le voyage, l'exil, l'ailleurs' (14) ('It's the departure, the fleeing, the travel, the exile, the elsewhere'). Kaurismäki's response to what constitutes melancholia is 'one's homeland. Or rather, the port' (Breteau-Skira 31). Such scripts propel us to a multiplicity of earlier histories, and the collapse of two temporalities: for instance, that of the French Occupation with present-day times. Of course, the ramifications of the Occupation in France extend beyond nationalist borders for a Finnish director whose country was successively occupied by the Germans and the Soviets. Other possible historical extensions and variations engage slave narratives and colonial history.

Another French film located in a port is *Transit* (1991), René Allio's filmic adaptation of Anna Seghers's *Transit* (1944). Seghers, a German-Jewish refugee, waited for a visa to take her family across the sea to safety in Mexico. She started writing the book on board the ship to Central America.[33] It spins a Kafkaesque tale of a long wait for visas in Marseille during the German occupation. Most of the characters consist of European Jewish refugees in hiding as they wait for their visas to escape by boat during the war. Allio's films denounce a society of entrapment, 'la société souricière'.[34] André Téchiné's *Les Temps qui changent/Changing Times* (2004) is a variation on the topic of immigration in its recurrent shot of a crowd standing facing the sea, gazing north, in a film that is set in Morocco and deals exclusively with a romantic triangle. More recently, Costa Gavras's *Eden à l'Ouest* (2009) covers the story of a clandestine immigrant who survives a Mediterranean crossing and passes for a worker at a Club Med vacation resort. The origins of the young man are never precise, highlighting instead the larger phenomenon of clandestine immigration.

The Surrealist film *La Fée* (Dominique Abel, Fiona Gordon, and Bruno Romy 2011) interlaces a cast of working class characters in the working class area of Le Havre, near the port. A one-star hotel night watcher, Dom, meets a woman, Fiona, who pretends to be a 'fairy' and can grant him three wishes. In the footsteps of Georges Méliès, Jacques Tati, and Charlie Chaplin, the tentative comedy turns to accommodate more current and tragic themes: clandestine migrants, incarceration, and mental health. In their fantastic adventures the hotel dwellers constantly cross paths with three African immigrants trying to 'hitch a ride' across the channel.[35] No communication is exchanged between them. In fear of possible expulsions, they hide in a car trunk to escape the police rounds and are seen intermittently throughout the film as comedic figures.

Inguélézi, similarly to *Le Havre* and *Welcome*, passes by the inevitable harbor on the way to England, the transposition of the film's Kurdish title. Calais is reached at sunset, with the large ferries with the SEAFRANCE logo in the frame of both *Inguélézi* and *Welcome* offering the lure of a one-way ticket to freedom.[36] *Inguélézi* passes by the port and a truck stop before reaching London by ferry.

Le Havre

Le Havre is the second French-speaking film directed by Kaurismäki, after *La vie de Bohème* (1992). In many ways, Kaurismäki pays homage to French cinema and Marcel Carné, Damia, and Arletty – his fetish actress (mostly remembered as Garance in Carné's *Les Enfants du Paradis*, 1945). In Carné's film *Quai des Brumes* (1938) the figure of the deserter (Jean Gabin) walks into town (Le Havre) with a lost dog in tow, his *doppelgänger*. Idrissa (*Le Havre*), a young African child, is the new comer, shadowed by Marx's dog Laïka. Dogs are omnipresent meaningful presences in Kaurismäki's films. *Les lumières du Faubourg* (2006) also casts a young black child who is close to a dog, who witnesses the demise of the main protagonist throughout the film and rescues him at the end.

In *Le Havre*, Marcel Marx is a shoeshine, an artist who took refuge in the city after leaving Paris, and lives with Arletty (Kati Outinen), a woman who took him in. He is a defector from the earlier film *La vie de Bohème* (Kaurismäki 1992), in which Marx (played by the same actor André Wilms) struggled as a writer in Parisian Bohemia. In *Le Havre* he is seen 20 years later as a down and out in Le Havre, yet now with a roof on his head and with Arletty as his companion (played by the director's Finnish fetish actress). Of Romanian origins in the script, she rescues Marx from a life 'in the gutter'.[37] The woman is the anchor for the more nomadic man. She is the nurturer and the savior. Marx's language and tone are extremely polished and courteous and help save the 'moral' compass of the narrative and its rather unsavory characters – evoked in the first sequence when cops aim their pistols at a fleeing refugee child. Echoes of the Calais transit camp named 'the jungle', dismantled in 2009 by the police, are broadcast in a televised news report watched by Tchang, a Vietnamese exile with forged papers, and Marx, two buddies in the shoeshine business who appear in the first noir-like sequence. The film spins a tale of the humanity surrounding Marx and Idrissa and the law of hospitality. Derrida interprets 'pure hospitality' not as a law, a program, or a behavior. In Greek society the foreigner (*xenos*) had a right to be heard, and have access to the legal system. He/she was therefore linked to the natives and treated with respect.[38] Yet the world is now so deprived of its hospitable traits that it renders the image of the *container* both visible and metaphorical, as in Bauman's expression of 'a container full to the brim with free-floating fear, and frustrations desperately seeking outlets' (Bauman 14).

The laws of hospitality toward the foreigner-traveler kick in when Marx decides to shelter Idrissa in his working-class bungalow before securing him a safe passage to England on a fishing boat. Through the combined efforts of the neighborhood community, the impossible becomes possible. 'The small community, bakers, "beur" grocery owners, a Vietnamese fresh immigré, and regulars from the bar, all collaborate to arrange the escape, the deserved happy ending.'[39] The marks of hospitality toward the foreigners are at odds with the cold bureaucratic, legal, and repressive attempts to deport migrants, and park them in detention camps or force them to scramble for makeshift refuges. Yet they play on France's past reputation. Next to the heavy colonial memories triggered by visions of African refugees arriving in France and the ensuing lack of empathy, reminiscences of wartime denunciations occur, especially with the shadowy neighbor (a sinister Jean-Pierre Léaud) and his manic anonymous phone calls to the police to report on his neighbor's actions.[40] There are 'no miracles in the neighborhood' yet by borrowing the genre of the fable or fairy tales the film reverses this fatalistic statement and offers a vision of miracles that unfolds in front of us as seen in Chapter 3 with regard to *La Légende du Saint Buveur* (Olmi 1988). Marx and Arletty's shabby bungalow, with its side window giving onto a brick wall and its sterile surroundings, constitutes a veritable gate to the outside world and a shelter. Marx reconnects not only with his neighborhood shopkeepers and friends, but also with his African counterparts, indicating that he lives in a world of relations, not a solitary one. Marx goes out of his way for Idrissa. In so doing, he seeks out his relatives in Calais, passes through a clandestine encampment on the coast and visits a detention camp to meet with his grandfather. These acts demonstrate respect and propriety. The police are relatively helpless when confronted with Marx's charismatic verbal brio. Amidst the chaotic situation, intensified by Arletty's terminal illness and bleak medical diagnosis given by Dr. Becker (played by filmmaker Pierre Etaix), the odds are not good. Yet personal woes do not deter Marx's resolution. A fundraiser is brokered with a rock concert headed by Little Bob, a legendary rocker and blues artist from Le Havre who describes his hometown as 'a tough rain-battered grey hole.'[41]

'The situation is desperate', as Kaurismäki reports in his usual pathos. The film expresses the untenable situation of France and immigrants, and reflects the pre-war anxiety that spectators found at the core of Carné's *Quai des Brumes* and duly recognized in Sadoul's film history notes (205). The sentiment resonates within today's European crisis. Europe has been the center of heated arguments regarding immigration from the 1990s and earlier. This in turn impacts the films discussed here and in other film histories. The utopian tale has a double happy end, when the spectator realizes that there is some hope left. The cherry tree in their tiny garden blooms again at the end, when Arletty, miraculously healed, comes home (unlike the tragic fate of Mimi at the close of *La vie de Bohème*, who dies at the hospital, leaving her man alone). The tree's symbolic presence is as strong as found in such songs as *Le Temps des cerises* or *Les lilas refleuriront*, both political odes to better times for working class heroes. It stands as the metaphor for Kaurismäki, whose films plant the seeds of future trees. Idrissa, the child (and the future), is 'free' to leave on a fishing boat when Inspector Monet decides to look the other way and lie to the harbor police with the complicity of Marx who arranged the 'sea-voyage', with a planned exchange in 'international waters' onto a British boat. The chain of solidarity is mapped out once more and solidified, and is performed in Rozier's film *Maine-Océan* (Chapter 7).

The director, who is deemed 'the European filmmaker most widely identified with cinema' (Mazierska, Rascaroli 13), shots of many port cities in his films, not just in *Le Havre*. Already *Ariel* (1988), *J'ai engagé un tueur* (1990), *La vie de Bohème* (1992), *Tiens ton foulard, Tatiana* (1993), *La lumière du Faubourg* (1995), and *Au loin s'en vont les nuages* (1996) all frame characters either living by, and/or departing from a port, by boat. Kaurismäki's protagonists, often victims of the system and unemployed, are fated to leave or escape the country. *Tiens ton foulard, Tatiana/Hold on to your scarf, Tatiana* is a road movie shot in black and white and set in the 1960s. Two young women from Estonia and Belarus are returning from Helsinki to Tallinn, across the Gulf of Finland by ferry (Estonia is located just across the bay from Helsinki). They meet two Finnish male rockers driving a Volga in Finland. The two men have never been 'abroad' and join them on the trip. In *Ariel* (1988), Taisto Kasurinen, an unemployed coal miner and the main protagonist, must leave Finland to escape being sent back to jail. He is able to do so on board Ariel, a ship he will board at night-time in the harbor with his wife and her child at the close of the film. Throughout the narrative, the port and its noises are a staple of the maritime landscape of Helsinki.

Le Havre displays a humanity of wandering characters, immigrants passing through town in locked containers, detained by the authorities, in the hope of making the crossing to the United Kingdom. For Kaurismäki, the port city signifies a border. Marcel Marx is acutely aware of the difficulty of being a wanderer after his earlier Bohemian life as an impoverished artist in Paris. Many characters belong to the world of itinerants, vagrants, homeless artists, and now immigrants – all of them at the margins of society. It is a reflection of Europe as it stands now, in the middle of the worst political and humanitarian crisis since World War II, at a crossroads between the affluent Western world and a new under-privileged class (economically poor, migrant, unemployed, jobless, homeless, etc.).[42] The issue is no longer national or European, but global; Thomas MacCarthy touches on immigration in the United States, with immigrants from the Middle East (Syria) in *The Visitor* (2007). Akerman approaches the Mexican side of the issue in *De l'autre côté* (2002). Similarly, Stephen Frears's *Dirty Pretty Things* (2002) casts a look at African and Eastern European immigrants and their predicament in London, and probes into human and organ trafficking. *Biutiful* (2010) by Mexican director Alejandro Gonzalez Inarritu delves into the world of Chinese and African immigrants and trafficking in the middle of Spain.

Little Senegal

The port is a visual reminder of the transatlantic slave trafficking orchestrated between European powers, African countries, and the Americas in the 18th and 19th centuries. The trope of ports and deportations looms large in this chapter; it encompasses the presence of ships, an integral starting point to Paul Gilroy's theory of the 'Black Atlantic'. 'I have settled on the image of ships in motion across the spaces between Europe, America, Africa and the Caribbean as a central organizing symbol for this enterprise' (Gilroy 4). The very image echoes Edouard Glissant's *Poétique de la relation* with his notion of 'la barque ouverte' (the open boat) of the slave ship (18). Rachid Bouchareb's *Little Senegal* (2001) opens at the place from where slave ships departed, Gorée being the gate to 'the journey of no return' (film script), an island off the port of Dakar (Senegal). The location featured prominently in *Sankofa* (Haile Gerima 1993), an Akan word and symbol used in the film, meaning a return.[43] Alloune (Sotigui Kouyaté), a historical tour guide of Gorée island, decides to trace some of his ancestry by traveling from Senegal to North America, landing first on the east coast in South Carolina, and moving north to New York (Figure 5.1). The film's opening and closing shots capture a vista of the sea, with an oncoming boat, from inside

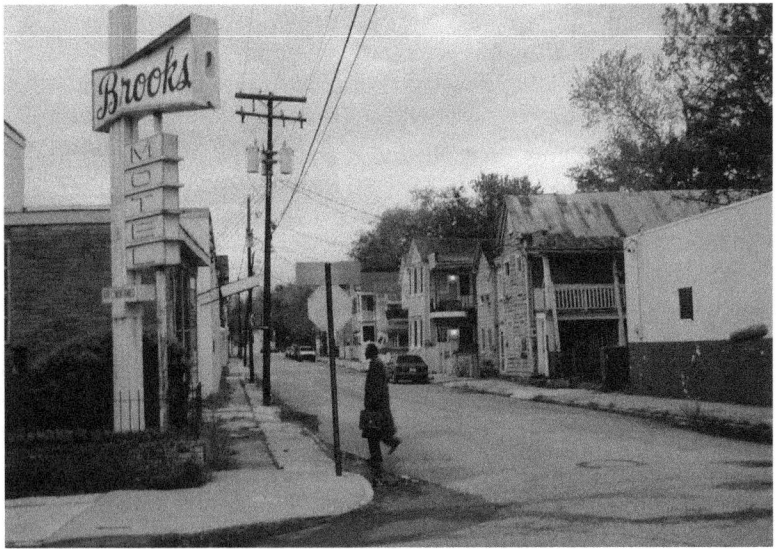

Figure 5.1   Rachid Bouchareb, *Little Senegal*
Note: 'Alloune (Sotigui Kouyaté) travels from Gorée, Senegal to South Carolina and New York to connect with family descendants.'
Source: 3B Productions.

the wall of the Maison des Esclaves at Gorée. These are subjective shots. The place is now a tourist site and a location of pilgrimage. Alloune is compelled to travel because of a dream he had, of an ancestor requesting his search for descendants in North America to appease the spirits. He maps out his journey with notebooks and pens next to a globe of the world on the side of his desk in Gorée. He confides the dream to his nephew Hassan who lives and works in New York as a mechanic and taxi driver. Composed as a circular trip to North America and back to Africa, Alloune's historical investigation is first based in South Carolina, on Sullivan Island. This is where it all started for some of his ancestors and the branch of the family that was uprooted. Bouchareb mentions 'Port de Caroline du Sud' as the port of entry. The traveler ends up in New York, confined to the African-American Harlem neighborhood called 'Little Senegal'. However, the narrative effectively concludes when Alloune returns to Gorée to bury his nephew, who is murdered in New York during his stay. His path covers the deportation routes taken by millions of slaves shipped to the 'new' continent, and the memory of 'the gouffre' (Glissant 19). Glissant compared and sketched the figure of the Slave Trade passing through the 'narrow gate of the slave ship, whose wake imitates the crawling of the caravan in the desert ... In the east, African countries, and west, American lands' (17). Alloune travels back in time and space. While he is able to reconnect with some of his distant relatives and even has a romantic relationship with Ida, the trip is tainted by the murder of Hassan. The director approached the issue of immigration earlier in the 1980s with *Baton Rouge* (1985), his first fiction film – a comedy – and recently in a more somber film *London River* (2009). *Baton Rouge* was structured as a round-trip to North America from France, with a trio of friends whose dreams to migrate to the USA come true but soon fall apart.

Bouchareb, a Franco-Arab filmmaker who was born in France of Algerian parents, is interested in the double identity of characters, and movement back and forth between two cultures (Arnaud 5).[44] Whereas the structure of the round-trip or the 'loop' is possible in *Little Senegal*, with a return to Gorée, slaves' travel and predicaments are best captured under the form of a beast that Glissant calls and describes as a *'fibrille'* – (a short fiber). The significance of the film lies in the geographical and historical ties between the two continents and the dialogue initiated between Africans and African-Americans. They are inseparable due to the nature of the immigration narrative. Alloune, the guide, reconciles their two histories. The whites are peripheral here. The casting of Sotigui Kouyaté is significant as he comes from a long line of griots, 'masters of words, and who were at once genealogists, historians, masters of ceremonies, advisors, mediators'.[45] Alloune painstakingly manages to draw the family tree, and shows it to one of the descendants he has tracked down. His task is made more difficult since the slaves were stripped of their (African) names when they were purchased. Visits to museums, historical societies, plantations, and cemeteries constitute his itinerary. The sea-voyage and the memory of the middle crossing visually and aurally stamp the narrative, making Alloune's task of gathering the descendants and caring for them more pressing. It is he who does the research, and patiently walks in the footsteps of the ancestors. He also transmits some of the family traditions, which dictate respect toward the elders and one's family, as well as resilience in all circumstances. Bouchareb's subsequent film *London River* pairs three different communities, African (Sub-Saharan), Arab, and White, this time relocated to London in a post 9/11 climate:

> Elisabeth and Ousmane are from different geographical places—Guernsey and Paris via Africa, respectively. They travel to London to seek their children Jane and Ali. From different race, religion, and linguistic communities, London becomes the space where they seek knowledge of their child's wellbeing (Reid 2012).

The narrative, like so many in this chapter, is based on the meeting of people from different origins and locations. In view of circumstances, they travel to London in order to locate their children who went missing after the 2005 terrorist bombing on the London Underground. Sotigui Kouyaté plays the role of a Muslim francophone African patriarch, Ousmane, alongside the white Christian English widow and mother Elisabeth Sommers (Brenda Blethyn). In their respective search for the missing children, they become close and respectful of each other. Once the search has unsuccessfully concluded, they return 'home' in separate ways; she returns to Guernsey, and he returns to West Africa, via Paris.

This chapter has underlined the urgency of the situation of migrants and refugees and the way France 'welcomes' them as they are passing through. I have closed with *Little Senegal*, a film that evokes former the colonial routes and displacements across the Atlantic of the slave trade. This last film departs from present day scenarios but retraces similar past transatlantic routes from Africa via Europe to the United States. Such accounts reactivate such memories and wounds. The present-day 'emergency' situation and crisis has led to new debates and laws everywhere in Europe, Asia, Africa, and North, Central, and South America.

6
Rebels and Flâneuses

J'ai souvent rêvé de lointains voyages. Les voyages m'auraient tentée si je n'avais eu le projet de vivre pour ma mère. Et dieu, voilà! Si ma mère ne veut pas de moi, quelque jour je partirai, j'irai au bout du monde. Je verrai l'Etna et le mont Gibel, j'irai en Amérique, j'irai dans l'Inde. On dit que c'est loin, que c'est difficile, tant mieux. On dit qu'on y meurt, qu'importe! En attendant, vivons au jour le jour, vivons au hasard; puisque rien de ce que je connais ne me tente ou ne me rassure, laissons venir l'inconnu (George Sand 128). ('I often dreamed of far-away trips. Travels would tempt me if I did not have the project to live for my mother. And God, here I am! If my mother does not want me, one day I will leave, I will go to the end of the world. I will see the Etna and Mount Gibel, I will go to America and India. They say that when far away, it's difficult, good! They say that one dies there, no matter! Meanwhile, let us live day to day, at random, since nothing that I know tempts me or reassures me, let the unknown come.')

My focus on women-based travel narratives and their displacement in uncharted territories is featured in this chapter. The mobility of strong female characters points to possible danger zones based on gender. I appropriate the term 'flâneuse', which I feminize in the context of my approach to establish a distinction between male and female travelers. New territories and geographies are explored. My corpus examines first Ella Maillart and Anne-Marie Schwarzenbach's trip to Afghanistan in 1939 in *Journey to Kafiristan* (Dubini brothers 2001). Maillart and Schwarzenbach are early (20th century) French-Swiss travel writers and photographers. I turn next to *La Salamandre* (1971) by Alain Tanner, a francophone Swiss director who projects a woman rebelling against the system, a woman in movement, as found in his subsequent road movie *Messidor* (1979). The mid-section reconsiders Chantal Akerman's film *Les Rendez-vous d'Anna* (1978), a European travelogue that frames Akerman's own story of a filmmaker on tour to present her film, and her encounter with people in Germany and Belgium. Although the film covers spatial displacement, it looks back at the history of World War II, the displacement of people, and its aftermath.

Continuing with the trope of nomadism, Agnès Varda's *Sans toit ni loi/ Vagabond* (1985) offers a 'wandering road' movie in which the nomadic character wanders aimlessly on the roads of southern France. The film is part of a depressive crop in French cinema that came out in the mid-1980s, and conjures noir elements.

The second part of the chapter tries to unpack a woman director's perspective on a female traveler with Laetitia Masson's *La Repentie/The Repentant* (2002). Masson's characters typically rebel against the male societal order. Isabelle Adjani's lead role is projected through the lens of studies of stardom. Her filmic characters usually fit within the category of 'dangerous women'. Masson's work undermines a traditional film noir reading. I conclude with two directors of Maghrebian descent and their films, Zaïda Ghorab-Volta's *Jeunesse dorée/Gilded Youth* (2001) and Mehdi Charef's *La Fille de Keltoum/Keltoum's daughter* (2002). The latter is configured as a North-South return to Algeria, from a feminine perspective.

The road east

Ces voyageuses non voilées faisaient sensation sur une terre musulmane où, les nomades mises à part, les femmes n'apparaissaient en public que le visage couvert, restant même invisibles la plupart du temps. (Perret 185–186) ('These unveiled female travelers created a stir in a Muslim country, where nomads aside, women would never appear in public without their face covered, and being invisible most of the time.')

During his long trip eastward to Afghanistan via Khyber Pass (1953–1954), travel-writer Nicolas Bouvier demystifies the concept of travel, 'On croit qu'on va faire un voyage, mais bientôt c'est le voyage qui vous fait ou vous défait'[1] ('One thinks you're going to make a trip but the travel makes or unmakes you').

In 1939, Ella Maillart took off on a journey to the valley of Kafiristan, an Afghan region on the eastern border of Pakistan. This was her fifth journey to the Orient. She had previously visited Afghanistan by bus in 1937 (Perret 180). She partnered with Annemarie Schwarzenbach for this trip; when they arrived, World War II had just been declared. Their path echoes the Leiningers' bicycle trip to Afghanistan in 1939 and anticipates their compatriot Nicolas Bouvier's trajectory in 1953. Fleeing Europe, with the 'impatience of the world', Maillart wanted to survey one of the last places on earth that had not yet been civilized: the Kafiristan Valley.[2]

Je voulais gagner une vallée non encore influencée par notre civilisation. Et là, je désirais établir une relation en profondeur entre mon agitation d'Européenne désaxée et la stabilité d'une tribu asiatique traditionnelle (Croisières 210). ('I wanted to reach a valley that had not yet been influenced by our civilization. And there, I wanted to establish an in-depth relationship between my European agitated state of mind, and the stability of a traditional Asian tribe.')

Maillart was a formidable sportswoman, a hockey player who also won the single's sailing competition at the 1924 summer Paris Olympics (and the only woman to enter the competition), later competing in skiing in Switzerland.[3] She had visited Russia, China, and Tibet earlier in 1935 with Peter Fleming, with both reporting on their trip in the book *Forbidden Journey: From Peking to Kashmir* (1935). She bankrolled her trips through writing and conference circuits. Unafraid to set off for another expedition, she actively prepared for it. The prospect of using a brand new Ford to cross Asia was alluring.

Fosco and Donatello Dubini's contemplative film *Journey to Kafiristan* (2001), a Swiss-German production, retraces the two friends' footsteps and the drive across Europe and the Near East between March and October 1939.[4] Informed by Maillart's version of the trip as well as Schwarzenbach's essay *Où est la terre des promesses?*, *Journey to Kafiristan* is a period piece, seen by some as a lesbian narrative although homosexuality is merely implied and not explored. It examines the first venture ever made by a Western woman to Afghanistan,[5] in the immediate pre-war moment, a time when negotiations with borders and maps were taking place (Voituret 126).

Both Maillart and Schwarzenbach were Swiss, from Geneva and Zurich, respectively Swiss French and Swiss German. Their interests differ. Maillart declares hers to be the scientific goal of researching nomadic tribes whereas Schwarzenbach, a recovering morphine addict, wishes to journey away from her melancholy condition and familial background. Under the supervision of Maillart, whom she befriended in 1938, she moves toward recovery from morphine dependence.[6] Maillart's ethnographic purpose was not fully tested since they never reached Kafiristan, and upon arriving in Afghan territory, at a British archeologist camp (Joseph Hackin), war was declared, dismantling an entire European team of now divided personnel and cutting their travels short.

The film opens on Maillart's visit to the Royal Geographical Society in London, which grants her authority to undertake the expedition. She first seeks permission to become a member. The society was closely allied to colonial geographical ventures in Africa and the Indian subcontinent and was mostly run by male members. Maillart and Schwarzenbach cut across different countries, taking turns at driving Schwarzenbach's new Ford Roadster along unpaved empty roads or trails. Both look boyish, dressed in loose fitting slacks with short haircuts, emulating the tail end of 1920s' flapper style; they do not wear headscarves. Although they must have attracted a lot of attention in the various places they crossed, as two unaccompanied white European female travelers, they manage to escape direct confrontation, and brandish diplomatic immunity papers secured through Schwarzenbach's French husband's diplomatic status in Tehran whenever appropriate. Only during the black sea crossing do they run into comments and questions about their status as female travelers and lesbians, when a man ponders 'one does not know where she belongs', pointing directly at Schwarzenbach. They move across a vast landscape captured in lush cinematography. Political and geographical borders and divisions appear as they forge ahead, yet the film emphasizes the inner journey over the physical one. In fact, the real dangers are the dark clouds of fascism rising above the European skies, and the Nazi sympathizers they run into at Tehran's German embassy. Maillart's philosophy is that we are all nomads. Schwarzenbach understands that the border crossing has to be internal, not on maps – and arranges her return to Europe. Their journey is historically dated, and places them as pioneer female adventurers at a time when Hitler's armies are marching on and trying to expand their territorial holds, thereby creating further ethnic and geographical divides. Moving through the Balkans, Turkey, Persia, and reaching Afghanistan in 1939, Schwarzenbach is perceived as a rebel, fleeing the Nazi regime as well as her bourgeois family background. She was a strong anti-fascist supporter, close to Erika and Klaus Mann. The two women financed the trip with advance contracts for a book and photographs. They also purchased 16 mm film material.[7] The contracts were obtained through meetings with different geographical societies in Paris, London, and Berlin, in order to prepare for the trip. Schwarzenbach was a photojournalist and writer. *Où est la terre des promesses? Avec Ella Maillart en Afghanistan* (1939–1940) and *La Voie Cruelle/The Cruel way: Switzerland to Afghanistan in a Ford* (1939) as well as a series of photographs are the fruits of their voyage. The film's aesthetics do not linger on the hard questions regarding women traveling alone at the time, yet *Où est la terre des promesses?* assigns an entire chapter and section to 'Two women traveling alone in Afghanistan'.

A travel theory emerges from their trip; for Schwarzenbach, who was seen as rebelling against her family values and those of Switzerland, the journey gives meaning to her life.[8] For Maillart, the impetus to escape European limitations and discover herself motivates her plans. As Sarah Steinert-Borella underlines in her book-length study devoted to Maillart's travel narratives, it is not to write about Afghan women, or to fight against the colonized gaze on women. The two women are eager to flee the impending war, rising fascism, and Western civilization in search of the world and themselves (Maillart *Croisières* 211). Added to this, Maillart is on a mission to save her friend and help her recover. Unable to fully prevent Schwarzenbach's ailment and a relapse during the trip after war is declared, they both part ways: Schwarzenbach returns to Switzerland, hoping to become a war journalist, whereas Maillart joins an ashram in Southern India.[9] Years later, she credits her friend for opening her to that 'interior' life (*Croisières* 221), which she formulates as another type of inner travel,

Aux Indes, j'étais au début d'un voyage tout nouveau qui devait me conduire plus avant vers la vie complète et harmonieuse que je cherchais instinctivement. Pour entreprendre ce voyage, il me fallait d'abord apprendre à connaitre les 'terres inconnues' de mon propre esprit (*Croisières* 224). ('In India, I was at the beginning of a new trip, which was to lead me further into a full and harmonious life that I was looking for instinctively. In order to undertake the journey, I needed first to learn to know the 'unknown territories' of my mind.')

Women passing by

Alain Tanner's 1971 film *La Salamandre* portrays a rebellious young woman, a free spirit who is caught in the web of a capitalist society specifically located in Switzerland. Shot in black and white, it chronicles a few months in the life of Rosemonde, and those who are looking to use her as material for a television film script, namely Pierre, a journalist, who hires his friend Paul, a writer. For those familiar with the Swiss director's later film *Jonas qui aura 25 ans en l'an 2000/Jonah who will be 25 in the year 2000* (1975), *La Salamandre* similarly combines Marxist art-critic John Berger's and Tanner's notions surrounding work and individual freedom in our society and has been perceived as a subversive film (Stam 1977). Berger and Tanner worked together on both *La Salamandre* and *Jonas qui aura 25 ans en l'an 2000*. *La Salamandre* was their first narrative feature collaboration (White 92). It is set in the post-68 era, and reflects some of its values. In *Jonas*, one recalls the spectacular classroom demonstration of the sausage as history by Marco Perly. Marco (Jacques Denis), a newly arrived high-school professor, begins his first history lesson with the slicing of a blood sausage into pieces on top of his desk to the beat of a metronome. The slices are a literal representation of bits of history. What matters is the way one perceives the future through the holes of time or, as Dudley Andrew puts it in his analysis of the sequence, 'history can be sliced up in many ways, but only when it is seen from the right perspective can one peer through its holes to the past and then prophetically into the future' (346).

In the circular shape of (the sausage of) history, in the Annales school tradition, the notion that time is circular and cyclical is conjured up, rich in revolutionary possibilities. Tanner involves another key character in *Jonas*, the retired railroad worker who witnessed the 1936 Popular Front era in France, as a living example of such moment. Raymond Bussières, a direct heir to Popular Front cinema, an actor in Duvivier's and Becker's films as well as a member of the agit-prop Octobre theatre group comprised of the Prévert brothers, J.J Brunius and Sylvia Bataille, plays Charles La Vapeur.[10] Charles' meeting with Marco signals the conjunction of history as theory and practice. The questioning between both men attests to the importance of agency within one's history. Charles, a locomotive driver, borrows the metaphor of the train for life's history lessons. Besides the fact that the train is a recurrent figure in our project, the question applicable to *Jonas*, with extensions to our present film corpus, is the following: Is a traveler or passenger on a train different from the train driver, and how is it different to travel on board a train than it is to drive a train?' As Charles indicates, 'the landscape goes by, like at the movies when you're a traveler, but when you are at the wheel, you enter the landscape, the landscape does not run by you ... and the railroad tracks never meet.'[11] These lines bring to life the spirit of 1936 and 1968 and yet by the time *Jonas*, a millennial film, was released in 1975 the mood had changed.

The ghost of May 68 haunts *La Salamandre*, with Rosemonde (meaning the 'rose of the world') as a character of passage or 'Rosemonde just passing through' and a woman in full r/evolution.[12] According to Alison Smith, 'In the ten years following 1968, Tanner made five films which show a clear, if complex, progression from film to film, and form, as a group, a reflection on 1968 and its implications.' *Jonas qui aura 25 ans en l'an 2000* concludes the May 68 chapter for Tanner (Smith 235).

La Salamandre revisits possible approaches to the filmmaking process, one being a sociologically inspired approach and the other being purely fictional. Both male protagonists and friends (Jean-Luc Bideau and Jacques Denis) are hired to write a script. The journalist previously involved in a travel article on Brazil for a Parisian journal turns to the piece on Rosemonde and the attractive lure of a quick payment. The character of the young woman is first 'imagined' by Paul (Denis), a writer and occasional house painter. At a loss for ideas, the sudden emergence of Rosemonde springs from a newspaper account of a crime that Pierre (Bideau), a journalist, selects for the story and is based on a *fait-divers* (a news item): a young woman is accused of attempting to kill her uncle with a shotgun. An initial documentary-style montage steers the spectator toward forming her own conclusion independent of the writer/journalist team. The journalist pursues a sociological mode of investigative journalism and seeks out witnesses to the event, before finally meeting with Rosemonde. Does Rosemonde exist through their imagination and journalistic search only as a character dependent on her authors or does she have a certain agency in the story?

The camera separately follows Rosemonde (Bulle Ogier) before the actual encounter. She is working in a mindless job filling sausages at a sausage factory. The task is mechanical and repetitive, and the camera focuses solely on her hands and face. The investigation, which starts with neighbors and former employers, tends to reveal that she is a bit 'off' or not 'normal'. However, any notion of 'normalcy' begs questioning in a Swiss film. The search locates her living in new housing projects. Rosemonde agrees to sell her story to Paul, the journalist. Meanwhile, in a parallel attempt, Pierre the writer reconstitutes her story out of his imagination without meeting her first.

As the opening credits roll, a long tracking shot (aptly named a 'traveling' in French) introduces Rosemonde walking by a river, in a long, floating, and stylish 1960s black coat. The film closes with the camera circling Rosemonde moving in the middle of a Christmas-time schizophrenic downtown Geneva crowd, in slow motion, smiling and walking away from yet another alienating job. Interestingly, twenty-five years later, Tanner remade the film in a modern version with *Fourbi* (1996) (*fourbi* means disorder, bric-a-brac, or mess) with a new Salamander-Rosemonde, played by Karin Viard. Viard incarnates the new rebellious woman in French cinema (Sellier). The director stages the same mise-en-scène with the Salamander as the young woman (Viard) in the exact same pose walking freely and decidedly by the river in the opening shots, leaving out the earlier fractured montage of the possible murder attempt on the uncle.[13]

The matter of Rosemonde's guilt initially drives the script. Did she or did she not attempt to kill her uncle with his military rifle or was she innocent? However, since it is removed from a classical Hollywood format that would otherwise be saturated with events and actions, the focus misdirects the search for a true portrayal of a young woman, her everyday routine, and her quest for something in life. More specifically it outlines the psychological and sociological paths that may have led to her act, without dwelling on them. Even when we find out about the actual event, it no longer matters. Her mystery attracts both men, and she seduces them with her personality. She resists any definition, sociological or psychological. Rosemonde is neither an extraordinary nor an ordinary woman; she is an independent woman. She fits the characterization and portrayal of women as mysterious and entirely enigmatic. Just as Freud, Lacan, Breton, Aragon, Irigaray, Nin, or Cixous pondered, along with countless theorists, the enigma of woman is present here, and somehow eludes everyone, including the probing eye of the camera. The 'salamander' harks back to medieval imagery, an animal able to walk through and survive fire.

Conveniently located in the Suisse Romande (Francophone Switzerland), Tanner's native country, a place of national pride, purity, and order, a series of events disrupt the usually unruffled surface and order of things. Switzerland is a constant metaphor for Tanner, who teases the notion of neutrality and sovereignty (Smith 253). Analyzed by Lieve Spaas in her chapter on Switzerland in *The Francophone Film*, Tanner's work 'reveals an insistence on the interaction between space and identity' (53). Each one of his films places the individual in a well-defined spatial context, which often takes on an identity of its own (53).

This is an 'unfilmable' town and country, a domesticated picturesque scenery, akin to Disneyland.[14] Another border film like *Jonas*, in it Paul rides his moped to the city for work, like the character of Mathieu Vernier (Rufus) does in *Jonas*. Actually Geneva is closest to France, and, figuratively speaking, turns 'its back on Switzerland' (Tanner).

'In Switzerland, as in so many other places, the Lumière Cinematograph made an early appearance at fairgrounds. The country itself soon attracted many European film companies and filmmakers because of its spectacular beauty, which provided a natural setting for those in search of pretty pictures' (Spaas 244). First, the extra-diegetic female voiceover narration (Anne-Marie Michel) informs of a sudden garbage collectors' strike orchestrated by the country's migrant workers. The camera veers to show garbage piled up on the sidewalks. Order is threatened in this otherwise orderly society. Second, the two friends engage in a disruptive public performance, on board a tram in Geneva, and harangue the crowd about Arab and migrant workers threatening the country. The sequence features Paul impersonating an Arab man, with loud singing and drumming in the tram while Pierre complains about the growing presence of migrant workers in the country. The improvised subversive theatrical skit compels people to intervene on the tram and some of them to display their latent nationalistic and xenophobic streaks. It addresses the growing fears of immigrants already present in the early 1970s that arose in an earlier Italian film *Pain et Chocolat/Bread and Chocolate* (Franco Brusati 1972).

The implicit third disruptive element in the film, as it is constructed, is the fleeting presence of Rosemonde. She is unruly and ungrateful to her uncle who helped raise her, according to the official version. He is after all a respectable bourgeois, a retired military man who took her in from her large rural family in order to give her an education; yet the thankless Rosemonde turned out to be a delinquent teenager, involved in car theft, teenage pregnancy, and near murder. She is of course a rebel. The opening segment illustrates her potential violence through a rough montage of these events, with a close up of an older man cleaning his shotgun, followed by the sound of a shotgun popping off in the frame and his subsequent screams. However, nothing is elucidated, and the montage deceptively leaves no clues. Not once does the camera implicate Rosemonde except that the editing produces a possibly incriminating version, reminding the spectator that cinematic montage is key in the fabrication of stories. Still, after the shotgun scene, a cross-cutting of Rosemonde's bewildered face, looking back, could point to her guilt, if we wish to interpret it as such. Even though the legal case is dropped, Rosemonde's reputation is tarnished and she is put under police surveillance. Her irreverence erupts in the last sequence at work when she is caressing the legs and feet of male and female clients in the high-end shoe store where she has finally found employment. The uptight shoe-store owner, who at first offered her a ride in his Alfa Romeo, which she refused, fires her at once. Rosemonde's disorderly conduct coupled with a free-floating sexuality and her refusal to engage with her employer's sexual advances mark her as a morally disturbing element in a society where order and cleanliness are legally maintained. Apparently, legislation and a 'little red book' are used to enact these national measures.[15] The script implies overactive sexual behavior on her part through disclosing at one point her use of birth control pills, a rather new product on the market at the time. The post-68 context is a key component of the character, evoking the legalization of contraception for women in Swiss society, who in 1971 finally gained the right to vote, after an initial referendum vote in 1959 was turned down.[16] One can speculate as to the reasons why Tanner and Berger propose a character caught between a child-like rebellious self and a woman in control. No matter how I perceive her, the character 'bounces all over the industrial landscape in her undirected rage' and is not a static figure (Wiener 3–4).

The writers (Tanner's and Berger's alter-egos) help Rosemonde and give her agency over her story. She narrates her life in the first person voice, instead of being invented, recorded, and written. The narration switches hands at a point that coincides with the recognition that they have reached a dead-end in their script writing. As Rosemonde escapes them, they are unable to finish the script. The concluding scene alludes to an emergent 'schizophrenic society' that produces elements like Rosemonde. The cinema-vérité sequence is conjured by a camera that dances around her, in slow motion, as the shot fades to dark.

La Salamandre anticipates Tanner's 1979 film, *Messidor*, although the tone in the latter film has turned dark and hopeless. *Messidor* is the pre-cursor to female road movies such as *Sans toit ni loi/Vagabond* by Agnès Varda (1985) on the French side, and *Thelma and Louise* (1991) by Ridley Scott, an American film. In *Messidor* two young women Jeanne and Marie, from two different social backgrounds, meet and decide to hitchhike together through the Swiss countryside in the summer. *Messidor* comes from the French revolutionary word signaling June-July, the months of harvest. The initial fun-seeking liberating trip turns into a nightmarish descent into delinquency and detention for the two women thanks to a series of events they experience over the course of three weeks. Tanner explains the film as an attempt to walk into Switzerland and discuss the place for the first time,

> *Jonas* ... était un film d'idées, de discours. Cette fois c'est un peu l'inverse. ...J'ai eu envie d'un peu de silence, d'écouter, me promener, d'aller dans la montagne. Mais ce silence n'est pas innocent non plus. Je n'avais jamais parlé directement de la Suisse. Je ne l'avais jamais montrée. Il existe dans ce pays une horreur un peu glacée que je voulais montrer (Mühlethaler). ('Jonah was a film of ideas, of discourse. This time, it's the reverse. I wanted a bit of silence, to listen, to go for a walk, into the mountains. But the silence is not innocent either. I never spoke directly of Switzerland. I had never shown it. There is a certain sense of frozen horror in this country that I wanted to show.')

The journey documents the boundaries of travel for women, in the 1970s, the possibility of enjoying actual freedom, and the repression of movement within society. The trip, game-like at the start, tests the boundaries of their travels. The two female characters wander off on the road, walking and hitching rides from mostly male drivers. Zones of danger threaten their sense of security and propel the story toward its bleak conclusion, off camera. Their journey becomes a crossing of the void. Framed as dangerous terrorists, with their profile displayed on national news, they are forcibly removed off the peaceful roads of Switzerland so that order be restored at the close of the film.

Chantal Akerman's passages

> I'm Belgian, a Polish Jew by origin. I was born in Brussels 6 June 1950 and I wanted to make films very young, after I saw *Pierrot le fou* by Godard. (The Innovators)

Akerman's interests lie deep in travel and borders. Her latest film *Almayer's Folly* (2012) is a personal study of a traveler.[17] *Les Rendez-vous d'Anna* (1978), a pre-fall film, looks back on the post-World War II years and the cold war in Europe. It examines 'female nomadic subjectivity' (Bruno 99). The main character, a filmmaker, is never static as she travels by train through different European countries in an effort to promote her films. The train rides across Germany, Belgium, and France focus on the uniformity of places, seen from the voyager's perspective.

In 1960s cinema characters evolve, and distance between them and the world becomes more pronounced, announcing a new era of the ballad in cinema. Goldmann's study of wandering in contemporary cinema examines films by Godard, Akerman, Jarmusch, and Wenders – all travelogues – to unveil each character's wandering mode.

> ... de lieux en lieux, dans les villes, dans la nature, prendre des trains ou des avions, faire des rencontres, sans qu'aucun événement ne marque réellement son existence (Goldmann 17).

('from place to place, in cities, in nature, taking trains or planes, meeting people, without any event significantly marking his existence.')

Aurore Clément plays the character of Anna; the actress had appeared previously in *Lacombe Lucien* (Malle 1974) and *Apocalypse Now redux* (Coppola 1979), and later in *La Captive* (Akerman 2001), *Paris Texas* (Wenders 1984), and *Demain on déménage/Tomorrow we move* (Akerman 2003).

Les Rendez-vous d'Anna raises the problematic of 'home': Is Anna ever home? Where and what is home for her? Is home where she is born, Belgium? Where is it now that she is a filmmaker? Is it France? This issue is not resolved when she reaches home at the very end of an arduous two-hour-long trajectory. Her Parisian apartment is empty and impersonal, and more like a place of passage.

For the duration of the film, Anna (whose name I infer from messages left on answering machines) is touring Europe, traveling from town to town, hotel to hotel in Europe before the fall of the Berlin wall. She introduces her newly made film, yet paradoxically, the camera does not go into theaters or capture spectators; the audience (us, spectators) never sees her film. *Les Rendez-vous d'Anna* can therefore be construed as the film 'I' am presently watching.

Nothing happens in the film, except for distance traveled from one town to the next and rare sporadic exchanges between people. Most of the 'action' is located in liminal zones, Marc Augé's *'non-lieux'* – nondescript and oddly uniform places all lit in the same brown color scheme: cities, hotel rooms, trains, or train platforms and stations match her single brown outfit; a few short sequences are located in café/restaurants. The majority of the film is shot at nighttime.

The camera's characteristic long takes are very static. Throughout the trip, Anna's encounters with others are impersonal, short-lived, unsatisfying. She attracts men everywhere she passes, although nothing develops out of these short encounters, except that most men confide in her as they would an analyst. She is a great listener, and draws confessions from different people. Yet she is distant, and does not seem engaged, except when she is with her mother.

Germany. First encounter

Anna's sexual encounter with a German man, Heinrich, whom she met at her evening screening, fails. When she asks him to get dressed, he wonders if something is wrong; she simply answers: 'We don't love each other.' He is the only spectator to emerge from her screening. He is a rather melancholic man. Their last exchange takes place in the hotel lobby (a recurrent location in the film), as he leaves her with his address. He is a teacher and wants her to meet his young daughter.

She visits him the next day, yet the camera stays statically outdoors, in a garden with a train passing in the distance, rejecting the intimacy of a house. The man converses with her, about German history and the war. The discussion of Germany, and its occupation by Allied forces, its division and reconstruction from its ruins, takes place outdoors in a wintery garden. The camera respectfully stays at a distance and does not go inside the house when he invites her to come. A woman (possibly his mother) and a little girl greet her, from a distance.

Outside/inside: outdoors/indoors

Indoors means home, family, comfort, and relationships. Since Anna is always on the margins of any relationship, she is framed outside or in neutral hotel rooms. She sleeps with men and a woman, but leaves the next day. In fact, she immediately leaves after visiting the German man's house. Anna avoids going home. Home could be located in Brussels if taken as hometown or birthplace. When Anna catches up with her mother (Lea Massari) during one of her stops, at Brussels Midi station they decide to go to a hotel, instead of the family house. They speak as close friends; a strong undercurrent of love runs between them. They both walk in the streets and end up in a hotel room. They have not seen each other in three years. Anna embraces her mother and they spend the night together in the hotel room.[18] Anna confesses her lesbian relationship with an Italian woman. The hotel room provides a space where she feels uninhibited enough to confide in her mother and tell her a secret they will share. The mother depicted is the 'idealized mother' that Akerman wants to see and remember: young, and with a slight foreign (Italian) accent. She is the woman who calls her and leaves messages at hotels.

The second encounter features Ida at the Cologne train station. Ida is a Jewish friend of Anna's parents; after living in exile, she is back in Germany. She urges Anna to settle down and have children. Ida is very conservative and unhappy about the way women are nowadays: free, yet lonely, not even trying to get married and produce children. When she is depressed, she thinks of the past and her sons. She is the link to Anna's mother and the family's Jewish roots. Ida believes that it is 'nice to be an artist' because they are 'always traveling'. If this is an attempt at matchmaking, and arranging a marriage between Anna and her son, Ida is unsuccessful in her quest.

The German man on the last train ride is the third significant encounter in the trip. He tries to strike up a conversation on the walkway. A non-committal Anna responds with curt acknowledgements as she did with Ida. The rather long train sequence passes through different cities with various track changes. The man talks to her about himself first in German, then in French. 'Vous allez à Paris?' ('You're going to Paris?'). He is from Berlin, yet is unable to stay in Germany, which he hates. He has lived as an expatriate in various countries in South America.

Landscapes

The trains traverse industrial settings and cityscapes glimpsed through the windows. When Anna arrives in Paris, it is the first time that the city is seen through a car, a taxi, and with her boyfriend Daniel (Jean-Pierre Cassel), who picks her up. The 'natural' surroundings are otherwise bleak with no sunlight, adding noir elements to the film. The modern, massive, impersonal, and cold architecture lit by harsh neon lights establishes a distance. Although Anna is constantly framed looking out windows, the outside does not seem engaging, despite the possibility of fresh air. Daniel depressingly talks about the ordinariness of his life. Instead of going 'home' they go to a hotel. He asks her to sing. Her Marguerite Monnod sentimental song, sung by Edith Piaf, 'Les Amants d'un jour', features the dark tale of a lovers' suicide in a hotel room, a prefiguration of *Hôtel du Nord*'s script by Marcel Carné/Eugène Dabit. It is the only 'live' music in the film besides the dull hotel radio's classical tunes and elevator music. Despite his initial sexual desire for her the reunion is anti-climactic as he literally falls sick, and she volunteers to pick up some medicine for him.

The film tackles gender issues through the woman's travel and occupation, and the various encounters she has. Expectations that are placed on women demand that they settle down and be housewives, raising children. Women are supposed to be sedentary. Yet Anna, an artist, is constantly moving, and does not live at 'home.' Ida recalls her transient position.

She faces the loneliness and alienation of people (including her herself), trying to make connections, in any possible ways, mostly on trains. This takes place before the age of the Internet and the cellphone. What ensue are dislocated temporary relationships, passages through topographies between women and men and among women.

Les rendez-vous d'Anna is visibly autobiographical. Akerman was twenty-eight years old when she made the film. The chronology corresponds with her departure from Brussels at age twenty or twenty-one. She keeps a distance between herself and the spectator, through the main protagonist. The entire subtext is about exile and one's land and about Jewish memory from the perspective of the generation of children born of Jewish survivors. The focus on Germany activates the return to history and origins; Germany is where orders for the extermination of Jews were issued and implemented. Anna's Polish-born parents had to leave their country and seek asylum in Belgium. The image of the train further contributes to the figures of displacement, migration, and exile.

> When I look at my parents, I see that they are very well integrated here ... they don't have this feeling of exile. In a way they have made a break with their past ... I think that we represent the generation in which the repressed comes back. Because they did not tell ... (Audrey-Foster 98)

Akerman's obsession with the past and her Jewish identity is conveyed through Ida's discussion of the war. It projects in most of her films. The inability to settle down echoes the difficulty of processing the past and becoming a sedentary type.

The perpetual feeling of displacement and rootlessness is linked to Jewish identity, estrangement and alienation between self and others. Akerman's cinema is a cinema of passengers (Bruno 100). Interiors are not shown, barring one from visiting the family home, the German friend's place, and the theaters. However, the camera follows Anna through her nomadic architecture (Bruno 100). The film's geography is exclusively composed of hotel rooms, streets, trains, train stations, cinemas, and car interiors.

Nomadism in Varda's Sans toit ni loi/Vagabond (1985)

J'aime à penser que Mona la campeuse, par-delà les décennies de 'revendications sociales', a été livrée par Varda au mouvement rageur et

instinctif de celle qui 'veille' au paysage comme sur un vague trésor.
A contretemps (Serge Daney 243).

('I like to think that Mona, the camper, after decades of social claims,
was delivered by Varda to the instinctual and raging movement of
the one who "watches" over the landscape like a vague treasure. In
counter-time.')

Road and travel movies deliver a statement on the globalized world
in relation to Europe's porous borders. Movies mirror increased mobility from one nation to the next, dangers of terrorist threats, and of
non-desirable immigrants, for instance in France, the growing number of Roma (Gypsies), Afghans, Pakistani, Turks, West Africans, and
North-Africans moving north or west to France, some of them trying
eventually to cross over to England. Some movies travel from within
the periphery, the margins of societies without ever leaving the nation,
and crossing borders and therefore focusing on *intra-muros* travels or
travels within.

Franco-French travels

Agnès Varda became a well-established filmmaker after her debut as a
photographer for Jean Vilar's theatre troupe followed by a first feature-
length film *La Pointe Courte* (1955). Like *Voyage to Italy* (Rossellini 1954),
La Pointe courte 'embarked on parallel unpredictable journeys' (Andrew
106).[19] As a precursor to New Wave cinema, Varda struggled to produce
her films throughout her career and was unable to secure *avance sur
recettes* (Tarr/Rollet 234) for *Sans toit ni loi* (1985). Two years before, the
release of *Tchao Pantin* (Claude Berri 1983), a film noir headed by national
comedian Coluche in the dramatic role of gas station attendant Lambert,
marked the pervasive *noirceur* of the moment. Maurice Pialat's film *Loulou*
(1980) and Michel Blanc's *Marche à l'ombre* (1984) reveled in the prevalent noir atmosphere. *Sans Toit ni loi/Vagabond* (1985) marks a significant
moment in French cinema – a somber film in the middle of a dark era in
French cinema. Much has already been eloquently written about Varda's
films, especially in terms of feminist analysis in Sandy Flitterman-Lewis's
study. *Sans toit ni loi* garnered a prestigious series of prizes: the best actress
César for Sandrine Bonnaire, along with Agnès Varda's nomination as
best director and Macha Méril as best supporting actress, and it won
the Golden Lion at the Venice film festival. It propelled actress Sandrine
Bonnaire onto the scene as one of France's upcoming and leading

actresses. She had appeared earlier as a teenager in Maurice Pialat's *A nos amours* (1983), her debut film, scripted by Arlette Langmann and Pialat. The film is set in the deep Southern (West) region of France, the Languedoc, near Montpellier, an area that is highly touristic and quite photogenic with postcard-like qualities. Varda returns to her childhood region, located not far from Sète.[20] However, the film opens on the vista of a harsh wintery terrain and the body of Mona found dead in a ditch. It will be structured in a series of flashbacks retracing the 'impossible portrait' of the last days of a young female vagrant.

> Le film est parti sur l'hiver, dans une région du Midi que je connais bien ... et l'émotion insupportable pour moi de tous les cas de gens qui meurent de froid ... A partir de là, c'était automatiquement un film sur les vagabonds en général. C'est une nouvelle génération de vagabonds et de sans abris qui ne sont pas les clochards d'avant, mais des plus jeunes qui prennent simplement la route (Dormoy, Lazar 78). ('The film started with winter in the South, a region I know well ... and the unbearable feeling that some people die of cold... from that, it automatically became a film on vagabonds, in general. There is a new generation of wanderers, and homeless people who are not like the bums from before, but younger people who just hit the road.')

The new generation of bums, according to Varda, is not intellectual, but motivated by a refusal to adapt to societal norms (Dormoy, Lazar 78). Mona is said to be from nowhere – she possibly came from the sea and left remarkably few traces behind her after her passage. Yet witnesses emerge and recount their sightings of Mona or their encounters with her. People define themselves in relation to her. The camera painstakingly documents and in a series of flashbacks reconstructs the last days of Mona's odyssey as she crossed the region, hitchhiked and camped alone, squatted with a road companion, found temporary refuge with a female tree-scientist, drank with an older woman, and bathed in a cold wintery sea. Varda's qualities as a photographer and documentarist *'documenteur'* – a pun on documentary film(maker) and liar that she returned to in a mockumentary made later in her career, *Documenteur* (1980–1981) – are deployed at their best, anticipating *Les Glaneurs et la Glaneuse/The Gleaners and I* (2000).[21] The latter, concerning the rubble of society in the year 2000, crowns her career, along with the autobiographical documentary *Les Plages d'Agnès/The Beaches of Agnès* (2008). Although the narrative spins different texts, styles, and genres, I choose to examine *Vagabond* as one of the few road-movies directed and written by a woman director and focus on the road motifs inherent to the structure of the film. From the start, the labeling is arguable. Technically speaking, David Laderman sees the film only as a semi-road movie, for it does not take place in a car although it 'deconstructs and reinvents the genre in terms of narrative structures, film style, and thematic tone' (265). European road-movies are less dependent on driving (265); in fact some film analysts question the genre (Aumont 222). Mona never drives, but hitches rides, is driven, or walks. Susan Hayward writes that 'the road movie unravels in chronological time and space and the point of view is that of the roadsters. The purpose of the trajectory is ideological (for example, by exposing a social injustice) and implies self-discovery' (Hayward 257). Of course, as the camera follows Mona throughout the region, it resists giving the spectator any *état d'âme* or introspection. Hayward situates the narrative outside of history and ideology. Varda named this film a wandering-road movie. As Flitterman-Lewis has argued,

> Varda refused to offer us the security of a fixed identity for her character; rather, through her careful orchestration of these diverse visions, she invites us to participate in the construction of meaning – of this woman, of her situation, of the necessary social contact for all of human activity. (243)

For some privately-kept personal reason, Mona chose the life of a vagrant, a vagabond, as the English title for the translation of *Sans toit ni loi* suggests, doing away with the notions and suggestions of roof, home, and law found in the French title, which is itself a pun on the common expression *sans foi ni loi* (lawless). The road is central to the narrative, and so are the accompanying markers of road movies or travel narratives paved with road signs, traveling shots, car rides, and hitchhiking.

–Baba cool: Tu campes par ce temps? (Are you camping in this weather?)
–Mona: J'ai pas choisi le temps. (I did not choose the weather.)
–Baba cool: Mais tu as choisi la route. (You chose the road.) (Hottell 686)

These lines, transcribed from the film, evoke the perils faced by female vagrants. One man labels such women 'rôdeuses' ('prowlers'), assigning them a sense of danger and suspicion that is prevalent to the nomadic condition. Their own safety is not even an issue. Viewed as a women's film, *Vagabond* is not empowering, but disruptive of common assumptions about women as caring, beautiful personas that are preoccupied with images of self-representation. Similarly, Varda questions the concept of cleanliness as it socially applies to women (Dormoy, Lazar 78). Mona Bergeron qualifies as the 'campeuse sale' ('the dirty camper') (Daney 242). Needless to say Varda already shattered the mirror in *Cléo de 5 à 7/Cleo from 5 to 7* (1962) with the on-screen metamorphosis of a doll (the equivalent of a *poupée de son* ('a wax doll'), a character and song by contemporary singer France Gall) into that of a mature and thoughtful woman.[22] Hottell views *Sans toit ni loi* as a remake of *Cléo de 5 à 7*, a point ascertained as well by Flitterman-Lewis: '*Sans toit ni loi* picks up where that film ended in terms of a path by the main female character' (Hottell 684).

Female wanderers are suspicious. 'Mona's chosen liberty makes traditionalists uncomfortable' (Hottell 686). Many witnesses subject Mona to tough questioning and at one time challenge her notion of freedom as if this element disturbed their comfortable sedentary life and had come back to haunt them. Mona's harshest critic is a young man who left the city to cultivate a piece of land, one of these marginal figures from the 1970s, raising goats and producing goat cheese. He is an ex-philosophy student – a 68er – who dropped out of school to return to the land and raise a family. The plot resonates with post-68 ideologies. The goatherder compares his life with hers at first, a mutual kinship based on the road, but soon tires of her lazy attitude once he has given her a chance to cultivate her own field and sees that she decides to do nothing but live off them, as he puts it as 'a parasite'.

Varda sketches an 'impossible portrait' of a woman traveling alone, a genre reversal of road movies that were first male-oriented, featuring at least two male companions and their friendship (Flitterman-Lewis 1996). A case example of such a film in earlier French cinema is René Clair's ending in *A nous la liberté* (1931), a buddy film in an era where friendship and social classes as well as a community of people were at the core of such films. Even the more recent American *Thelma and Louise* (Ridley Scott 1991) pairs two women as buddies, but they cannot survive and die a 'heroic' death. An early female wanderer film *It Happened One Night* (Frank Capra 1934) quickly sets a single woman (Claudette Colbert) traveling alone with a male companion (Clark Gable) and has a happier resolution.[23] Class differences are important yet not necessarily central in American ones. More recently in French cinema, the case of Virginie Despentes and Coralie Trinh Thi in *Baise-Moi/Fuck me* (2000) exemplifies what can go wrong in a female road movie, by using the slasher/horror/porn genre in an adaptation of their novel.

Mona Bergeron (the protagonist) rarely encounters friendship, nor she does care to pursue it (*Sans toit ni loi*). A woman professor, Ms. Landier (Macha Méril), thinks back to her encounter with Mona and recounts that she could have done more for her. A university professor, specializing in plane trees, Landier is researching the fungal epidemic affecting the trees imported during the arrival of American G.Is after World War II. The ecological discourse about the disappearance of a species so common to French roadsides raises parallels with Mona, who is also endangered and disappears by the film's end and whose death is foretold in the opening sequence; she is viewed as parasitical by some because of her homelessness and wandering. In retrospect, Landier observes that Mona marked her. Yet Mona is/was a pessimist at heart. She has no drive and no interest. She will not accept compromise. She does not care if the trees are cut or disappear from the planet. Before her progressive decline, Varda indulges in a few brief comedic moments celebratory of women's complicity, such as when Mona meets an elderly woman, aunt Lydie, whom Yolande (Yolande Moreau) cares for and who is a potential victim of her nephew's inheritance schemes. Assoun (Yahiaoui Assouna), a Tunisian farm hand who gives her shelter and shows her how to trim vines in the vineyards during winter, has compassion for her. Assoun is the only person who in the post-mortem interviews keeps a respectful silence.

Otherwise, the road provides a zone of male-dominated danger where Mona successively meets her rapist, is pelted by grapes in the wine harvest fest, starves, and freezes to death. It does not have the redeeming qualities that one would expect to find for a free individual. The road is not open to freedom as shown in *A nous la liberté* (René Clair 1931) or more recently *Western* (Emmanuel Poirier 1997), two male buddy road movies; instead the film captures the dead-end ditch, the image of the open grave that awaits and threatens excessive female mobility at the end of the trip. The death imagery crisscrosses the narration as it did in *Cléo from 5 to 7* and, as usual with Varda, is done with many pictorial indexical references such as the inclusion of Hans Baldung Grien's paintings. (Ungar 88–90).

Yet Mona awakens liberating aspirations in people, especially housewives who envy her life. However, nomadism in the film passes through exclusion. The female wanderer navigates the panoramas in beautiful panning shots that are tableaux-like and are inspired by the paintings of Van Gogh for instance.[24]

Road movies and westerns are in general male genres, whereas costume dramas are usually regarded as the suitable genre for women (Doane, referenced in Pidduck 172). The road movie enables men to freely traverse geographies while strengthening the notion that a woman's place is that of stasis, at home, by the fire, like Penelope in Homer's *Odyssey*, as best demonstrated in the characters of Yolande and Aunt Lydie. As Zingarina does in Gatlif's *Transylvania*, Mona sets fire to such preconceived notions, and by rejecting such values is in turn rejected and endangered by those she meets on the final road-trip to death. Mona becomes part of the terrain, statue-like, and resists capture. She escapes her fate as a clerical worker in an office (the only clue we have of her past) for a life of mobility, yet her trajectory is circular. She goes around a circle, and crisscrosses a limited regional area for the duration of the narrative. The same wine region at one point becomes claustrophobic, especially during the wine harvesting celebrations when Mona is surrounded and harassed by the male wine harvesters' ritualistic celebrations preceding her actual death. The script does not give her a past, or a future; she is a mysterious creature, who in the end is just as mysterious as she was at the beginning. She resists objectification in the cinematographic sense, and resists a psychology that would expose a childhood trauma. Jurij M. Lotman's analysis of characters and plot development distinguishes between

> those who are mobile, who enjoy freedom with regard to plot-place ... who can change their place in the structure of the artistic world and cross the frontier, the basic topological feature of this space, and those who are immobile, who represent a function of this space (Lotman 167).

Mona epitomizes mobility, marginality, and chosen homelessness in the mid-eighties, yet she does not deliver a viable model as a modus vivendi. Varda develops her as a symbol, although she claims that she met someone like Mona, a young woman of Arab descent, traveling along the Southern roads. She was fascinated by Settina's rebellion and her total independence (Dormoy, Lazar 79) and even gave her a cameo appearance in the film:

> *Sans toit ni loi* is a reinscription of an original and real text. Varda's initial idea – to make a film about road people/vagrants (male and female) in the winter who perish from the cold – became substantially modified when she encountered a hitchhiking vagabond, Settina. (Hayward 285)

Wandering becomes a central element in 1960s films. New Wave cinema has had a determining impact on the orientation of films depicting the road such as Jean-Luc Godard's *Week End, A Bout de souffle,* or *Pierrot le fou,* films in which a main protagonist is on the loose. The proliferation of films dealing with the open roads and travel epitomizes the postmodern era and functions as a cultural critique. Laderman has observed this on the following levels:

> Cinematically, in terms of innovative traveling camera work, montage, and soundtrack; narratively; in terms of an open-ended, rambling plot structure; thematically, in terms of frustrated, often desperate characters lighting out for something better, someplace else (2).

Goldmann formulated a preliminary commentary on the emerging *problématique* of wandering roads and movements in contemporary French and/or European cinema. She conveys her point through such filmmakers as Godard, Hopper, Loden, Akerman, Duras, Wenders and Jarmusch – a perspective that goes beyond the regimented national borders of French or American cinema. Investigating films made between 1960 and 1985, she stops short of Varda's *Vagabond,* not released at the time of her writing. In European movies, space is more limited – it is not really about crossing vast areas and therefore it cannot be construed rationally and imaginarily in the same way as it is in American texts. In the French imaginary, the desert plays a strong role. Unlike American movies, the road is not a refuge from 'home'.

The repentant one

La Repentie (2002) participates all of a sudden in a return narrative, unannounced to the spectator. A woman's film, the script was written and directed by Laetitia Masson, who started with *En avoir ou pas/To have or not* (1995), followed by *A Vendre/For Sale* (1998), a road movie.[25] *En avoir ou pas* focused on unemployment and women's work in Brittany's fishing factories. Sandrine Kiberlain played the lead roles in both films. *La Repentie* loosely borrows Didier Daeninckx's eponymous novel.[26] Masson supplemented the script with a Maghrebian background and a Riviera setting for the character that Daeninckx located in a witness-protection program in Brittany.

A woman (Isabelle Adjani) wheeling her suitcase arrives at a Paris train station and changes from a jogging suit into a long gaudy black lace dress that will stay with her for the duration of the film. After shoplifting a pulp-fiction novel and dark sunglasses, she boards the first fast speed train to the seaside, and ends up in Nice, on the Riviera. She has different aliases, all pointing to the 'path' undertaken: Alice Duchemin, Alice de la Route, and Charlotte Desmoulin. It is only at the end of the narrative that she reveals her true name, Leïla. Ashamed of her Maghrebian origins, and tired of her wandering, she confesses her life story to Paul Viard (Sami Frey), a man who initially hired her to be his escort.

Leïla-Charlotte's past clings to her and catches up with her. Yet she lives in the moment and immediately celebrates her newly acquired freedom by dancing solo and barefoot on the Croisette, undisturbed by onlookers. A man (Samy Naceri) tracks her down back from Paris, possibly a former boyfriend, commissioned by her husband (Jacques Bonnafé), who is now in jail. After five years in jail, she had traded her release in exchange for his arrest since he was on the lam; together they had committed petty crimes eight years before, yet when he killed two police officers she did jail time for him. Because of his arrest, he signs her death warrant and dispatches his friend to locate her. Reversing roles, she is what he calls a 'killer' – metaphorically speaking, a *femme fatale*.

Her newly found freedom is painful, as she is down and out in Nice, rejected from luxury stores where she seeks employment as a sales person. She is ready to live in the shady, mythical, and kitsch world of palaces, rescued by Paul, a wealthy widower whose gives away his money to noble charity causes. He hires her as a companion for his social life. Their encounter takes place at the Negresco hotel, a palace that she frequented before with her boyfriend.

She reveals her background to Paul, in front of his middle-class parents, and talks about her origins: she comes from the *banlieue* (the suburbs), her father married a Moroccan woman, they were poor and unemployed, and her sister went astray; she fled that life as a youngster when she met Joseph, with whom she went on a stealing spree. The camera lingers on her face, in a long take, as she tells her story, never once providing a reverse shot of the parents and their reaction. Yet we see glimpses of Paul's face upon hearing the news. Paul supports her decision to travel to the end of the road and accompanies her to North Africa where her mother resides.

The film performs a triple return: one metaphorical, the return of Isabelle Adjani, a now mythical French film star, to the French screen after a hiatus in her career, a second the return of the character (Leïla) to her place of origin, the suburbs and North Africa (the latter in fact being her mother's origin), and a third Leïla's return to the place of her earlier career as a thief. In all instances, the return is unhappy and fails to satisfy its intent. The return of Adjani itself in this film is controversial as it provoked a barrage of negative critical responses in the press. If Leïla is ultimately looking for peace (as the repentant one) she does not find it and is unwelcome in both cases. If Adjani was looking for a 'comeback', the critics defused any chance of it. The film skirts the issue of mixed heritage, and mixed origins for the mother is Maghrebian. Adopting a chase mode, Leïla leaves again and takes a train north, stealing Paul's money. She revisits her parents' neighborhood, checks her family's place, and encounters an aphasic father (José Giovanni) and a half-crazed sister (Maria Schneider) who talks about her in the third person, rejecting her. Leïla leaves them some money. The mother (Farida Amrouche) abandoned them and returned to Morocco. Paul rescues Leïla from the former boyfriend who has been commissioned to kill her, and accidentally kills him in self-defense in a motel room. The last part of the film is situated in Morocco, to where they both flee in an attempt to visit the mother. She lives in a small desert-village and pretends not to recognize Leïla. Leïla collapses but is rescued by Paul once more. They both go to the city and stay in a hotel, where she is ultimately arrested for the murder of the tracker back in France. She turns herself in, saving Paul, whereas he is unable to convince the police of his guilt, reinforcing a racial and gender reading. As an Arab woman Leïla is the designated culprit. The last image shows Paul hopelessly waiting for her on a staircase outside a Moroccan police station.

The 'repentant' one waits until the end of the film to repay a debt. She recognizes her past and drops the mask. The reality of her suburban family who no longer accepts her in the last segment is hard to grasp and is destructive. Both father and mother, though separated now, no longer acknowledge her, and the sister voices their rejection. Paul accepts her for what she is, and 'wants her to be happy', regardless of her past or origins.

La Repentie, in direct lineage with Masson's earlier film *A vendre*, was criticized for showing 'a hopeless wandering, full of clichés'.[27] Both films share similar features; in *A vendre*, two men are looking for a woman who vanished in lieu of attending her wedding. The fiancé (Jean-François Stévenin) hires a man to locate her and bring her back to him; the investigation provokes a long journey on the back roads of France and into the past. Luigi, the investigator (Sergio Castellitto), interviews people she knew, her parents and some of her acquaintances. He starts getting inside the character's mind, and empathizes with her, in tune with a feminine psyche. In his quest, their trajectories parallel each other, and she leaves France for the United States as she always longed to do. However, while homeless in New York she calls Luigi and asks for his help to repatriate her to Europe.

Masson's filmic narratives follow women who live on the margins of society and attempt to negate their past. France (*A Vendre*) comes from a rural background she despises. She will not return to the Champagne *pouilleuse* (the name of the region). Rejecting a conventional life-style, the repentant Leïla (*La Repentie*) tries to erase her roots in order to make amends with her past. The female protagonists meet men who try to be good to them, out of charity and love. They rebel against any model of conventional bourgeois lifestyles. Both characters attempt to find regular employment but one is easily led into prostitution, whereas the other becomes an escort girl ('minus the sex'), defining the unstable place of women in society and a rather quick descent into prostitution. Both films take the spectator to the Riviera, with Nice or Marseilles as a backdrop to such legal or illegal activities.

Coming across writer Christine Angot's review compelled me to revisit *La Repentie*, despite or maybe because of the harsh negative criticism it garnered.[28] Angot reminds readers that some critics went as far as to talk about the film as this 'thing', disavowing the term 'film'. Similarly, bloggers have described Adjani's comeback as the 'sinking' of a boat.[29] As the film preview states in its opening sentence, borrowing from the dialogue between the two men from her past: 'we missed her' (*elle nous a manqué*), playing on the ambiguity of the pronoun 'her', indicating that both men are simultaneously referring to the character of Leïla or Adjani, the actress, and possibly both raising the possible inclusion of viewers and their infatuation with her.[30] Early star studies point to the fact that audiences confuse the life of stars with their roles, to the point of not distinguishing between the two. They are inextricably merged. Edgar Morin, in what constitutes the earliest study of stars, refers to the 'two lives of stars' – the one lived in their films and their own life ('La star a deux vies: celle de ses films, et sa vie réelle') – their substance being literally 'seized' by the camera (47–48). Regarding French stars such as Jean Gabin, Alain Delon, Jeanne Moreau, Catherine Deneuve, and Louis de Funès, Chris Holmlund proposes that 'stardom is different in France than in the UK or the USA; stars play a larger role in cultural life and are more often politically involved' (Holmlund in Vincendeau 452).

Film critics overlooked the point of the film by focusing on Adjani and her career and mixing them together. An interesting amalgam of such criticisms occurs in Hélène Frappat's interrogation: 'How does one film the working of time on the miraculously smooth and round face of an actress?'[31] The same interrogation of ageing actresses can be found in recent studies of Catherine Deneuve (Lisa Downing, Sue Harris). Located in the noir genre, the film's opening sequence preceding the credits immediately faults the woman, while pairing the two men who were ever close to her (with the exception of the new person she meets). The incarcerated man, calling for revenge, announces: 'She killed us. We are dead.' Yet the film pokes fun at the markers of the genre for its full two-hour duration. If she 'betrayed' the man she once loved, she paid for five years of her life in jail, and now trades her freedom for his incarceration. The past returns and haunts her; she is not 'free' until the end, rejected by her family and her relations but incarcerated again in the finale. Like Rosemonde in *La Salamandre* (Tanner) she rebels against bourgeois conformity and its lifestyle and rejects everything. She wants to live her life fully and not grow old, as she once confesses to Paul. Her style is definitely anti-fashion; she does not imitate any current common taste, and avoids clichés, such as the customary sunbathing and swimming in the sea, bikini-clad on the Riviera. Instead, she wears an all-black gown (although I discovered that it is a stylish Tom Ford outfit), a black umbrella, describing what the director and costume designer envisioned as a nomadic look.[32] So much for the wardrobe and what critics singled out as Adjani playing a model. The only baggage she retains from her past life is the wheeled suitcase, a souvenir of her past journeys (Halberstadt 51).

Adjani fits the category of 'dangerous women' (Tarr, Rollet 204), after playing the role of a murderess in *Mortelle Randonnée* (Claude Miller 1983), not to mention her casting in the American remake of Clouzot's *Les Diaboliques* (1955) with Sharon Stone (Jeremiah S. Chechik *Diabolique* 1996). She plays a small-town vixen, and troubled women (LaSalle 27). Similarly, she is often 'on the run' (Carr, Rollet 230). Therefore her appearance in *La Repentie* as a criminal on the run matches her customary roles.

Throughout the 1980s, Adjani made the headlines and cropped up on multiple covers of *Elle* magazine (both *Elle* France and *Elle* USA). Adjani 'embodied the face of France for the past two decades' (Baudot 16). The thriller *L'Eté meurtrier/One Deadly Summer* (Jean Becker 1983) owed its success to her lead and 'pulling power' (Austin 69). In the footsteps of Catherine Deneuve and Brigitte Bardot, whose personal lives suffered from relentless scrutiny, Adjani was hunted and subject to many rumors in that decade. Partnering Adjani with Sami Frey, a charismatic actor whose reputation was solidly anchored in the 1970s film and theater world, especially as a film companion to Deneuve (*Manon 70* 1968) and Bardot (*La vérité* 1960), indicates his return to the screen. Both Frey and Adjani are stage actors, albeit of two different generations. Adjani was a teen actress (Comédie Française), like Sophie Marceau, Charlotte Gainsbourg, and more recently Ludivine Sagnier (LaSalle 15), introduced in Claude Pinoteau's *La Gifle* (1974).

La Repentie is noticeably one of the first films to embrace Adjani's Arabic background. In her analysis of the later film *La Journée de la Jupe* (Lilienfeld 2009), Geneviève Sellier notices that Adjani's ethnic identity had been occluded until recently – 'her star image has been built at the antithesis of that identity' – which she reads as connoting Frenchness: 'Her blue eyes and white skin, as well as her classical training ... all give credence to the viewer's belief in her "'Frenchness"' (Sellier 146).[33]

In a rare 2001 interview, shortly before *La Repentie*, Adjani, then forty-five, confides to journalist Annick Cojean about her German mother and her Algerian Kabyle father:

I was completely incapable of doing anything about my parents' unhappiness, their failure to integrate, their financial problems. One is impregnated for life by the suffering of one's parents. (Cojean)

The headline reads 'Adjani tells Annick Cojean of the price she has paid for being a maverick.' Conscious of the fact that 'actors occupy a position in the public imagination, so they necessarily play a political role', her career suffered some consequences, with interruptions and many rebirths (Cojean). *La journée de de jupe* provides another career change (2009) and is described in Sellier's previously mentioned article. The interview and press reactions merely underscore the misogynist and ageist world of cinema when it comes to the position of actresses and their roles. Of course, none of this is foreign to the disproportionate reception Adjani provoked when *La Repentie* was released a year after Cojean's interview.

Away from the cité

Jeunesse dorée/Gilded Youth (2001), directed by Zaïda Ghorab-Volta, casts two young girls (one is seventeen and the other one eighteen) who cross France and leave home for the first time.[34] Gwenaëlle and Angela are from Colombes, a suburb near Paris, a familiar area to the filmmaker.[35] They are determined to escape their respective families and channel their creativity into a photo-reportage project they both have designed, which consists of crossing France and taking pictures of buildings, in *cités* outside of Colombes. Their neighborhood *Maison des Jeunes* (a youth cultural center) subsidizes their project and fully endorses their artistic talent. An exhibition of their photos is scheduled to take place at the city hall upon their return. The film is composed of the many still portraits they snap of people, who they sometimes direct into happy or sad poses, in front of their places. The young women share a positive outlook on life and an openness toward others. They move south to the Pyrenees after initially going north and east to the Ardennes area, driving a car they borrowed. Gwenaëlle wants to get an impression of borders. Maps are deployed during their trip. Still shots of their pictures show buildings (housing projects) in the midst of nature – some of them remote from all city centers and shopping areas, beyond all rational urban planning. They witness the destruction of a huge project in the St-Etienne area and meet different inhabitants who, charmed by them, warm up to their questions. They are open to other people's lives. The director displays the different facets of France today, and the way it is composed of different countries (Nouchi).[36] Most people are not aware of the outlook of the *cités* and their pictorial compositions note an interesting architectural facet. Carrie Tarr views the film as a cross between *cinéma de banlieue* (films about the suburbs) and a road movie (Tarr 2005).

> It subverts dominant expectations of both road movies and banlieue film. People are hospitable. The car never breaks down; groups of potentially threatening black-beur youth turn out to be friendly and nice ...(Tarr 183–185)

According to Tarr, Ghorab-Volta chose white women as her nomadic subjects, and the possibility of women of beur or black origins to accomplish such feats was not imagined (183–185).

Despite all expectations, the film does not embrace the stereotypes associated with *banlieue* films and the director is opposed to such typecasting. Her first film *Souviens-toi de moi/Remember me* (1996) 'challenges the masculine perspectives found in Kassovitz's *La Haine* (1995)' (O'Shaughnessy).[37] Such expectations are thwarted, and the film instead offers,

> Un film de cinéma, ou une approche de la vie de deux filles de la région parisienne. Une réflexion sur les individus qui l'habitent et l'habitat qui les abrite. (Review *Jeune Cinéma*)[38] ('A cinematic film or an approach of two girls from the Parisian region. A reflection on individuals who live in it, and their sheltering habitat.')

The title has a deceptive and ironic ring to it. *Jeunesse dorée* or 'gilded youth' is misleading since the two women are neither privileged, nor stylish and fashionable types. Their lifestyle, as reflected in their fifteen-day tour, is nothing but low-key and simple. The format is diary-like. The focus steers clear of their life at home; enough brush strokes combine to give a view of fatherless families, with one father (Gwenaëlle's) hospitalized, and a depressive mother raising her three daughters in the project. The other family is less defined; a trailer-home appears briefly at two different points. One of the introductory segments opens on the funeral of a young friend from the project but eschews details about it. As the narrative progresses, Gwenaëlle reveals a somewhat more hostile outlook toward people and her environment; her strong protective shell compels her to reject love when it appears in the form of a woodcutter they meet in the mountains. Angela is more receptive and outgoing; the women's joint presence helps smooth out some of their rough edges. They are both dedicated to each other.

The trip through France serves as a catalyst for them to reflect on their lives and meet people who have left home (the *cité*) for good, for the return to the countryside that originated in the 1970s. Friendships form along the way, and conviviality plays the most important role. The journey opens their eyes onto other environments and lives, leading them gently into another rhythm as previously seen in Sarah Petit's (Léonor's) nomadic films.

Ghorab-Volta is credited as the first woman director of Maghrebian (*beur*) origins to make a film in France.[39] The fact that she did not involve *beur* characters and moves away from the *banlieue* surprised the critics. Ghorab-Volta rejects all labels, which critics tend to apply easily:[40]

Je hais cette mentalité qui implique que, puisque je suis Maghrébine, il faudrait que je filme des Maghrébins. S'il y a bien une chose que je déteste, ce sont les ghettos, cette logique qui fonctionne sur la division. (Diatkine 32)

('I hate this mentality that implies that, since I am of Maghrebian origins, I have to film Maghrebian people. If there's one thing I hate, it's ghettos; and the logic that operates on division.')

Such a decision affected her career. She remains outside the system as an independent filmmaker (Ghorab-Volta).[41] Nothing can effectively inform the viewer that she/he is watching a *beur* character or not. The identity of the two characters and their ethnic background is hazy and not defined. All we know relates to the geographical space that is tied to the women, which they leave for a fortnight, as well as the new places they discover. The script engages with friendship between two women, their encounters with others, artistic creativity, and the claustrophobic space they inhabit and escape. The overall positive outlook is similar to *Drôle de Félix/Adventures of Felix*, (Ducastel, Martineau 2000), which retraces the adventures of a young gay *beur* through France (on foot) and his encounters with different situations and people. However, Félix is alone in his trip, unlike the two heroines, who rely on each other for support.

Keltoum's daughter

Charef injects a feminine trajectory of a return into a typically male-centered narrative. *La Fille de Keltoum/Keltoum's Daughter* (2002), Charef's sixth fiction film, ushers in a bold path engaging a young westernized woman's return to her native land of Algeria, reversing the route of the director, who left the country thirty years before.

> One must believe in cinema in order to dare tell this story of a woman who little by little discovers that nothing was as foreseen; that she is immersed in a destiny that she no longer controls. Just like this filmmaker who returns to Algeria thirty years later and renounces the film he had in his head in order to adopt the topic that imposes itself. This man will speak of women rather than about the war, of women forgotten in the most remote corners, women who can only be silent and sacrifice themselves (Barlet).[42]

The timeline is set during the Algerian war of independence – a period when Charef and his family left Algeria. Charef migrated to France in 1963 with his parents, lived in a Parisian suburban area, and worked in an automobile factory before writing scripts, novels, and plays, and directing films. He focuses on the plight of women and migrants in narratives that deal with new immigrants living in France. His filmic trajectory started with *Le Thé au Harem d'Archimède* (1985), *Miss Mona* (1988), *Marie-Line* (2000), and *Cartouches Gauloises* (2007). Charef objects to the ethnic (and *beur*) filmmaker label: 'I don't have any desire to be labeled immigrant filmmaker. I'm a filmmaker, that's all' (Naficy 98). Charef is at the forefront of *banlieue* cinema in France; he shot one of the first fiction films about second-generation youths of North-African origin living in housing projects within the periphery of Paris. *Le Thé au Harem d'Archimèdes/Tea in the Harem* (1985) foreshadows 1990s French films that revive the *banlieue* theme, and belongs to the 'cinema of the margins' (Beugnet).

Rallia (Cylia Malki), a young woman, arrives by bus in the middle of the mountainous region of les Aurès in Southern Algeria; she is looking for the mother who abandoned her as a baby and gave her away for adoption to Swiss parents. She plans to confront her mother with the tragic scenario of abandonment at birth. The story constructs a gender-based view of a world partitioned along gender lines.

In *La Fille de Keltoum/The Daughter of Keltoum* and *Le Thé au Harem d'Archimèdes/Tea in the Harem* the director empathizes with Algerian women (like his mother) and pays homage to them. The film *L'Autre Monde/The Other World* (Merzach Allouache 2001), which follows a young French woman of Algerian descent to Algeria, influenced Charef's script. In both films, the issue of language erupts each time the protagonist cannot speak the language of her parents. This issue, which is central to *Le Grand voyage* (Ferroukhi), isolated the son from the father. The north clashes with the south as they both collide in the person of Rallia, a modern emancipated Swiss woman on a mission to find her biological Algerian mother. In *La Fille de Keltoum* the harsh Algerian mountainous environment is gendered and can be read according to a male-female grid. On the one hand, the café in the middle of the desert for example is a male location from which women are excluded; on the other hand, Rallia's aunt Nedjma is a water-carrier and provider in the middle of an arid desert. In her function, she navigates the masculine landscape but does not stop for refreshment. The emancipated Europeanized Rallia is at odds with the culture she encounters that requires her to wear a headscarf in order to travel freely. The exhibition of one's body to photographers and readers pertaining to Rallia's profession, presumably that of a top model in glossy fashion magazines, conflicts with her native culture.

> We will wait for Keltoum, the mother and we will understand along with her daughter that she will not come, that one must leave and that, whatever the outcome, what is important is the travel (Guilloux).[43]

The same system is tested by Naïma (Gatlif's *Exils*) once she is in Algeria and is pressed to wear a djellaba over her short skirt. She temporarily complies but quickly sheds her robe in an angry gesture. Similarly, Rallia abandons the headscarf. The spectator is familiar with the flow of images of Arab women at home or veiled if they are outside, the images being the direct heirs of (post)colonial representations. Ida Kummer points to the fate of women immigrants who have to adapt to a new space and/or a non-space once they arrive in France, giving the example of Zouina in *Inch' Allah Dimanche/Inch' Allah Sunday* (Benguigui 2001),

> Each of these films examines the difficulties that these women encountered in trying to find their own space in a reality constructed by others, for others. For clearly, there is no public space for them in these films. In Maghrebian cafes, a public space par excellence, the only women one sees are considered prostitutes (Kummer 50).[44]

Benguigui's film, set in the 1970s, presents a South-North scenario, with the departure from the home country and arrival of migrant women in France to join their husbands. It is set during the 'family reunification' implemented by the Giscard d'Estaing government, a time when male migrant workers in France were finally allowed to bring their wives and children to join them. *Inch'Allah Dimanche* is further complicated by the northern location of the newly regrouped family in the small town of St-Quentin, in Northern France. Benguigui previously authored a three-part documentary on the history of migrants in France, *Mémoires d'Immigrés, l'héritage maghrébin/Immigrant Memories* (1997), which retraces the different steps of the migratory history inclusive of the fathers, the mothers, and the children.

Charef singles out Rallia, a Europeanized woman of Arab origin who is traveling back to her birth country – a country she does not know. Rallia's aunt (Baya Belal), a rather 'wild' woman, tries to warn her many times against the dangers of an excessive free circulation, a concept that is unthinkable in the geography traveled as far as it relates to women in the Mediterranean regions. Women who travel freely are in danger and risk being brutally punished, sometimes just for the act of gazing at a man. These risks appear in recent cinema in an Algerian woman director's first feature film *Barakat!/Enough!*] (Djamila Sahraoui 2006). Actually, the danger is present in the West as well as, as supported by the films discussed in the present chapter, from Varda's *Sans toi ni loi* to Tanner's *La Salamandre*. Female travelers have to constantly negotiate through their travels, 'defend' themselves, or justify their journey.

Whereas Schmitt/Dupeyron, Ferroukhi, and to a lesser extent Gatlif conduct searches for the father in male-inflected scenarios of growth and healing seen previously, and in which movement is never inhibited, Charef transposes a male scenario (as a male script-writer) onto a female trajectory that embraces the feminine and searches for the mother.

7
Dérives

Crossing to the other side. Jacques Rozier

I create an opposition between writers inspired by history and writers inspired by geography. I'm definitely on the side of the geographers. (Tournier 97)[1]

Thus I had to give up at six years old, a magnificent career as a painter ... I had to choose another profession and I learned how to drive airplanes. I flew a bit everywhere in the world. Geography, for sure, helped me a lot. I knew how to recognize at first glance, China and Arizona. It's very useful if one gets lost at night. (Saint-Exupéry 2)[2]

This last chapter begins with a study of Jacques Rozier's films, with an emphasis on two films that directly plunge into the travel motif at the core of my focus: *Les Naufragés de l'île de la Tortue/The Castaways of Turtle Island* (1976) and *Maine-Océan* (1985). I make a distinction between filmmakers who (like writers) are indebted to geography as opposed to history. Rozier's films unlock new ways of looking at the 'open road', and the call for an elsewhere, away from predetermined patterns. I examine Rozier as a traveler within French cinema, part of the New Wave but also a loner and an artisan. I borrow the term *'dérive'* from Situationist theories although I apply it to a rural landscape. Rozier advises a new outlook on travel and time, like Jacques Tati, with an emphasis on slowness.

The second part of the chapter marks a return to the 1970s with key director Jacques Tati in one of his last films *Trafic* (1971), a unique plot that deals with cars, speed, communications and the European market. Falling into the comedic type, the character of Hulot makes his last screen appearance. Now an engineer/designer, responsible for the creation of a new futuristic camping car, Hulot is dispatched to Amsterdam for a large international automobile show, in order to exhibit and sell his product. However, his arrival in Amsterdam is constantly delayed due to unexpected circumstances, which allows Tati to promote his theory on leisure, slow speed, and life at its best. The film takes us on an improvised road trip, where side roads and deviations are more important than the newly created interstate that links Paris to Amsterdam. *Trafic* is a return to the past and Tati's origins in Holland.

The distinction between writers as historians or geographers extends to filmmakers whose work exhibits an interest in the topography of places visited by their camera. Rozier is firmly grounded in the realm of geography and travel. His films pull the trope of travel and displacement in an unconventional way. In the following pages, my argument relies on *'dérive'* as formulated by the Situationists – applied to unplanned journeys through an urban landscape, but which I extend here to a more rural and folkloric setting. The term denotes 'drifting' and occasionally subversive activities. Rozier unlocks new ways of looking at the call of the open road. *Adieu Philippine* (1962), *Du Côté d'Orouët* (1973), *Les Naufragés de l'île de la Tortue* (1976), and *Maine-Océan* (1986) all build an 'invitation to the voyage' in a Baudelairian sense. I propose to examine Rozier as a traveler of French cinema as well; he refuses to adopt a mainstream approach to filmmaking yet he is very much in the tradition of the French realist film school. Although his original film style and approach to filmmaking have slowed down and affected most of his film production and distribution throughout his career, the present essay stays away from quantitative aspects. I plan to reinterpret his films as open voyages.

A direct heir to Jean Vigo, and generally designated as the main figure of New Wave cinema before the youth generation was baptized as such by *Express* journalist Françoise Giroud, Rozier stands out as a loner and artisan.[3] At the crossroads of different paths, his productions tackle the complexity of communication between people and the poetry of the everyday. Some if not most of his films are untranslatable to a spectator who has not yet watched them.

The Ballad-form: the impossible voyage and geographies

L'impossible voyage, c'est celui que nous ne ferons jamais plus, celui qui aurait pu nous faire découvrir des paysages nouveaux et d'autres hommes, qui aurait pu nous ouvrir l'espace des rencontres. (Augé 13)

('The impossible voyage, the one we will never take again, the one that could have shown us new landscapes and other men, that could have opened up the space of encounters.')

At some point in his career, roughly in the 70s, Rozier moved away the location of his earlier films set in Southern France, the Riviera, or the Mediterranean area. These films comprise two shorts *Rentrée des Classes* (1955), *Blue Jeans* (1958), and a feature-length film *Adieu Philippine* that entails a long episode in Corsica (1962). Rozier opted for the Atlantic side, and the coast of Vendée, South of Brittany. All his films contain a liquid element such as the sea or a river, as in *Rentrée des Classes/Back to School* made two years before Truffaut's *Les Mistons* (1957). The main protagonist, a young boy, refuses to go to school on his first day of class and spends most of his time outside, idly swimming down the stream that runs through a Southern village.

Most of the films adopt the topography of an island, with l'Ile d'Yeu, or a Caribbean island in *Les Naufragés de l'île de la tortue/The castaways of Turtle Island* (1976). Water and travel are at the root of Rozier's creativity. The main protagonist – usually a working-class urban character (male or female), mostly trapped in an office job (as a secretary, supervisor, TV technician) or, more specifically, stuck on a train (*Maine-Océan*) – decides on some impulse to drop everything and travel to a distant location in order to escape the boredom or routine of their job or to go on a prescribed vacation. Most pressingly, *Adieu Philippine's* main character leaves his job as a television camera operator in order to take a short vacation before departing for the war in Algeria. The time spent in Corsica constitutes a temporary respite, a suspended time before his engagement in war and an uncertain future.

Les films de Rozier sont, de toute évidence, des manifestes successifs en faveur de la géographie, lignes de fuite, parcours nomades, espaces hasardeux. (Bouquet 92)[4] ('Rozier's films are evidently a succession of manifestoes in favor of geography, fleeting lines, nomadic wanderings, and random spaces.')

In *Les Naufragés de l'île de la Tortue/The Castaways of Turtle Island*, Jean-Arthur Bonaventure (Pierre Richard), along with his friend (Jacques Villeret), is a 'tour operator;'[5] he works in a travel agency and decides to revolutionize the organized travel concept he sells for a new form of travel:

Nous pouvons aller beaucoup plus loin ... dans la vie moderne, il faudrait créer des émotions inoubliables, uniques. (*Les Naufragés de l'île de la Tortue*) ('We can go much further ... in modern life; one should create unique and unforgettable emotions.')

The avant-garde concept Bonaventure presents his boss is that of a packaged tour without a program ('un programme sans programme').

Whereas his job usually condemns him to a static/pedestrian clerk position of selling packaged tours to future vacationers, his proposal to take people and drop them off on a desert island precipitates his own departure to scout for possible locations and lead the first group. The realization that there 'are no more desert islands' to be found comes very early in the narrative, but does not deter Bonaventure. In reexamining the theory of tourism proposed by Dean MacCannell, George Van den Abbeele writes,

> Authenticity is what the tourist is supposed to find in the presence of the sight itself ... Tourist attractions are also supposed to supply an authenticity which is felt to be lacking in the modern world (Abbeele 6).

The script relies on the archetype of the modern-day tourist, his/her predicament, and the exploitative nature of the tourism industry. Rozier, like Tati, is interested in leisure time. Tourism studies as a nascent field emerged in 1968 in North America with research conducted by Dean MacCannell. It allows for a multitude of explorations in diverse areas ranging from social sciences, an umbrella term for such diverse fields as the study of human behavior and society, geography, economics, law, criminology, and psychology. Tourism touches many areas, such as fashion, for example, as it inspires designers' annual vacation collections and world travel clothes; sexuality, with sexual tourism; psychology; magazine spreads; culinary trends; and the publishing world.[6]

The word *tourist* started in 1800 in England and was adopted in France in 1816, whereas 'tourism' was only used in 1876 (Fernandez 33). 'Tours' were already in practice in the 18th century and were aimed at young educated upper-class people who would do 'the grand tour of Europe'. It was initially a male-dominated venture.

> Young English elites of the seventeenth and eighteenth centuries often spent two to four years traveling around Europe in an effort to broaden their horizons and learn about language, architecture, geography, and culture in an experience known as the Grand Tour. (Rosenberg)

Modern tourism became more widespread in the 19th century and was transformed by the creation of the Thomas Cook first travel agency in England, industrialization, and the development of the railway system.

Writer and traveler Paul Morand remarked in his early volume on travel (first published in 1927 by Hachette) that collective journeys were becoming more frequent than individual ones (Morand 16). Attesting to the democratization of travel in the 20th century, he lamented the fact that due to the Popular Front's *congés payés* (paid holidays for workers) mass travel soared, depriving the traditional traveler of his comfort zone. In his own words: 'everything travels'!

Hier, le voyageur s'agitait dans un monde immobile. Merveilleux moment, ces années 30, en pleine crise économique, où l'on sautait, sans avoir à retenir ses places, dans des trains toujours vides, où l'on trouvait à prix réduits les plus belles cabines! Aujourd'hui tout voyage (Morand 12). ('Yesterday, the traveler was agitating himself in an immobile world. Marvelous moment, the 1930s, when in the middle of an economic crisis, one could find at reduced costs, the best compartments. Today everything travels.')

In short, the travelers' backgrounds are wildly diverse, ranging from bakers to watchmakers, assembly-line workers, and hardware store employees. They all decide to travel in order to 'assert' themselves (Morand 2). This overlooks travel undertaken by workers who used to peddle their services around the community, going from village to village like seamstresses, chimneysweeps, or artists such as musicians and actors. The remark that 'L'Europe est "bourrée comme une rame de métro à midi'''[7] ('Europe is "packed like the underground at noon"') establishes the upper-class tensions about the democratization of travel modes, privileging as an alternative the happy few of the 18th and 19th centuries in a rather reactionary nostalgic view.

Most tourists select their destination on the basis of cost. Social tourism thrived in the 1930s, with trips organized by (and for) workers, as well as educational and religious institutions (Morand 22). Many travel writers inaugurated their travel theories or journals then, as Paul Morand did, and although the genre is not new, the notion of 'modern travel' definitely is.

Earlier I introduced Swiss-born Ella Maillart and her companion Annemarie Schwarzenbach, who left Europe for Afghanistan in 1939 by car. Maillart had been on the roads of China and India before in 1935, and took to the road again to flee a ravaged Europe:

Oui, j'entendais l'appel de la Terre vaste et sauvage! Incapable de comprendre ce qui se passait dans l'Europe chancelante, accablée par l'anarchie latente dans toutes nos capitales, je n'avais envie que de fuir (73).[8] ('Yes, I heard the call of the vast and wild Land. Unable to understand what was happening in a vacillating Europe overwhelmed by the anarchy controlling all our capitals, I had one desire: to flee.')

Most travel writers respond to the urge to leave their country and see the world, as Bouvier would later do in the 1950s.

Less known, as their narrative has never been reprinted, Nicole and Raymond Leininger's *La Route sans borne. En campant, de France, aux Indes, à bicyclette/The Limitless Road: Camping from France to India, by bicycle* chronicles a journey from France to India that started on a bicycle in 1939.[9] The couple's adventure passed through Afghanistan, yet was cut short because of the declaration of war that was made just as they reached the country. They dedicated their book to the memory of Léo Lagrange. Under-secretary for sports and the organization of leisure under the 1936 Popular Front government, Lagrange promoted tourism, sports and leisure, and helped start railway fare reductions. He also implemented youth hostels in France. Filmmaker and explorer Samivel's preface to *La Route sans borne*, an epic travel-narrative, summarizes their adventure as going against the precepts of the organized tour:

Deux bicyclettes, deux paires de bonnes jambes endurcies aux travaux alpins. Quelques hardes et c'était tout ... Un matériel à la portée de tout le monde. Rien de commun avec ces voyages plus ou moins 'organisés', comme disent les agences, où les interprètes, les liftiers et les barmen élèvent une muraille infranchissable entre le monde vivant et l'infortuné boyard. Ces deux jeunes gens avaient choisi volontairement d'être pauvres, de vivre en pauvres, de dormir et de manger comme mangent et dorment les pauvres de tous les temps et de tous les pays du monde. (Leininger 9).

('Two bicycles, two pairs of good legs, toughened by Alpine work. A few belongings and that was all ... A material affordable to everyone. Nothing in common with these more or less "organized" travels, claimed by agencies, where interpreters, carriers, and barmen raise insurmountable barriers between the world of the living and the unfortunate noble. These two young people had willingly chosen to be poor; to live as poor people, to sleep and eat as poor people have always done in all the countries of the world.')

France witnessed a veritable transformation in the nature of travel in the 1950s. The Club Méditerranée revolutionized the nature of mass travel in the 1950s. Started in 1950, 'vacation innovator' Gilbert Trigano, then in charge of camping vacations[10] ran the company from 1963 to 1993. 'Quintessentially French', it devised the setting of a village, circulating the feeling of friendship and camaraderie 'in contrast to the stiffness of French urban life', and according to Trigano provided 'an annual liberation' (meaning a vacation) in what at first were 'tented villages' (Lewis 1985).

The initial concept attracted singles and couples to a resort that functioned on shared interests in an autarchic village-based community setting. The staff of 'nice organizers' – GO's or *gentils organisateurs* – advertises the spirit and gentle message of the formula that is an integral part of the family. As professional staff, they are 'lively professional helpers who pretend to be as much on vacation as the guests' (Lewis) and mix with the paying guests in all their activities, from dancing to other sports and actions – the difference being that they are paid to do this. To that extent, Trigano's background and innovative ideas are compelling:

> The Club Med formula he created has a nearly universal appeal: It is a unique mixture of stylishness, sensuality and utopian fantasy – offering the lure of a primitive Gauguin island paradise where everyone is friendly, innocent and equal (Lewis).

The club became a favorite destination for families with children. The company adopted the Parisian fitness center formula ('Un corps sain dans un esprit club', 'A healthy body in a club spirit') and applied it to its restaurants and cruise ships. The villages spread globally, starting with the Baleares, Florida, Tunisia and China. The former CEO of Euro Disney Philippe Bourguignon, ran it until 2003. A 2008 advertising campaign launched its new motto: 'Where happiness means the world.' Previous slogans ranged from: 'Club Med vacation: the antidote to civilization' to 'Club Med: Life as it should be.' The 1970s advert ran: 'Club Med invites you to spend your holiday in a little grass hut.'[11] These ads reveal the 'return' to primitivism promulgated by Club Med.

Les bronzés/French Fried Vacation (1978)

French cinema immortalized the club formula in a series of popular films made about tourists (singles) vacationing in the resort. *Les Bronzés/French Fried Vacation* (Patrice Leconte 1978) and its sequels were comedic hits and to a certain extent the earlier Rozier film critiques such packaged group vacations and anticipates such films. The slogan 'Sea, Sex, and Sun' – a 1978 Serge Gainsbourg song – opens Leconte's film, a farcical comedy, poking fun at the club activities set in a remote African country, where the natives are barely shown except in a highly racialized frame. Since the Club Med is its own village, contact with the native population is limited; tourism (or sightseeing) does not constitute the drive of such packages. Contact occurs once in the first *Bronzés* film, during a small shopping tour at a nearby African village, when one of the characters purchases a native mask after trying to bargain for it. The level of sexist jokes, gags, and activities is infantile and betrays a return to children's summer camp mentality.

Les Naufragés de l'ile de la tortue/The Castaways of Turtle Island (1976)

Nostalgic undertones as well as colonial inferences taint *Les Naufragés de l'ile de la tortue* in terms of the location itself – L'Ile de la Tortue, a former French colonial island close to Haiti – and the use of ships, which recall colonial times and maritime navigation routes, reinforced by the constant references to *Robinson Crusoe*.

The travel form that Bonaventure (Rozier) envisions predates the reality television shows that took over in the 1990s and 2000s, yet brilliantly predicts them in an ironic and futuristic way:

-Je prends des gens et je les fous dans une île déserte ... Nous forçons les gens à se débrouiller et nous appelons ça le 'produit Robinson Crusoé' ... Les passagers doivent se débrouiller sur place pour subvenir à leur existence. (Film dialogue, *Les Rescapés de l'île de la Tortue*)

('I take people and dump them on a desert island ... We force people to get by and we call it 'the Robinson Crusoe product.' The passengers must manage on the spot in order to survive.')

The concept is akin to the *Survivor* reality TV series and its spin-offs, which in its summary defines the principles of the 'game' as follows:

... Average Americans are abandoned in the middle of some of the most unforgiving places on earth. Divided into teams, they participate in challenges and every three days, the losing tribe must trek to Tribal Council to vote out one of their own.[12]

Bonaventure and his colleague Gros Nono sell the concept to an agency director who is more interested in the three 'S's' (sea, sex, and sun), and shows no consideration for the travelers who sign up, and worries instead that the profit margins might not be very substantial at 3,000 francs a trip. As in most of Rozier's films, boats, and particularly sailboats, are predominant. Nautical terminology pertains to our study of travel in film. The trope of the boat is as important as that of the road or train for the travel narrative, and is a major topos in the contemporary migration narratives under discussion. The organized drifting away (*dérive*) at the core of Rozier's films corresponds to the language used for sailboats (a '*dériveur*' is a name for a specific sailboat) and for wanderers. The organized tour does not fare well from the start, despite the initially enthusiastic responses and applications for such an adventure. People of middle-class origins sign on, in the belief that their vacation will be about leisure and fun. The publicity lured them into thinking that they would be daredevils in their vacation plans, reminiscent of Paul Morand's concept of the traveler as a rebel for whom 'travel is an antisocial gesture' (Morand 13). The 'organized tour' group is disorganized at best, if not eclectic. The location is one of France's overseas islands. One young woman arrives wearing a fur hat; some travelers never arrive. Another woman wants to rest. A couple bickers. Most of the travelers share a desire to break with their urban lifestyle, and dissatisfaction with their jobs on the mainland.

> Given the present sociohistorical epoch, it is not a surprise to find that tourists believe sightseeing is a leisure activity, and fun, even when it requires more effort and organization than many jobs. ... In being presented as a valued object through a so-called 'leisure' activity that is thought to be 'fun,' society is renewed in the heart of the individual through warm, open, unquestioned relations, characterized by a near absence of alienation when compared with other contemporary relationships. (MacCannell 55–56)

Bonaventure's wish to follow Daniel Defoe à la lettre falls short; his demand for *le pittoresque jusqu'au bout* ('nothing but the picturesque') is no longer appreciated by the crew on board the sailboat, who after two days of trekking across steep mountains and jungle-like terrain, arrive exhausted and hungry at a beach littered with debris. The main organizer (Bonaventure), in the Crusoe spirit, wants to emulate a shipwreck and throws all the passengers' belongings into the sea. As one fellow traveler remarks, the notion is 'interesting but a bit theoretical'. The organization unravels; it now appears more disorganized than those who signed up had bargained for. The film becomes increasingly chaotic from this point, and suffers from weaknesses. The main organizer, who becomes more and more disheveled as the trip progresses, is presumed lost at sea, while two passengers, his new assistant Little Nono/Petit Nono (Jacques Villeret), and the young woman who writes a travel diary of these events, team up for a search and rescue trip. Most of the tour members have vanished to return to mainland France. Eventually, the remaining two rescue Bonaventure from jail for having stolen bananas, a survival strategy most likely adopted from Robinson Crusoe's survival book but not appreciated by the local police.

   Les Rescapés de l'île de la Tortue functions as a metaphor for Rozier's adventures in French filmmaking: 'We advanced in the bush, literally and figuratively' (Villeret).[13] Watching a film by Rozier is to advance into la Roziérie or Rozierland (Trémois 260). It is an adventure with its own grammar, geography, and different sense of time. Rozier critiques packaged exoticism and adventures peddled to contemporary travelers as well as the concept of 'organized travel' – all indexes that travel and activities must be prepared, thereby not retaining any spontaneity. This speaks to film productions as well, then and now. The creation of 'unforgettable and unique emotions' cannot be prepackaged. Everything in these films moves according to a law of disorganization, impromptu decisions, and improvisation or the semblance of such. Surrealist notes are inherent to the psychogeography of the 'dérive'.

Sea travelers/earth travelers

Maine-Océan (1986) is a 'balade impromptue, décousue et terriblement étirée d'Angers à l'Ile d'Yeu' (Copperman 1986) ('an impromptu ballad, scattered and terribly stretched from Angers to Ile d'Yeu'). Rozier dates the original idea for the script to a train ride he took on the *Maine-Océan*, the name of the train line from Paris to Nantes, in 1974, followed by another ride during a beautiful winter light on the Loire.

J'ai dû prendre le Maine-Océan vers six heures du soir, à l'heure où le soleil traverse presque horizontalement le compartiment quand on va vers l'ouest. C'est la fuite vers l'ouest, vers le soleil couchant et, à ce moment-là, j'étais dans le Maine-Océan. J'ai ressenti une espèce de choc et je me suis dit: je veux faire un film qui s'appellera Maine-Océan (Vigo). ('I had to take the Maine-Ocean around 6pm, a time when the sun almost traverses the train car horizontally, when you go west. It was the escape west, toward the sunset, and at that precise moment, I was in the Maine-Océan. I felt some sort of shock and told myself: I want to make a film that will be named Maine-Océan').

Train stations, like ports, are places of passages, of transits, where people come and go. The film historian Siegfried Kracauer was fond of train stations, and wrote about them and travelers, with allusions to port cities as transient places,

Mon amour pour les gares est resté inchangé. Comme les ports, ce sont des lieux où l'on ne demeure pas. Ici les gens ne s'attardent pas, ici ils ne se rencontrent que pour se séparer. Si partout ailleurs ils ont des attaches, à la gare, malgré leur bagage, ils sont libres de tout lien. Tout est possible, l'ancien est derrière eux, le nouveau est indéterminé. Pour un laps de temps, ils redeviennent des vagabonds; même si l'horaire régule strictement leurs errances. C'est pourquoi il est peu de plaisir comparable au séjour prolongé dans les gares. Au milieu du désert du quotidien, elles sont les oasis de l'improvisation (85). ('My love for train stations remains unchanged. Like ports, these are places where one does not stay. Here people don't linger, here one meets only to leave each other. If everywhere else, one has ties, at the station, despite their luggage, they are free of these ties. Everything is possible, the old is behind them, the new is undetermined. For a short time, they become itinerant again; even if the schedule strictly regulates their wanderings. Hence, there are relatively few pleasures that compare with the prolonged stay in train stations. In the middle of the everyday desert, these are oases of improvisation'.)

Rozier is fascinated by the name of the train, *Maine-Océan*, the last generation of Express trains before high-speed trains (TGV) were launched in 1976.[14] The TGV *Atlantique* line that replaced the Maine-Océan train would be built later, between 1988 and 1992. It is likely that Rozier, a Parisian who vacationed in Vendée as a child, remains attracted to the place that for him is associated with freedom and filters a superb light, with Atlantic winds, as a region Luce Vigo perceives at the crossroad of two areas:

Un pays de vent, un pays atlantique, donc la mer avec des vagues, un grand espace ... un point de rencontres: c'est le pays de Loire, le nord et le sud de la France, plus la composante atlantique, c'est à dire le vent d'ouest (Vigo). ('A land of wind, an Atlantic country, with a sea of waves, a large space, a place of encounters: it is the Loire region, the north and south of France, and its Atlantic component, that is the Western wind.')

The premise of *Maine-Océan* lies in the encounter between people from different worlds, thrown together in uncanny yet comedic situations. The camera follows a young Brazilian woman (Rosa-Maria Gomes) who rushes to board a train at the Montparnasse station (it appears at it was before its renovations) in Paris, only to be hassled by two finicky train inspectors because of her illegal situation: first she did not punch her train ticket before boarding the Express Paris-Nantes train; second, she is sitting in a first class car and does not have the proper first class ticket to show for it. The basic circumstance at the onset of the film branches out into radically unexpected directions. It follows the play of life and ordinary people caught in ordinary circumstances, and chance meetings. Any (French) person who watches the first ten minutes will smile at the familiar situation they have experienced at least once in their life on board a train in France.

Linguistic trip – Maine-Ocean

The film concentrates on orality and speech patterns intrinsic to the French, as, for instance, the Vendean sailors at l'Ile d'Yeu. One of them, called Marcel Petigas – literally 'little buddy' (Yves Afonso) – has an unmistakable accent that cannot be explained or translated in any subtitling format.[15] Yet, when heard on the soundtrack, the sailors provide a distinctive speech pattern recognizable to any French person, denoting different sentiments. Another example of the importance of language is articulated in the Parisian female lawyer's defensive speech about Chomsky's linguistics and the various levels of language. Her defense speech made at the Petitgas's trial fails to convince or impress the Maine et Loire courtroom or the judge. Instead, the demonstration appears snobbish and out of place in the context of her client's drunken episode in Anjou. Accents designate class differences. All of these peculiarities form some of the epic moments of *Maine-Océan*. The techniques used by the director range from improvisation to the spontaneous adaptation of a radically transformed script. Rozier mines the encounter, the mixing of different social groups, and different languages (such as regional French from Vendée, Luso-Brazilian, and Spanish), which turns out to be the most humorous and poetic event of the film itself. The director engages in a trip through language.

Trains and lifelines

Maine-Océan articulates the shared elements between people and the bonds between them, despite all geographical, physical, and linguistic barriers. To say that the two inspectors end up on an island (*l'île d'Yeu*), and meet up again with the Brazilian woman, the lawyer, and the feisty man who decides to protect them, Marcel Petigas, is to present a rapid summary of an episode that does not do justice to the script. Language, as presented earlier, is central to the narrative, but as I argue further it goes beyond language. The Brazilian native Déjanira does not speak a word of French, and barely understands the rough English spoken by the train controlers. A young French woman, Mimi de Saint-Marc (Lydia Feld, the co-scenarist), pleads her case. She corrects the situation, and takes the traveler under her metaphorical lawyer's robes. The lawyer speaks Brazilian and Spanish; she acts as the interpreter and defense lawyer of Petigas at the Baugé (Maine & Loire) courthouse. Her defense consists in brandishing the specter of language and miscommunication that plagues people, especially in instances like that of the drunken Petigas, who is sued over a fight he had with an Anjou resident on his drive back to the island (Anjou is on the way to Vendée). Clearly, within France, regional languages and customs are not shared or appreciated by all. Saint-Marc loses the case yet gains a friend for life, Petigas, who takes the Brazilian woman who followed the lawyer under his wing and invites them to l'Ile d'Yeu, his kingdom. Informed of the unhappy accident that took place earlier on the *Maine-Océan* train ride between her and the inspectors he vows to avenge her.

Through a series of coincidences, the second part of the narrative brings all five characters to the same location: the two train inspectors and friends search for a healthy break by the sea *'pour remettre les pendules à l'heure'* ('to rewind the clocks'); Lulu was invited by the two women, who themselves were invited by Petigas, who back at home on the island is celebrated by his local mates, sailors at the Bar de la Marine. The characters contribute to the setting's local flavor.

The immense appeal of the sea weighs on much of the French film school – a trait Gilles Deleuze described in *Cinéma 1. L'Image-Mouvement*. Renoir, an adept of this movement, was fascinated by water, especially the passing flow of rivers, which is found in many of his 1930s films, if one recalls *Boudu sauvé des eaux*, *Une partie de campagne*, and much later, his Indian epic *The River*. Rozier stands in the footsteps of Renoir,[16] Grémillon (with for instance *Remorques*), and Vigo (*L'Atalante*, or *Taris, roi de l'eau*), and is a direct heir to this school:

Dans l'école française, c'est tantôt la rivière et son cours, tantôt le canal, ses écluses et ses péniches, tantôt la mer, sa frontière avec la terre, le port, le phare comme valeur lumineuse. (Deleuze 112) ('In the French (film) school, it is sometimes the river and its flow, sometimes the canal, its locks, its barges, sometimes the sea, its borders with land, the port, the lighthouse as luminous value'.)

Rozier plays with all the above motifs. His films (*Maine-Océan, Du côté d'Orouët*) are anchored in the Vendean coastal landscape, infused with a certain quality of light that is noticeably different from his Mediterranean films.

On board the Maine-Océan. Vanishing point

Il y a des gens qui prennent le train, il ne leur arrive jamais rien. D'ailleurs ils ne voyagent pas, ils se déplacent. D'un point à un autre. De plus en plus vite.... La SNCF, reconnaissante, les a baptisés "usagers". C'est affreux, mais ce n'est pas faux : à force d'aller et venir, on finit tous par l'être usagé. (Remy 30) ('There are people who take the train and nothing happens to them. In fact, they don't travel; they just go from one place to another. From one point to another point. Faster and faster. The SNCF (French train company), gratefully baptized them "users." It's terrible but not wrong. After all these comings and goings, we all end up being "used"'.)

The above description of passengers as worn-out (a pun on '*usager/ usagé*', transportation user/used, that does not quite work in English) users of a transportation system does not apply in Rozier's *Maine-Océan*. It follows the precise route of the train as it leaves the Paris Montparnasse station located Avenue du Maine and ends by the ocean in St-Nazaire, the port city of Nantes (Roux 17). Nantes was the main departure gate for colonial ships. All disturbances on the line and stopovers are digressions for passengers and filmmaker alike. Of course, a Rozier narrative cannot follow a straight line or a fixed schedule; it derails to the delight of most spectators. It goes against the concept of speed. The grumpy and finicky train inspector Le Gallec (Bernard Menez, playing against type a serious Breton inspector) is tied to a job that he does not relish. Like most train employees, he travels for his work and not for pleasure, yet the narrative affords him the opportunity to get off the train, take a break, and dream. His colleague and friend, inspector Lucien Pontoiseau, or Lulu (Luis Rego, who played one of the

Club Med's *Gentils Organisateurs* in *Les Bronzés*), is a good influence on him. The two female passengers stop in Angers to appear at the Baugé courthouse for business, pass by a mysterious mansion in the middle of the night – a friend's place – for dinner, and catch another night-ride on the *Maine-Océan* train they pick up in Angers the next day.[17] They resume their travel westward, and arrive at L'Ile d'Yeu by ferry.

As evident in Jean-Claude Guiguet's film *Les Passagers* (1999) or in André Delvaux's *Un soir, Un train* (Delvaux 1968), the train is the perfect vector for mirroring people's lives. Early on, the railways practically invented mass spectatorship, with passengers sitting in front of the panoramic landscape scrolling in front of them, which was later reproduced in film houses. Jacques Aumont compares the spectator to an 'immobile traveler', 'assis, passif, transporté, regardant le spectacle par le cadre de la fenêtre' ('sitting, passive, transported, gazing at the spectacle through the frame of the window') (Aumont 221). Train travel would later be replaced by the road motif, and picked up in films. In Delvaux's film the train is a metaphor for life. Returning to the social history of railroads, Wolfgang Schivelbusch writes that 'Rail travel introduced a number of new sensory and psychological experiences in human history.'[18] Trains have been well represented in French cinema, embodying not only modernity but also the psychological aspects of their passengers or drivers. The station is 'a place of passage', recalls Nicole Lapierre in *Pensons ailleurs*, recounting an inventory of spy films located on board trains (77). Renoir's *La Bête humaine* (1938) personnifies *la Lison*, adapting Zola's novel. It represents Popular Front workers' aspirations and sympathies. Patrice Chéreau uses transportation as a vehicle for interpersonal communication for passengers on their way to a funeral in *Ceux qui m'aiment prendront le train/Those who love me can take the train* (1998). Tanner's *La Salamandre* references a train conductor's work with the character of Charles La Vapeur (Bussières). Rozier directs the same metaphor to boats. Two trains will be involved in the narrative, yet they meet up with boats. Boats embody aspects that go beyond transportation from one place to another, like trains. Their function, along with the landscape surrounding them, manifests another temporality and appreciation of time.

All workers exhibit a form of solidarity and humanity that moves beyond nationalism, work fraternities, and borders. The train employees are self-described as *voyageurs de la terre*, 'earth travelers', when they land at the Bar de la Marine of l'Ile d'Yeu, a land reference that stands in sharp contrast with that of sailors, *voyageurs de la mer*, or 'sea travelers'. The visitors are all housed at the *Hôtel des voyageurs*, the 'Travelers' Hotel' on the island, a rather generic name for many hotels in France.

Two different modes of travel and two (biological) rhythms intercon-nect; the group is solidified by the positive presence of Petigas ('little buddy') who, after an initial scuffle with the train inspectors, drinks with them and elicits the tearful confession of the main inspector Le Gallec (a Breton name), whose true vocation was to be a pilot – an air traveler. Both men sympathize as workers, and become fast friends. The rest of the narrative feeds on human qualities asserting that com-munication, friendship, and solidarity exist in an insular community of people who are like Petigas. In addition, despite different regional or national accents and languages, people get to understand each other. Cohabitation is possible in the intercultural world of the island. It becomes a melting pot. The last part of the film unlocks a musical dimension that mobilizes artistic talent from common people. This combination creates an impromptu musical performance that lingers aurally until the last shots. Most of the film relies on musicality and is symphonic (Roux). At one point, close to the end, the film switches genre and tempo for the musical form.

Transformations can happen in people's lives. The main ticket inspec-tor is pressed to become a singer, a new Maurice Chevalier; the Brazilian dancer who had broken away from her routine hesitates about return-ing to her life as a star dancer during a walk by the lighthouse. In the early hours of a Monday morning – since the film spans over a weekend and a weekday – order has to be restored. The ticket inspector, lured to a new career, is instead stranded on the island, abandoned by the others who took off on a small plane; Le Gallec must find a way to return to the mainland. In the last segment the forces of nature and workman-ship organize to make this happen. Sea tides are gauged, the community of local seafarers from different fishing boats (and fishing style) all pull together to return Le Gallec safely to Nantes-St-Nazaire, to his job on board the train and the different schedule imparted to earth-travelers. Overnight, everyone mobilizes in what turns out to be the most effec-tive sequence of the film, half-realistic, half-fantastic, between darkness and fog, shot with superb cinematography by Portuguese cinematogra-pher Acacio de Almeida. Le Gallec, forced to acknowledge and discover the nature of the sea, its tides and fluctuations, is 'moved' from boat to boat across different geographies (high sea and shallow waters at low tide to name just two) and witnesses the sunrise over the ocean. Fishermen take turns rescuing him and dropping him off on a sliver of land above water in what appears to be the early morning hours. The state of grace and weightlessness particularly adapted to the traveler's realm, and which we will glimpse next in *Trafic* (Tati), is injected into

Maine-Océan – an in-between space Onfray calls the in-between in his travel theory:

> Flottant, vaguement relié à deux bornes dans un état d'apesanteur spatiale et temporelle, ... le voyageur pénètre dans l'entre-deux comme s'il abordait les côtes d'une île singulière (37–38).
> ('Floating, vaguely linked to two mileposts in a state of spatial and temporal, ... weightlessness, the traveler penetrates the in-between as if he was landing on the coast of a special island.')

The space and temporality of the island are uncontrollable; they escape the law of the land. For instance, the Paris-St-Nazaire train line exemplifies the law of a tight, land-locked schedule, which is totally discarded once the characters 'land' on the island. Instead, the island is ruled by maritime navigation and sea tides, governed by the moon and imagination and fantasy.

Stepping off the train and its rigorous schedule for a weekend on the island instigates a new temporality and rhythm. What Bakhtin calls the 'chronotrope of the train' is divided here between the two modes of train travel and sea travel. Time on the island is no longer linear. As far as one can tell, it follows the lunar phases in accordance with the rise of the tides. 'L'abstrait liquide est aussi le milieu concret d'un type d'hommes, d'une race d'hommes qui ne vivent pas tout à fait comme les terrestres' ('Abstract liquid is also the concrete milieu of a type of men, a race of men who do not entirely live as earth people do') (Deleuze 113). The islanders are thus enrolled to act their own roles and are credited as *'les pêcheurs de l'Ile d'Yeu'* (the Ile d'Yeu fishermen). Bernard Menez and Luis Rego play dutiful train employees, bent on obeying rules and disciplines. The script in the second part of the film destabilizes their roles. What could have been at mid-point a dramatic revenge scenario is diverted towards friendship and a peaceful resolution involving a shift in temporality and new ways of seeing life. The train ticket inspector is not familiar with the vast space and the horizon displayed by the ocean. Nor is he accustomed to singing and playing the king of the samba in the middle of the night with a Brazilian dancer, her Mexican agent, and a local folkdance group. Rozier devotes the last segment of the film to a single character, Le Gallec, in a long outdoor sequence by the sea where his lanky Hulot-like silhouette is seen running, and touches land. At some point, land and sea become undistinguishable from each other in the shimmering light of dawn.

Inspired by the concept of travel, Rozier embraces his role as that of a traveler/sailor/filmmaker and relies on sea navigation terminology to explain his position:

Je suis un peu comme mes personnages, c'est vrai. Je lève l'ancre dans ma tête. Il m'arrive de monter sur le bateau, et aussi d'en redescendre, retrouver mes amarres, les larguer encore, ramer jusqu'à ce que j'embarque à nouveau. ('I'm a bit like my characters, that's true. I lift the anchor in my head. I happen to walk onto a boat, and also to get off the boat, to find my moorings.') [19]

In order to make his films, he maps them out, as 'great auteurs, inventing new space and time, make maps of their films first' (Conley 21). When the film stops, the spectator has undergone a long sea voyage and literally needs to shake himself/herself off. As Philippe Delerm remarked so pertinently in his essay on cinema, informed by Barthes' own reading of the cinema experience, the spectator becomes one with the film, and leaves in a state of weightlessness, a bit like a sleep-walker (Delerm). Le Gallec's long way back home crosses different seascapes that open his eyes to a new territory. By the end of the film we are unmistakably no longer in the tight space of train cars. At the same time, Le Gallec's successful trip back to his post was made possible through the help of the community of seafarers coming together. The 'voyage' is not solitary, or single, but plural. He had to travel with others. The spectator witnesses another temporality; while the rest of the group took a small airplane to leave the island, Le Gallec's improvised trip back imposed a new slower temporality, suggesting the importance of the crossing itself, the different stages, with his arrival reminiscent of a Gracquian approach to the departing traveler:

Cette image du départ-de l'instance du départ- traduit à sa manière sans doute un certain goût du dédoublement que je ne nie pas ... le besoin d'être à la fois acteur et spectateur, de prendre du recul, de se détacher constamment de ce qu'on fait, en même temps qu'on le fait. Car l'homme qui va partir jette un regard neuf sur ce qui l'entoure, il est là encore et déjà il n'est plus là. (Gracq 851).

('This image of a departure, of the instance of departure, translates in its way, without a doubt, a certain taste for a dedoubling, that I do not deny ... the need to be both actor and spectator, the step back, to detach oneself constantly from what one does, while doing it at the same time. For the man who is about to l.eave casts a new gaze around what surrounds him, he is still here, yet no longer here').

Side roads

Jacques Tati: Trafic. The modern improvised road-trip

Je regarde vivre les gens, je me promène. J'écoute les dialogues, j'observe les tics, le détail, la manière d'être qui révèle de chaque individu la personnalité. (Laufer 19) ('I watch people live, I stroll around. I listen to dialogues, I observe people's tics, the detail and way each individual reveals his personality.')

Trafic (1971), Jacques Tati's fifth feature-length film, marks the last appearance of Mr. Hulot, Tati's invented character. In comparison with *Playtime*, or *Les Vacances de Mr. Hulot*, the film was not extensively critically discussed. Tati's career was at that time affected by financial and personal woes. He had been bankrupt since *Playtime* and not on good terms with the critics. David Bellos's study of Tati describes the years of the film production as 'Confusion 1970–1982'. The three chapters devoted to *Trafic* are also the shortest ones in his study of the filmmaker's career.

Trafic is firmly rooted in the 1970s and incorporates the influence of the youth and the women's liberation movement, especially through the incarnation of the public relations agent, Maria, a young American woman who drives a sports car. It is also marked by fashion and the world of advertising.

Trafic relies on the recently opened *Autoroute* A1 (1954) the Northern route (and its adjacent side-roads), a newly-built interstate highway that links Paris to Lille, connecting France to the Belgian border. The 503 km that separate Paris from Amsterdam now take five hours and ten minutes, with the A1 connecting with other Belgian and Dutch highways. The connections between road transportation and airports in the film are further reinforced in the use of Schiphol's warehouse for the Internationale auto expo – the centerpiece of the film. Schiphol is the name of the international Dutch airport. In 1968, Tati negotiated with Dutch filmmaker Bert Haanstra over the making of film five (*Trafic*). Haanstra asked a cartoonist to come up with a series of sketches on the theme of 'modern travels' (Bellos 294). A series of sketches of cars and so on drafted by the Dutchman – a painter and sketch artist – predates the script. Tati also negotiated with Svensk film (Sweden) at the same time, which complicated things when they got into the project.

Shooting started in 1968 and stopped in 1969. Haanstra shot some of the sequences. Tati resumed shooting in summer 1970. By the time of the last days of shooting in Amsterdam, he had run out of money. There is somehow a parallel between the film's budget and the story within. The film highlights a new Europe in its formative boom years (during the CEE) and its attempts at communication and trade.[20] Common market ideology runs deep. The film resorts to a polyglossia: multiple (European) languages are used, and yet not a single subtitle appears in any shot. French, Dutch/Flemish, and English are all heard. A sense of disorientation appears at the beginning of the film, as we sometimes do not know where we are, aurally or visually.

Tati pushes his concept of commercialism and visually plays with the tyranny of brands: ALTRA is the name of the car-making company where Hulot the inventor (architect/designer) works. The car sports a rather avant-garde and popular design. ANTAR shows up as the logo for a gas station and was at the time a 'real' brand, followed then by DAF, another (real) car company, which Hulot runs into at the end of the film. Interestingly, *Antara* means 'inner' or 'supreme soul' in its Sanskrit etymology. The increased use of the lettering *A* did not go unnoticed as Michel Chion devotes a fascinating Chapter 11 to the use of the two letters A.R. in Tati's oeuvre.

In order to sell the idea of what the French then called a 'camping car' (a mobile home) – a new concept in Europe at the time – one must go to an auto-show, transport the model, travel, and run the risk of accidents. This parallels the work of a filmmaker who in order to see his/her film project take off, has to sell it to highest bidders (idea, script, then film produced, and distributed) and does not just stay behind the camera or in the director's chair. Thus the *Trafic* project mimics the actual task of the filmmaker, who not only has to secure funding, but also must pitch his/her product nationally and internationally on tour with the product. The credit sequence picks up the process of an assembly line at an auto-plant. It mimics the film industry.

Tati is interested in people and draws inspiration from mere observation. He constructs an entire world that is rather more complex than the surface image he proposes. *Trafic* shows his most intimate side as he communes with nature and people, his characters being closest to real people.

Despite the iconography and multiple attempts to display the practical side of modern technology and the efficiency of machines, a return to the village and the countryside is effected, achieved through the bucolic Dutch canals, side-roads and a more painterly vision of the landscape. Tati reclaims the nostalgia of *Jour de fête* (1949) and its dialectic between modernism=speed=efficiency, and the celebration of old time values and personal communication, as well as his maternal Nordic roots in Holland.

The vehicle, an early version of a camping car, is fully equipped, including a bed for two, cooking gear, a shower stall, and a television set – it is a home away from home. Hulot, the homeless vagabond uncle, has morphed into an engineer who devises such models. The film toys with the use of technology and jokes about the Citroën DS – a then futurist space-age car that popped up in many 1950s and 1960s films – abound during the car pile-up. The car that is bumped into and the one gliding on its two wheels is after all a DS, a universal dream car, a 'goddess' (literal translation or pun on *déesse*) yet unmistakably French. It is the same car that became the subject of an entry in Barthes' *Mythologies*:

It is obvious that the new Citroën has fallen from the sky inasmuch as it appears at first sight as a superlative object. We must not forget that an object is the best messenger of a world above that of nature: one can easily see in an object at once a perfection and an absence of origin, a closure and a brilliance, a transformation of life into matter (matter is much more magical than life) (88).

Tati prioritizes leisure and vacation time, especially when his main character is sidetracked on back roads and never makes the auto-show, only to arrive once the fair has closed and the crowd dispersed. He is an inventor and cultivates 'leisure time' as opposed to 'constrained time'.

Trafic unfolds as a journey gone wrong. Its own production background is marred by a long series of problems just as mechanical problems plague the drive to Amsterdam, at a time when technology and infrastructure have improved and one would assume that a straight ride north, to the neighboring countries of Belgium, then Holland, should be easy.

Peripheral visions

In the 1950s, French cinema adopted American cars 'to reinforce the idea of singularity – in fact, the most effective way to indicate an object from another planet, the effect of intrusion, is to use a foreign, preferable American car' (Ross 33). Of course, the concepts of speed, car chases, and accidents run in such films as *Un homme et une femme/A Man and a Woman* (Lelouch 1968), *Week end* (Godard 1967), and *Pierrot le fou* (Godard 1965). Cars are presented for their looks, and their foreignness in, for instance, Jean-Pierre Melville's films noirs, such as *Le Samouraï* (1969). Roadside problems still occur in late 70s films with *Le Grand embouteillage/L'Ingorgo: una storia impossibile/Trafic Jam* (Luigi Comencini 1979), inspired by Tati's *Trafic*, a rather horrific tale of a major traffic jam on the outskirts of Rome, in which drivers are immobilized for twenty-four hours on the interstate and mayhem ensues.

The omnipresence of cars in *Trafic* is intrinsic to the Hulotian character's life since he designs them for a living. In his past life, he was satisfied with his bicycle and moped. However, the graphic artist at work on the white page is a dreamer and straight lines can be interrupted, or curved, or simply zigzag and go off the page. Laufer interprets the main line of the film as the void (89).

The trip starts at point A in what seems like Paris and its *périphérique* (beltway) – the suburban belt designed and built under the 1970s Giscard d'Estaing government. Modern-day congestion and the difficulty of communication lie at the heart of the plot. Parallel sequences alternate between the auto-show in its preparatory stages and then in full swing in Holland, and the traveler unable to reach his destination due to unforeseen technical problems and 'side road attractions'. Yet the spectator is privileged to attend the auto-show at the Schipol warehouse, which makes room for some of the most humorous segments in any Tati film.

The film frustrates many viewers who want to see a successful journey north, since most of the gags rely on the combination of the auto-show and the side-trip, or the disturbances provoked by the non-arrival at point B. However, another reading of the film observes the inventiveness that occurs when a trip goes wrong: cultural misunderstandings, and the uncanny encounter of a French man with his European neighbors, or the provocative sequence of the moon walk of the Apollo 11 mission, which is witnessed by chance during one unexpected stop one evening by a canal. Tati asks us to take 'la clé des champs' – literally to take the key to pastures, to flee, to take off and follow him.

In a Europe whose frontiers have now exploded but were then still in place, the journey crosses invisible borders; if these are invisible to the eye, they come alive at intervals when the car/truck is singled out and inspected by a series of Belgian border police officers. Tati sought to make a film that would map out borders, and show a geographic, cultural, and linguistic *dépaysement*, or 'change of scenery.'

J'ai choisi la Hollande parce que je voulais un trajet, avec des frontières ... et aussi un dépaysement tant sur le comportement que sur la langue. (Langlois). ('I chose Holland as I wanted a trajectory with borders ... and also a disorientation vis-a-vis behavior and language.')

The border patrol is on full alert since the Altra truck did not stop, as is customary at any border – probably because the border did not stand out on the side road. Two motorcycle cops escort them to a patrol garage where Hulot and the truck driver again lose time, yet 'unpack' and display the car to the authorities.

When arrested, Hulot feels obliged to give a demonstration of the car to the intrigued Belgian border patrol police. It turns out that the model transported on board the truck is a 'camping car', what is now called a 'van' (the French term is the modern version of the '*roulotte*', or the Gypsy carriage); the rear opens into a tent and can house a double bed, a television, a stove, a barbecue grill, a lighter, a soap dish, a razor, and a television. Hulot's assistant and driver clarify the product in poor English: 'In common market, success' and 'Like at home.' The working television set presents a glimpse of the preliminary sequence to the moon landing. Incidentally *Trafic*, over its entire duration, parallels the shuttle lift-off, moon landing, and first moon walking, one of the key events in 20th-century world history.

As in most of Tati's films, the structure is choreographic. The multiple car crash sequence leaves people miraculously untouched, yet stretching out and walking in a daze. Ironically, it is a traffic cop planted in the middle of the countryside who provokes the collision. The accident takes place at an intersection. The Altra truck happens to be near the scene but is not hit. A charitable Hulot recues an older man who is injured; he drives at night him to his house, in a residential neighborhood.

Shots of the canal and passing boats constitute the first real interlude in the film. The protagonists finally eat breakfast together at the mechanic's place, where they have stopped over. The garage owner and the driver witness the first televised moonwalk. The two men emerge from that night 'moon walking' or mimicking the moonwalk in slow motion. This dreamlike sequence is composed of the camera pan over the canal/boats at dawn; the sequence of the men in space can be seen as a 'proliferation of Hulot characters' (Deleuze 2: 90). Tati brings together characters and separates them, as in some form of modern ballet (Deleuze 2: 90–91). Deleuze referenced the scene of people walking on passageways/and stones in *Mon oncle*, or the weightlessness sequence in *Trafic*, or as Serge Daney would write in his homage to Tati, 'the passage of the luminous stroke (painting stroke) from *les Vacances* that ends in a genial ending in *Parade'* (Daney). The sequence provides an in-between, a moment that Michel Onfray describes elsewhere as in between the desire to leave and travel, and the actual arrival itself. The first step has been made. Botton defines the state where the traveler finds himself as the third realm (48):

> There was no, apart from the motorway, no road linking the service station to other places, no footpath even; it seemed not to belong to the city, nor to the country either, but rather to some third, travellers' realm, like a lighthouse at the edge of the ocean (48).

The scenery, no longer located in a recognizable urban setting, is remote. This episode is transformative: the public relations woman, who until this point had been complaining all the time and trying to keep a tight schedule, now laughs and takes things lightly all the way until the end. With the car repaired in this most unlikely setting, the protagonists have formed a community of friends through the shared moon-landing episode. Once Hulot finally makes it to the auto-show, the CEO of Altra fires him on the spot, yet the car triumphs among the gathered crowd.

Trafic is a road movie. Yet the final destination is constantly postponed, as if it was never the main focus of the narrative. The great question of the 20th century, noted Chris Marker in *Sans Soleil/Without Sun* (1983), is the coexistence of different concepts of Time. Tati stresses the concepts of in-between time and space despite the fact that the itinerary should logically follow an arrow shooting straight to the north. The time it takes for Hulot to transport the camping car in the truck to Amsterdam is part of his work time. How long is the trip? We are now inside time and duration, not so much just space as in *Playtime*. In order to be marketable, the time it takes to transport the car is important, and must be 'fast'. Despite the efficiency and speed demonstrated by the public relations woman at the wheel of her sports car in the first part of the film, nothing she does facilitates the transport and speedy delivery of the product. Tati gladly emphasizes the time it takes away from the interstate, idling or drifting through the countryside, and meeting with Dutch people away from any plan.

The trip to the moon

A parallel trip spans the entire duration of the film. This is 'the trip to the moon' – the launch of the Apollo mission, the landing on the moon, and the first step of humankind onto the moon. The span of the movie roughly fits the time it took to land and walk. Tati cleverly clips salient episodes from the adventure to the moon, which he intersperses at intervals in the film, almost unnoticed.

The seemingly trivial events in the film are therefore strongly dated and have a historical frame: 20 July 1969. Other gags resulting from or echoing the lunar landing are the factory workers who look like astronauts at the beginning or the objects in the camping car that have spaceship qualities similar to floating objects in space, such as the soap dish. Why rely on such an event? For one, it dates the film. Yet it also establishes a statement about the possibility of humankind reaching the moon in the time it takes a Parisian engineer to reach Amsterdam. Communication routes in Europe are somewhat fragile and prone to delays, despite the grandiose roadwork and creation of the A1 Autoroute from Paris to Belgium. The film could pass for a commercial for the new motorways of Europe that link different capitals together, or a critique of them. However, in the end, when Hulot walks away, he leaves for the train station, dismissing any individual transportation system for the collective, older, and more reliable train system.

Tati always features cars (sports cars, collectible cars, and vintage cars), buses, bicycles, trucks, and rockets, but never really champions the train, except with the exceptional shot of the arrival of the train at the station in front of the beach resort in *Les Vacances*. The gags never play out on board a train (the most democratic way of traveling in France). In fact, Tati's films never venture inside trains.

The link between man and machine stands at the center of Tati's films. Visions of the aging of cars and of wrecked automobiles and pile-ups crop up. The similarities between men and cars (machines) appear in several sequences. Cars that resemble man (at the gas stations), complete with sounds and visual gags, the windshield wipers that mimic the cars' owners, the gas stations that have become 'historic galleries'. On the way north, the crew starts to 'take its time' and adapts to a new rhythm, surrendering to the vision of a bucolic picnic straight out of Renoir's *Une partie de Campagne* (1936–1946) and celebrated by Tati. Freed from the car and the high-speed interstate, man is able to be more introspective, to go inside himself.

The Hulotian invention of the camping car should in fact belong to nature, away from towns and cities. However, the evocation of its true purpose takes place at the auto-show in its absence, with a fake-forest of trees and recorded sounds of birds. It is a simulacrum. As a true 'star' (like a cinema star) she (the car) does not arrive on time! Its appearance is delayed. Forced instead to reveal its beauty to a group of policemen, the leisure car turns into a representation of home away from home. Tati's notion of 'home' is always elastic, reinforcing the nomadic treatment of the main character. Hulot's house is represented in one film, *Mon Oncle* (1958), albeit at a distance from the outside, before he is banished and exiled to the provinces. Examples of domesticity abound in a camping car for two, conjuring the image of a utopian couple who can sleep and watch television, use liquid soap, and barbecue at leisure. It is not until *Trafic* that Hulot is paired with a companion and can fulfill the dream encapsulated in this image of domesticity.

Leisure time is associated with commodities and the society of consumption. However, unlike the Salon des arts ménagers featured in *Playtime*, the auto-show embodies work time. In a final ironical note, the camping car never makes it to the floorshow, the ideal floor plan where it is supposed to attract consumers. Instead, it creates a sensational attraction while parked on the street outside the show. The director has managed to disrupt the codes once more, and forced a debate on speed and slow time, at a moment of intense European industrial activity.

The film signals the final installment of the Hulotian character. But as in all Tati's films, if Hulot is a character, he is never the star of the show. Here, the character is self-effacing, like his initial sketch for the new car. He disappears but his world – based on everyday people – remains. After all, he is just a passenger. The bachelor, known to viewers since *Les Vacances de M. Hulot* (1953) and *Mon Oncle* (1958), is still nomadic and homeless, and becomes jobless at the close of *Trafic* as he stylishly walks away with Maria in order to take a train to an unknown destination. He can roam around at leisure. On a happier note, Tati releases the character and frees him from any further narrative constraints.

Conclusion

Films travel and transport the spectator to an elsewhere. Writing a book on travel in cinema is a process. I have presented some of the tropes that are at the core of the spectator's experience, and used a specific segment in time. George Méliès plunges us onto the moon, the Lumière brothers expanded on the travel motif with trains and 'live events' commemorating coronations and banishment. There has been a frenzy of movement and displacements since the 1950s on screen. Festivals devoted to travel literature, which acknowledge filmmaking as well, exemplify this passion. One example is *Etonnants voyageurs*, organized in Saint-Malo (Brittany) since 1990 by Michel Le Bris, a proponent of world literature.[1]

Travel literature inspires film projects. Tourism has become an area of studies not far from leisure studies since the 1970s, with the work of Dean MacCannell initiating multiple interrogations on the socioeconomic conditions of travelers. Such areas are usually dismissed by scholars and tucked away in a parks and recreation category. Writers like Montaigne, Rousseau, Voltaire, Claudel, and Gide had the most influence when Paul Morand discussed travel literature (Morand 110). I prefer to extend this list to include Simone de Beauvoir, Marguerite Duras, Alexandra David-Neel, Ella Maillart, Nicolas Bouvier, and more. Passionate travelers (such as Bouvier, Morand, Schwarzenbach, and Maillart) agree that travel does not win freedom and it can be a painful adventure. However, the person finds his/her compass in the world through displacement. The encounter with the Other and the Self is accomplished en route.

Despite the large presence of the archetype of the traveler in our society, travel has lost some of its early aura and meaning, and acquired new ones instead. The advent of cars, electricity (late 19th century), cinema (1895), computers, Internet connectivity, and high speed are the high marks of (post)modernity and progress in the 20th and 21st century; affordable tourism followed. The praise of 'slowness' infiltrates people's mentality. Sansot, Maffesoli, Delerm, Rozier, and even the 'hurried man' Morand in the 1960s, advocate a slower pace and rhythm.[2] Their messages are heeded.

One must appreciate the elsewhere in the desire to leave home. Whereas many travelers left home and travelled out of *ennui* – especially in the 19th century – the desire to explore 'new territories' is still strong. The traveler in search of himself/herself can travel at home on their computer and tablets, through social media broadcasts, becoming a spectator and actor in and of the world, watching world events unfold and traveling vicariously through all sorts of films:

> Depuis quelques années, je pratique à ma manière l'art du peu.... Je ne gambade plus avec les jambes, mais avec le regard (Sansot 118). ('For a few years now, I practice the art of the 'few' in my own way ... I no longer frolic with my legs, but with my gaze.')

Virtual travel (simulation) or 'travel without traveling', also termed 'immobile travel', is widespread through the projection of oneself on screen, in what are named 'home-theaters' (living rooms). or in training rooms with 360-degree 3D and audio. Many of us become armchair travelers then, projecting telekinetically elsewhere, deserting collective screenings and film houses.

The inability to stay still is at the heart of the human experience (Pascal).[3] What some call 'the immobile voyage' – people traveling by proxy or virtually – takes place through computers or television screens, images, novels, and films.

A thriving market economy surrounds travelers, offering packaged tours around the world. This continues an old tradition, but at a low cost and always in search of new marketing strategies by which to sell trips. Travel writing is a profession, soliciting all kinds of writers to report on their jaunts abroad. In search of thrills, the traveler looks for some authenticy that is lacking in the modern world (Abbeele 6). Some people travel to get paid, others pay to travel, while still others pay to read or watch these travelogues or reality shows on film, television, or in print. If a travel narrative is successful, a film adaptation will soon ensue. I am of course thinking of the memoir *Eat, Pray and Love* by Elizabeth Gilbert (2006). Film since its inception has always invited spectators to travel, and it took them along on board trains, planes, spaceships, and other vehicles.

Nomadism is used to package tourism; for instance, *Nomade Aventure* proposes original adventures with home stays 'far from the hordes of tourists'.[4] Other enticing lines among travel brochures play on the appeal of the 'nomadic spirit' of travelers. Some mottos advocate 'intelligent traveling', promoting wild adventures such as 'stress-free safaris ...'. Van den Abbeele notices that tourism is an

> institutional practice which assures the tourist' s allegiance to the state through an activity which discreetly effaces whatever grievances, discontent or 'alienation' that the tourist might have felt in regards to society. (3)

Travel is still an enterprise that requires multiple preparations. One cannot just up and go. Active preparations occur prior to a trip, down to reading much of the literature that has been published, and asking amongst peers and acquaintances for their own experiences. French bookstores devote entire shelves to travel literature and tour guides, if not entire stores. Yet some filmic narratives do just that: people just drop out and hit the road. A character suddenly leaves everything behind, sheds all their belongings and family for the road and the unknown, as is the case for Erick Zonca's *Julia* (2008) or Sólveig Anspach's *Lulu femme nue* (2014), not to mention the fate of the American businessman in Pascale Ferran's tale *Bird People* (2014), and as witnessed in Tony Gatlif's *Transylvania* (2006).[5] For others the road and the unknown may be a pretext for some open air and 'cleansing', as *Mammuth* (Delépine, de Kervern 2010), *Old Joy* (Reichardt 2006), or *Wild* (Vallée 2014) have shown. These scenarios allow us to project ourselves away from our daily routine, into the unknown and into another flow.

The globalization of our world impacts the experience of the traveler and the viewer. The transformation of borders, at least in Europe, has contributed to mass movements; however, these never deterred yesterday's travelers, in a time of horses, donkeys, and buggies, from turning Europe into a well-traveled space.

Modes of travel have changed our perspectives. Traversing a country by plane, train, or on foot constitute different types of experiences. Aimless wandering is almost a luxury, for time is precious. 'Flânerie' has become an ideal. The figure of the 'flâneur' may have died with the advent of the modern city (Mazierska, Rascaroli 71) but it endures in narratives, especially the 'flâneuse.' Free itinerant spirits roam the screens such as Sansa (*Sansa*), Mona (*Sans toit ni loi*), Stéphane (*Gadjo Dilo*), Andréa (*La Légende du Saint-Buveur*), or Cheryl (*Wild*, Vallée 2014).

Their paths cross those of the migrant in search of asylum and a better life, or the figure of the worker in search of employment in another country, or going to work, casting aside national boundaries and braving multiple dangers (*Nulle part, terre promise, Inguélézi, Welcome, Le Havre*). They may cross paths with criminal and horror elements as in *Feux Rouges* (Cédric Kahn 2004), *The Vanishing/Without a Trace* (George Sluizer 1988), *Eldorado* (Bouli Lanners 2008), or *Baise-moi/Fuck me* (Virginie Despentes, Coralie Trinh-Thi 2000).[6] I did not follow the latter paths, nor did I venture into science fiction with the possibilities offered by time travel, or into porn or erotic cinema.

Many travelers sense an urgent need to leave in order to renew themselves, as do Maillart, Bouvier, the Leiningers, Morand, and Gatlif's and Rozier's characters. Displacement is their way of feeling better and being at one with the world. Many of them rethink their place within the world, doing away for some with 'national' identity. Still the notion of home lingers throughout our approach. The journeys undertaken correspond to an inner one, and a search for roots and experiences. Film taps into unchartered territory, along with music, dance, photography, or any other art form. To leave, to let go, and to roam the world is a recognizable moment, detached from any moorings. Pilgrimages are very much present in contemporary cinema, yet in a revamped form (*Le grand voyage, Saint-Jacques ... La Mecque, Emmenez-moi*). Sightseeing as envisioned by MacCannell is a modern ritual (43). International tourists, in droves, are once more taking the road to Santiago de Compostela, a holy place during the Middle Ages; likewise Mecca, Lourdes, Jerusalem (the Holy Land), or Aznavour.[7] Such journeys are 'rituals'.

My work attempts to locate contemporary forms of travel in French films, and to pinpoint some of the existing tropes within the field, distinguishing between different practices. I remain acutely aware that this area is like a vast forest, with many trees and many paths, and curves, or to stay within previous nautical terminology, a vast sea. Different roads and profiles strongly emerge along the chronotropes of departure and return, the figure of transit and migrations, the nomadic trope, the importance of speed or slowness, the theme of the chase or the fugue, the figure of the holy beggar, and so on. All film genres and styles crisscross each others, from detective fiction to comedy or science-fiction, from horror to erotica or the chase, homecoming narratives, the aimless *dérive*, and so on ... I do not pretend to cover all genres but engage with a trend that goes beyond a nation-centric space and cinema and to invite the reader to take up some new forms of wandering in his/her sedentary life.

Notes

Introduction

1. This is an approximate translation found in English. (not mine) 137. *The Journal of Montaigne's Travels in Italy by way of Switzerland and Germany. 1580–1581.* London: J. Murray. 1903. E-book.
2. *En Famille* was suitably adapted into a Japanese anime version *The Story of Perrine (Periïnu Monogatari* 1990). The narrative follows the fate of a young 13-year-old girl, orphaned, of mixed heritage (Indian/French), who travels some distance to join her blood relatives in the Somme area of France, as a vagabond, after a long trek to her father's native country of France.
3. Ella Maillart. *Croisières et Caravanes (Cruises and Caravans).*

1 Departures

1. Laurent Fabius, a Socialist, was part of the Mitterrand government. First a minister of the budget in 1981 then minister of the Industry, he was prime minister between 1984 and 1986. François Hollande, French president, at the head of the Socialist government, appointed him foreign minister in 2012.
2. For a clear description of Erasmus see http://www.britishcouncil.org/erasmus. Web. 19 January 2014.
3. In several instances, the narrator (Xavier) addresses 'us': 'je vais enfin tout vous raconter' at the end of the film. ('I'm finally going to tell it all').
4. http://goeurope.about.com/cs/publications/a/auberge_film_3.htm. Web. 31 July 2014.
5. Etienne Mougeotte, TF1 channel vice-president, declared on 2 April, during a colloquium on French television at Paris-Dauphine university: 'Nous allons réunir six garçons et six filles de douze pays d'Europe pour essayer de reconstituer un microcosme européen. Nous allons regarder comment ces jeunes peuvent vivre entre eux, ce qu'ils ont de commun'. ('We're going to gather six boys and girls from twelve European countries in order to reconstitute a European microcosm. We are going to look at how these youths can live together and what they have in common.') The show started in summer 2004.
6. http://www.actustar.com/actualite/200303/20030325b.html. Web. 19 May 2012. The information is no longer there. 'M6 avait son loft présenté par Benjamin Castaldi, TF1 aura son *Auberge espagnole* à partir du mois de mai.'
7. Introduction to Montaigne's journal by S. de Sacy, v. 'Les uns, joyeux de fuir une patrie infâme; D'autres, l'horreur de leurs berceaux.' 'Pour lui [Montaigne] aussi, voyager, c'est, d'abord, fuir.' (Montaigne, 1954, v). ('For some, happy to flee the infamous homeland. For others, the horror of their cradle.' 'For Montaigne too, to travel, is, first of all, to flee.')

8. Timothy Corrigan's Chapter 5 is devoted to 'Genre, Gender, and Hysteria. The Road Movie in Outer Space.' 137–160.
9. C. Klapisch. 'La vie de Xavier dans le film est une vie en vrac parce qu'il se sent instable dans une époque instable. Son parcours se cherche, il n'existe pas encore, il est en chemin, il n'y a pas encore d'autoroute tracée pour lui' (*press kit*). ('Xavier's life in the film is a disordered life because he feels shaky in a shaky period. He is looking for a trajectory, he does not yet exist, he is on the path, there is no highway traced for him.')
10. The term 'gaulois' is raised by the French neurosurgeon friend while speaking to Xavier: 'Entre Gaulois il faut s'entraider.' ('Among people of Gaulois ancestry, we must help each other').
11. Vincent Malausa's review is the only review of a Klapisch film to ever appear in *Cahiers du cinéma*, as the journal seems to boycott all his films.
12. Cédric Klapisch's detailed published press kit for the film announces, 'He will discover the world, Europe, social life, autonomy and sexuality.' (3)
13. Klapisch. *L' Auberge espagnole*. presskit 10.
14. The ranking lists #1 *Astérix et Obélix*, #2: *8 Femmes*, and #3 *Le Boulet*. Statistics and figures from Octavi Marti, 'France. La fin d'un mirage?' *Cahiers du Cinéma*. Hors-Série (April 2003): 63.
15. Olivier Aubert. 'Sangatte, un non lieu pour des non-gens.' *Uzine* 20 October 2002. Web. 25 April 2015. http://www.uzine.net/article1184.html.
16. The 'hexagon' signifies France. The term has been adopted to reflect the geographical contours of the country.
17. I presented *L'Auberge espagnole* as a euro-trip film at the fifth annual French Studies conference in London (30 March 2005).
18. *Exils* by Gatlif received the Cannes award for best cinematography in 2004.
19. Sylvie Forbin is Senior Vice-President of Public and European Affairs at Vivendi Universal. This is based on a one-day symposium on the state of European cinema held in 2005 (Paris), organized by Confrontations Europe.
20. Initially Klapisch wanted to locate part of the film in Turkey.
21. 'Ces Français qui veulent changer de pays.' *Le Nouvel Observateur* 22–28 September 2005. Cover-page. http://www.pbaudry.com/presse/presse_64.php. Web. 25 April 2015.
22. 'Vieille et moderne, à l'image de l'Europe' ('Old and modern like Europe'). 'Cédric Klapisch commente sa filmo.' dvd #8. *Studio* June 2005. DVD.
23. Arnaud Gonzague. 'Changer de pays.' *Le Nouvel Observateur* 22–28 September 2005: 7. 'Aujourd'hui grâce au programme Erasmus, plus de 20,000 étudiants jouent les Romain Duris dans 'L'Auberge espagnole' film générationnel s'il en est – en passant un an dans une université européenne.' (7). http://www.nouvelobs.com/articles/p2133/hebdo.html (this link is no longer operational).
24. Aurélien Férenczi. 'L'Europtimiste.' *Télérama* 2892. 15 June 2005: 48.
25. 'In fact, I think that in all my films, I try to lose myself! I always try to surprise myself by choosing a very different topic from the previous film. Here, in order to surprise myself, there was the fact of going geographically far away and arriving there through foreign languages, I manage to no longer know where I am.' (Klapisch. *Les Poupées russes*. press kit. n.p.)

26. The budget figures may be found at www.imdb.com.
27. The young actor Ovidiu Balan is Romanian Gypsy.
28. *Mondo et autres histoires*. Gallimard, 1978.
29. 'Après avoir voyagé longtemps dans la soute d'un cargo, ou dans le dernier wagon d'un train de marchandises ...' (*Mondo* 12).
30. 'Il n'était pas d'ici.' (*Mondo* 12).
31. 'Unlike the Gypsies, whose allegiance was familial, and at the outer limit tribal but never national in the sense of aspiring to a territorial state, the Albanians I met were acutely aware of themselves as dud Europeans.' Isabel Fonseca. *Bury me standing. The Gypsies and their Journey*. New York: Vintage Books. 1995. I am grateful to Moses Iten for suggesting this fascinating book for my research.
32. Azabal's debut in Téchiné's *Loin* (2001), situated in Morocco, most likely prompted her casting in *Exils*. She subsequently played an interesting role in *Viva Laldjérie* (Nadir Moknèche 2004). *Loin* takes on the dynamics of the road and truck traveling through France-Spain and Morocco.
33. For further reading on the use of Gatlif, travel, and music, see S. Blum-Reid 'Gatlif's Manifesto: Cinema is Travel.'
34. A similar ceremony of rebirth will be performed in the middle of *Transylvania* (Gatlif) in a different context, but also with a female character. This is further analyzed in Chapter 6.
35. Nancy Huston's reflection on writer Romain Gary, whom she aptly analyzes as having 'a planetary identity' and as a citizen of the world. *Tombeau de Romain Gary*. 40, 97.
36. For a lengthier discussion of the sequence, see S. Blum-Reid's article in *Portal*.
37. The lyrics of the song 'Ceux qui nous quittent' ('Those who leave us'): 'ceux qui nous quittent nous reviennent toujours.' The lyrics and tune were written by Tony Gatlif and Delphine Mantoulet. *Exils*. Original Soundtrack by Tony Gatlif. Princes films-Pyramide distribution, 2004. CD.
38. The Men's Fashion volume features Duris on the front cover. For Klapisch, Duris is very much like a new Belmondo. Klapisch paired Duris and Belmondo in the futuristic film *Peut-être* (1999).
39. Actually Klapisch spotted him and recruited him for his film when he was a teenager. Duris was not then an actor, and wanted to be a musician.
40. 'Ce qu'on aime chez Romain Duris, finalement, outre ses qualités de comédien, c'est que l'adulte qu'il est devenu n'a pas trahi l'adolescent d'hier. L'homme est multiple, se dévoile petit à petit et trace sa route comme Zano, son personnage d'*Exils*, l'esprit constamment en alerte, prêt à accepter de nouvelles conquêtes et à s'imprégner d'autres cultures.' ('What one likes in Romain Duris, finally, besides his acting talent, is that the adult he has become has not betrayed the teenager from yesterday. The man is multiple, reveals himself little by little, and traces his road like Zano, his character from Exiles, his mind in constant alert, ready to accept new conquests and to immerse in other cultures.') Thomas Baurez. 'Portrait Romain Duris. Nouvelle dimension.' *Studio Magazine* 213. June 2005: 64.
41. This is particularly true in the films discussed, but also in a film, which I left out of the analysis *Dix-sept fois Cécile Cassard/Seventeen Times Cécile Cassard* by Christophe Honoré, 2002.

2 Rituals: The Unlikely Journey

1. Screened in October 2012 during the France through Asia retrospective (Singapore museum summary). Web. (the link no longer works).
2. 'Inde – Nocturne Indien D'Antonio Tabucchi.' *Le Cartographe*. Web. 28 July 2014. http://www.le-cartographe.net/dossiers-carto/asie/44-mon-travail/asie/94-inde-nocturne-indien-dantonio-tabucchi.
3. Antonio Tabucchi. *Nocturne Indien*. Paris: Christian Bourgois, 1987.
4. Thierry Guichard and Philipp. 'Nocturne Indien.' *Le Matricule des Anges*. Web. 29 July 2014. http://www.lmda.net/din/tit_lmda.php?Id=3363.
5. Antonio Tabucchi. 'Author's note.' *Indian Nocturne*. Trans. by Tim Parks. New York: New Directions, 1989 (from *Notturno Indiano*. Sellerio editore. 1984).
6. 'J'ai rencontré Tabucchi à Lisbonne ... Je me suis dit que le film est autant à Lisbonne qu'à Bombay' (Corneau). Michel Buruiana and Alain Corneau. 'Alain Corneau.' *Séquence: La Revue de Cinéma* 144 (1990): 37–43. http://www.erudit.org/culture/sequences1081634/sequences1146392/50433ac.pdf.
7. Tabucchi. *Indian Nocturne* 13.
8. Corneau in della Coletta. Note 14.
9. Antonio Tabucchi. *Little Misunderstandings of No Importance*. New York: New Directions, 1987.
10. Tabucchi accepted that Corneau use his other 'short' story for the film script. Buruiana and Corneau. *Séquences* 37–43, 40.
11. Short story. Corneau's script uses the exact same line found in Tabucchi's short story.
12. In the novel, the seer is a distorted and disfigured twenty-year old man, cared for by a younger brother.
13. Antonio Tabucchi. *Petits Malentendus sans importance*. Paris: Christian Bourgois, 1987.
14. The Baedeker India edition is apparently a rare book now, and would be an expensive item. Tabucchi's trip to India was made with the Baedeker. 'Dans une chambre je garde les livres que j'ai achetés lors de mes voyages. Un secteur est réservé aux guides Baedecker dont celui que j'ai utilisé lors de mon séjour en Inde. Les livres de voyage, je les considère comme faisant partie d'un genre littéraire avec Stevenson, Loti, Stendhal en Italie, Henri de Monfreid etc.' Tabucchi. *Matricule des Anges*. Web. 6 June 2012. Guichard and Philipp. 'Nocturne Indien.'
15. 'Les trains qui vont à Madras' (short story).
16. Jack Turner. 'Antonioni's *The Passenger* as Lacanian Text.' *Other Voices. The (e) Journal of Cultural Criticism*. 1.3 (January 1999). Web. 23 November 2012. http://www.othervoices.org/1.3/jturner/passenger.php.
17. Isabelle Eberhardt. *The Passionate Nomad. The Diary of Isabelle Eberhardt*. Boston: Virago/Beacon, 1988. Cagliari, 1 January 1900 entry.
18. Les Acacias. 'Farid Chopel: Un si beau voyage.' Press kit. Web. http://www.farid-chopel.com/dpsibeauvoyage.pdf.
19. From an interview I conducted with the filmmaker in Paris, June 2011.
20. Isabelle Regnier. '"Un si beau voyage." Le bel adieu de Farid Chopel.' *Le Monde*, 17 February 2009. Web. http://www.lemonde.fr/cinema/article/2009/03/17/un-si-beau-voyage-le-bel-adieu-de-farid-chopel_1168862_3476.html.

21. Michel Amargen. '"Un si beau voyage" de Khaled Ghorbal. Chronique d'une descente au désert.' *Africiné*. 22 March 2009. Web. http://www.africine. org/?menu=art&no=8475.
22. Jean Rabinovici. 'Rencontre avec Khaled Ghorbal.' *0 de conduite. Revue de l'union française du film pour l'enfance et la jeunesse 72*, 9–12. April–June 2009. Web. http://www.wobook.com/WBAW6U42ZG1e-2-a/0-de-conduite-n-72/Page-2.html.
23. *Casting* aired on Arte television in 2001.
24. Emmanuel Finkiel. *Madame Jacques sur la Croisette*. Assistant Director Julie Bertucelli, Les films du Poissons, La Sept Cinéma. Ministère de la Culture et de la Francophonie. Paris, 1997.
25. *Casting* is now included in the DVD version of *Voyages* (France).
26. Emmanuel Finkiel's commentary of the film (DVD version/ Arte) reveals that the video camera sequence was actually shot in Birkenau. It gives much information about the director's thoughts and the way the film was made.
27. *Casting* features a segment when some of the persons who answered the casting call refused to go 'back' to Poland.
28. I recall seeing a list of sites to visit in the Czech Republic that included the Theresienstadt concentration camp. I am assuming that the same goes for Poland, which I have not visited.
29. Finkiel has called the Association and its spirit 'l'Esprit Carpe-farcie.' (see DVD's film commentary). Such an association is also behind the life of the movie.
30. In Finkiel's own commentary on his DVD.
31. *No sex last night* 1995. Made in its video version in 1992, entitled *Double-Blind*, released in 1995 its 35 mm version, screened at theatres in January 1996.
32. Simone de Beauvoir. *L'Amérique au jour le jour*. Paris: Gallimard, 1948.
33. I started writing about Sophie Calle in 1988–1990 in my dissertation entitled *Memory and Nostalgia: Photography and Texts*. University of Iowa, December 1990. I placed her alongside Christian Boltanski's work, in an analysis of the nostalgic and photographic texts of three writers: Duras, Modiano, and Perec.
34. She recalls the day he took a bath in her bath water in Kyoto. He told her that it was the most erotic experience he had ever had with a woman.
35. Film. My own transcription.
36. It was still shown in 2004 (MK 2 Beaubourg).
37. Art Wiki. 'Sophie Calle, Un art urbain.' Web. http://www.artwiki.fr/wakka. php?wiki=SophieCalle.

3   Vagabondages

1. *The Concise Oxford Dictionary of Current English*. Edited by H.W. Fowler and F.G. Fowler based on *The Oxford Dictionary – Fifth Edition*. Revised by E. McIntosh. Etymologies revised by G.W.S. Friedrichsen, Oxford at the Clarendon Press (1964).
2. See Maffesoli's *Nomadism*.
3. *New World Encyclopedia*, http://www.newworldencyclopedia.org/entry/ nomad. Web. 29 March 2015.

4. For an interesting definition of the new term and a map of internment camps see http://romafacts.uni-graz.at/index.php/history/persecution-internment-genocide-holocaust/internment-in-france-1940-1946. Web. 29 March 2015.
5. This is effectively demonstrated in Tony Gatlif's early film *Les Princes* (1983), which satirizes all these traits.
6. Quoted by Sarah Petit in press kit. 1.
7. Interview with Sarah Petit. http://www.commeaucinema.com/film/le-lac-et-la-riviere,16789. Web. 28 April 2015.
8. Both are produced by Michel Klein. Unfortunately not released on DVD format, except for *L'Arpenteur*, as recently as 2010, they are however available for download or streaming.
9. Due to their rare nature, and the fact that these films were never released commercially on any DVD support, or circulated abroad, I only saw both films once, at a movie house. I have wanted to see them again ever since; however I am relying on my once-taken notes in the dark. It is only recently that *L'Arpenteur* was released on a DVD format. It is available from the French film library, BIFI.
10. Lines of this exchange: 'Qui es-tu?' she says. He answers: 'J'erre sur cette terre depuis 1800, et j'ai vu tous les malheurs du monde, et j'en ai marre.'
11. In a four page-film dossier graciously given by Shellac distribution. Michel Klein states that 'L'arpenteur est le hors champ du lac et la rivière, et le lac et la rivière est le hors-champ de l'arpenteur.' (np)
12. Walter Benjamin. *One-Way Street & Other Writings*. London: New Left Books, 1979.
13. Joseph Roth. *The Legend of the Holy Drinker*. London: Granta, 2001.
14. I have taken the liberty of borrowing the term Jack Kerouac used in *The Dharma Bums* (1958).
15. This is Siegfried's second feature-length film, after *Louise (Take 2)* (1999) with Roshdy Zem and Elodie Bouchez. Siegfried is a music composer as well as a director.
16. Produced by Arte and Vagabondages film, *Sansa* is a Franco-Spanish co-production.
17. Jacqueline Dutton presented on 'The travel ideal in *Sans Soleil* and *Sansa*' at the Australian French Studies annual conference (December 2013).
18. Of course, the French pun would work best in the association of the two words: *pour/suivre* meaning to follow (amorously) and to chase after.
19. I prefer the French alternative for this title: '*Embrasement du récit.*'
20. This is reminiscent of *Gadjo Dilo*'s itinerant character as an adopted Gypsy who purchases a dilapidated car, which soon becomes unmanageable.
21. My own transcription of the lyrics.
22. Catherine Breillat exhibits Asia Argento's tattoos in her film *Une vieille maîtresse* (2007). Argento had just made the film *Marie-Antoinette* with Sofia Coppola (2006) right before her performance in Gatlif's *Transylvania*.
23. Michel Rebichon. 'Tony Gatlif en transe.' *Studio*, June 2006: 134–135.
24. Varda (quoted in Darke 2001: 30) in Ewa Mazierska and Laura Rascaroli, 125. Varda's labeling also fits *Les Glaneurs et la Glaneuse/The Gleaners and I.*
25. '"Transylvania": Romance Tsigane sur les routes de Transylvanie' 10 April 2006. Web. 3 June 2012.
26. Marc Augé. *Un Ethnologue dans le métro*, op. cit.

27. Louis Guichard. 'Un tramway nommé destin.' *Télérama*, 2 June 1999.
28. Jacques Mandelbaum. 'Grandeur et décadence du film choral.' *Le Monde*, 26 June 2007. http://www.lemonde.fr/web/recherche_breve/1,13-0,37-994444,0.html. Web. 29 March 2015.
29. His health concerns on top of his world concerns. Interview with Jean-Claude Guiguet, *Les Passagers*. DVD supplement. K Films.
30. Jean-Claude Guiguet. Interview. *Les Passagers*. DVD supplement. K Films.
31. Stéphane Rideau first appeared in André Téchiné's *Les Roseaux sauvages* (1994), Bruno Putzulu, a theatre actor, in *Emmène-moi* (Michel Spinoza 1994), Véronique Silver was first cast in Sacha Guitry *Si Versailles m'était conté* (uncredited 1954) and Fabienne Babe in Jacques Rivette's *Hurlevent* (1984) and *Souvenirs Souvenirs* by Ariel Zeitoun (1984).
32. Philippe Roger. *Les Passagers* de Jean-Claude Guiguet. Grigny: Editions Paroles d'Aube, 1999.
33. Véronique Silver is an actress who appeared in François Truffaut's film *La Femme d'à côté* (1981).
34. Jean-Claude Guiguet. Interview. *Les Passagers*. DVD supplement. K. Films.
35. BBC Music Magazine, April 2008, quoted at http://www.prestoclassical.co.uk/w/116500/Michel-Richard-de-Lalande-Troisi%E8me-Le%E7on-de-T%E9n%E8bres-du-Mercredy-Saint. Web.
36. Indeed Vigo did not survive the film and died before its release in Paris.
37. William Aggeler. Translation of *The Flowers of Evil*, 1959, *Spleen*. http://fleursdumal.org/poem/161. Web. 18 June 2012.

4   The Return or the Nostoï

1. *Le Voyage de Louisa*. A young Tunisian girl who has a genetic disease is taken clandestinely to France by her older brother for medical treatment, in a failed northbound trajectory.
2. The director when asked about the meaning of the title referred to the land: 'le pays d'origine ... la terre demeure vitale.' ('the land of origin ... The soil is vital'). Personal Interview. Montreuil. July 2009.
3. http://www.cineuropa.org/interview.aspx?lang=en&documentID=68311. Web. 22 May 2012.
4. Carry Tarr 2009.
5. Naficy 2001.
6. Anne Feuillère. 'The origin of the world. Rabah Ameur-Zaïmeche director.' *Cineuropa* 11 October 2006. http://www.cineuropa.org. Web. 11 February 2013.
7. Higbee 2009: 226.
8. Julien Welter. Actualité DVD-Bled Number One. http://www.arte.tv/fr/cinema- fiction/Actualite-DVD/1447722,CmC=1447730.html. Web (no longer available).
9. 'Etre vivant et faire du cinéma.' Interview Rabah Ameur-Zaïmeche. 7 June 2006. http://www.critikat.com/Rabah-Ameur-Zaimeche.html. Web. 22 April 2012.
10. Rodolphe Burger was born in Colmar in 1957 and became a philosophy professor in 1980. He belongs to the collective 'Dernière Bande' that became Kat Onoma. He sings and plays the guitar. He worked on Jeanne Balibar's

first album *Paramour,* and has also worked with Pierre Alfieri, and earlier Françoise Hardy. Web. No longer accessible http://www.rodolpheburger.fr/index.php/capitol/rodolphe_burger/no_sport/biographie.

11. The same actor (Bruno Abraham-Kremer) played alternately the three roles of a forty-year old Momo, a younger Momo and Mr. Ibrahim.

12. 'Car Monsieur Ibrahim passait ... pour un sage. Sans doute parce qu'il était depuis au moins quarante ans l'Arabe d'une rue juive'.

13. Ajar's novel *La vie devant soi* (Mercure de France) received the Prix Goncourt in 1975.

14. 'Arabe, Momo, ça veut dire ouvert de huit heures du matin jusqu'à minuit et même le dimanche ... dans l'épicerie'.

15. 'Close to one fourth (23.1 per cent) of Europe's Turkish immigrants thus live in this German state.' Figures/statistics obtained through the Medea institute. http://www.medeainstitute.org/index.html?page=&lang=&doc=1160. Web. no longer accessible.

16. http://www.allocine.fr/film/fichefilm_gen_cfilm=43960.html. Web. 22 May 2012.

17. Omar Sharif is an Egyptian actor of Lebanese descent.

18. 'L'Europe, je ne l'ai pas vue, je l'ai entendue'.

19. 'Nous nous refusons tous les luxes, sauf le plus précieux : la lenteur'. My translation unless otherwise specified.

20. 'Le temps d'Asie coule plus large que le nôtre'.

21. 'La lenteur ... c'est ça le secret du Bonheur'.

22. 'C'était incroyable. J'avais la haine qui se vidangeait'. Momo's sentence translates into: 'My hatred was being purged'.

23. 'Dans quinze jours, je serai mort'.

24 'Ne bougeant jamais, telle une branche greffée sur son tabouret' (Schmitt 1999: 12). The complete sentence is the following: 'Sans doute parce qu'il semblait échapper à l'agitation ordinaire des mortels, surtout des mortels parisiens, ne bougeant jamais, telle une branche greffée sur son tabouret, ne rangeant jamais son étal.'

25. http://en.unifrance.org/news/617/monsieur-ibrahim-turns-up-trumps-from-east-to-west. Web. 29 March 2015.

26. It was shown at the Seattle International film festival (May 2005) and through the FACSEA (now FACE) festival tournées series, promoted by the French foreign affairs ministry in the United States, an agency that actively encourages the distribution of French and Francophone cinema by offering competitive grants to different campuses.

27. '*La terre au ventre* ce n'était pas un film sur l'Algérie, les Algériens ont dit: c'est pas un film sur nous; c'était un film sur les Gitans et je n'ai pas voulu le dire à ce moment parce que ça ne m'intéressait pas de dire mes origines; maintenant je dis. Je dis tout. Pendant des années j'ai caché mon identité, je disais que j'étais Français, que j'avais fait les Beaux-Arts ... je dis que je ne suis ni Français ni Arabe. Je n'ai plus aucun frein.'

28. 'Lo spettatore è costretto al viaggio, un viaggio in cui il luogo di arrivo diventa subito il luogo di una nuova partenza: la rappresentazione di un determinato mondo che un film produce viene subito immediatamente rimessa in discussione nel film successivo. Gatlif invita a scoprire il potenzialità del transito'. I wish to thank Sophie Ganachaud for the translation of this quote from the original Italian text.

5 Transit

1. Anne Laffeter. *Les Inrockuptibles.* 31 March 2009. http://www.lesinrocks. com/2009/04/05/cinema/actualite-cinema/les-sans-   papiers-nouveaux-heros-du-cinema-1142541/. Web. 14 May 2013.

2. Matéo Maximoff is seen as the first writer of Roma origins in France; his works draw from his ancestry, for instance *Les Ursitory*, and his biography, *Le Prix de la Liberté.*

3. Régis Debray. Paris: Gallimard, 2010.

4. For the complete text of the law, see http://www.legifrance.gouv.fr/affich-Code.do?idSectionTA=LEGISCTA0000061 47789&cidTexte=LEGITEXT00000 6070158&dateTexte=20090408. Web. 10 August 2014.

5. Philippe Lioret. 'Welcome, Philippe Lioret, réalisateur' *L'Humanité dimanche* 12 March 2009: 1.

6. 'Ce film est une fiction. La réalité des transporteurs est autre. SEAFRANCE s'est efforcée, aujourd'hui plus que jamais de lutter contre le transfert des clandestins en Grande Bretagne.' This disclaimer by François Dupeyron opens the film.

7. Dominique Wideman. 'Entretien avec Emmanuel Finkiel'. *L'Humanité,* 1 April 2009: 21.

8. Mireille Rosello. *Postcolonial Hospitality. The Immigrant as Guest.* Stanford: Stanford University Press, 2002.

9. *Le Havre.* CNDP. http://www.cndp.fr/mag-film/films/le-havre/paroles.html. Web.

10. Jean Vigo Prize 2008.

11. Apparently Michael Gott observed four different trajectories in his essay. Due to the nature of my viewing of the film, from a single upload in France, since the film has never been commercially released on DVD format, I am presently unable to verify this and can only refer to what I saw. As some film theorist writes: we all see films differently, and may even construe our own films.

12. Michael Gott. 'Under Eastern Eyes: Displacement, Placelessness and the Exilic Optic in Emmanuel Finkiel's *Nulle part, terre promise/Nowhere promised land,* 2008.' Crossings, frictions, fusions: 20th and 21st century French and Francophone Studies International colloquium. Long Beach, 2011.

13. Michael Winterbottom's film *In this world* records the 2002 journey of two young Afghan men – one is only 16 – sent from their refugee camps to London. The film captures their harrowing journey across the continent on board trucks, cars, boats, and trains. One of them does not survive the trip, suffocated in a locked truck container. He is no 'longer in this world' as the younger one reports by telephone to his uncle back in the camp. The film is shot in a near documentary style.

14. Finkiel was assistant to Kieslowski.

15. In fact, the event in the original script shows that the woman was condemned and fined.

16. Antoine de Baeque. 'Drôle de voyage pour une rencontre.' *Libération,* 26 May 2004.

17. Yves Angelo worked with Dupeyron as his cinematographer in the more recent film *Mon âme par toi guérie* (2013).

18. 'J'ai refusé le "Sangatte film."' For Dupeyron, recent cinema is often based on news events (*faits-divers*). He wanted to move beyond that. Antoine de Baeque. 'Dupeyron dans la clandestinité.' *Libération*, 26 May 2004. http://next.liberation.fr/cinema/0101490181-dupeyron-dans-la-clandestinite. Web. 3 August 2013.

19. Dominique Wideman, op. cit. 22.

20. 'le délit de solidarité n'existe pas, c'est un mythe.' http://fr.wikipedia.org/wiki/Éric_Besson. Web. 2 June 2013.

21. Eric Besson, a socialist, joined the Sarkozy UMP government and became minister of immigration, integration, and national identity from 2009 to 2010. He then became minister of Industry, Energy, and Numeric Economy from 2010 until May 2012, under the Fillon government.

22. (n/a) *Le Monde* 11 March 2009.

23. Agathe André. 'Welcome dans un pays de merde.' *Charlie-Hebdo*, 18 March 2009.

24. 'undignified reality.' Jean-Claude Raspiengeas. *Welcome*. 'J'ai terminé ce film en citoyen révolté.' *La Croix*, 11 March 2009.

25. Claire Dupont-Monod. 'Enfin le cinéma français se mouille.' *Marianne* 7 March 2009.

26. Henry Rousso. 'Comparer les clandestins de Calais aux Juifs est une preuve d'ignorance.' *20 minutes.fr*, 11 March 2009. http://www.20minutes.fr/cinema/309573-henry-rousso-comparer-clandestins- calais-juifs-preuve-ignorance. Web. 5 August 2013.

27. Samira Ahmed's blog. http://www.samiraahmed.co.uk/from- casablanca-to-calais-refugees-on-film/. Web. 10 August 2014.

28. Marie-Noël Tranchant. 'André Wilms, entre Marx et Jesus.' Interview with Aki Kaurismäki: 'Je parle d'une humanité en miettes.' *Le Figaro* 21 December 2011. http://www.lefigaro.fr/culture/2011/12/20/03004- 20111220ARTFIG00519-andre-wilms-entre-marx-et-jesus.php. Web. 29 May 2013.

29. Kaurismäki plans on filming in Spain and Germany for the next installments. http://blogs.indiewire.com/theplaylist/aki-kaurismakis-le-havre-the-first-of-a-trilogy-director-plans-future-entries-in-spain-germany. Web. 9 June 2013.

30. Aki Kaurismäki by Peter von Bagh. http://www.the-match- factory.com/catalogue/libraries/items/library-aki- kaurismaeki/details/introduction.html. Web. 9 November 2013.

31. Sadoul notes that Prévert changed the year from 1912 to 1938.

32. Francois-Guillaume Lorrain. 'Le Havre, mon amour.' *Le Point*, 15 December 2011.

33. Nicole Bary. Preface to *Transit*, 1995: 7–11.

34. 'L'unité de l'oeuvre d'Allio tient à ce besoin de dénoncer la "société-souricière", devant laquelle il lui semble indispensable de préserver la fidélité à soi-même'. http://cinema.encyclopedie.personnalites.bifi.fr/index.php?pk=13500. Web.

35. Actors Willson Goma, Vladimir Zongo, and Destiné M'Bikula Mayemba are credited as 'clandestines'.

36. Apparently the Seafrance company has closed down in 2012, after declaring bankruptcy. The line is now replaced by My Ferry Link. http://www.directferries.fr/sea_france.htm. Web. 8 July 2013.

37. According to Kaurismäki, the character of Arletty was Romanian (Levieux).

38. Jacques Derrida. *De l'hospitalité*. Anne Dufourmantelle invite Jacques Derrida à répondre. Paris: Calmann-Levy, 1997: 25.
39. Yvette Biro. 'Two irregular fairy tales.' *Anachronia*, 11/2012: 106–112.
40. Kaurismäki is fond of Jean-Pierre Léaud, an actor in one of his favorite film-maker's films, François Truffaut. He uses him in the film *J'ai engagé un tueur* (*I hired a killer*), set in England, showing a dark French immigré, a victim of the capitalist system.
41. The story of Little Bob. http://www.littlebob.fr/littlebob_pagesHTML/littlebob_annees_biosHTML/bioe nglish.html. Web. 11 August 2014.
42. BBC world news report in October 2013, after the tragedies at Lampedusa and elsewhere, deemed this situation as extreme. Chris Morris, 'Sweden's asylum offer to refugees from Syria.', 23 October 2013. http://www.bbc.co.uk/news/world- europe-24635791. Web and radio.
43. *Sankofa*, an Akan word and an African symbol, meaning 'to get back and take'. http://ctl.du.edu/spirituals/Literature/sankofa.cfm. Web .
44. 'Bouchareb, cinéaste des origines.' In *Little Senegal. Un film de Rachid Bouchareb*. Ed. Alain Arnaud. CNC. Dossier BIFI. La bibliothèque du film. 2002, pp. 1–24, p. 5.
45. 'Sotigui Kouyaté: The wise man of the stage.' *The UNESCO Courier*. October 2001: 47–48. http://unesdoc.unesco.org/images/0012/001237/123798e.pdf. Web. 6 August 2013. Kouyaté was a Malian-born Guinean actor with a Burkinabe nationality. He performed in France and worked with Peter Brook on the production of the epic play: *The Maharabhata.* (1983) He acted in two of Bouchareb's films: *Little Senegal*, and *London River*, his last film (2009).

6   Rebels and Flâneuses

1 Bouvier. *L'Usage du Monde*.
2. I am borrowing a term that applies to Nicolas Bouvier, who always wanted to travel based on his childhood reading of Jules Vernes, Jack London, and Alexandre Dumas, used in Christine Jordis's preface to N. Bouvier's *Oeuvres* 10.
3. Ella Maillart discusses her childhood and sports practices in *Croisières et caravanes*.
4. Both Swiss-German directors/brothers are particularly known for their documentary film work.
5. Denis Voituret. 'Ella Maillart, un nouveau "genre de voyageuse": 1923–1935', TÉOROS. *Revue de Recherche en Tourisme*. 29. 2 (2010): 119–127. (126). http://teoros.revues.org/943?file=1. Web. 1st August 2014.
6. Biographical elements are culled from a website dedicated to A. Schwarzenbach: http://www.annemarieschwarzenbach.eu/french/vie3.html. Web. 5 October 2013.
7. Footage and photographs by both artists appear in *Une Suisse rebelle: Annemarie Schwarzenbach 1908–1942* (2000), directed by Carole Bonstein.
8. Annemarie Schwarzenbach. *Une Suisse rebelle*, documentary film by Carole Bonstein, 2000. http://www.youtube.com/watch?v=N6kbfB_e7BI.
9. Unfortunately, Schwarzenbach died of a head injury after a bicycle fall in Switzerland in 1942.

10. Raymond Bussières acted in Julien Duvivier's *La Belle Equipe* (1936) and Jean Becker's *Casque d'or* (1952).
11. The line comes from *Jonas qui aura 25 ans en l'an 2000* (Tanner, 1975).
12. As one character calls her 'Rosemonde qui ne fait que passer ...' (Rosemonde who is just passing by).
13. Both rivers Arve or Rhône pass by Geneva.
14. Interview with Tanner. DVD. Montparnasse editions (2006).
15. The inspector of the Civil defense pays a visit at Pierre's apartment to 'inspect' his morality.
16. Switzerland is a place where abortion was legal, and where European women would travel to in order to undergo the procedure.
17. Nicolas Rapold. 'Trapped in a Jungle and a State of Mind', *New York Times*, 9 August 2012. http://www.nytimes.com/2012/08/10/movies/almayers-folly-directed-by- chantal-akerman.html?_r=0.
18. The scene and presence of Lea Massari is a direct reminder of Louis Malle's film *Le Souffle au Coeur* (1971), which contained an incestuous relationship between a mother and her son.
19. Dudley Andrew 2010.
20. Although Varda was born in Brussels, she and her family moved to Sète (France) during World War II.
21. I am referring to *Documenteur*, a film she made while in Los Angeles, in 1980–1981.
22. Watching *Cléo* at the beginning of the film, I am invariably reminded of the 1965 hit- song 'Je suis une poupée de cire, une poupée de son' ('I'm a wax doll, a rag doll'), sung by France Gall and written by Serge Gainsbourg.
23. I thank John Van Hook (University of Florida Libraries) for indicating this film to me years ago.
24. For a discussion of paintings and their inclusion, see Sandy Flitterman-Lewis's chapter on *Sans toit ni loi*.
25. Sophie Grassin. 'Des filles qui se réalisent.' *L'Express*, 24 February 2000.
26. Didier Daeninckx. *La Repentie*. Vendôme: Verdier, 1999.
27. *L'Humanité*, 17 February 2002.
28. Christine Angot. 'Je préférerais qu'ils y fassent attention'. *Epok* 27. June 2002.
29. 'L'oeil sur l'écran.' *Le Monde* cinema blog. http://films.blog.lemonde.fr/2006/03/03/2006_03_repentie/. Web. 28 April 2015.
30. Preview of *La Repentie*. http://www.youtube.com/watch?v=fmhRiAPW9SA. Web. 21 December 2013.
31. 'Comment filmer le travail du temps sur le visage lisse et bombé, miraculeusement conservé d'une actrice?' Hélène Frappat. 'La Repentie.' *Cahiers du cinéma* 568 (May 2002): 121–122.
32. 'Une silhouette sexy en jupe noire longue et fluide. Une allure de danseuse, de nomade. Isabelle est enchantée. C'est tout de suite un personnage' (Halberstadt 51).
33. Geneviève Sellier. 'Touche pas la femme blanche: *La Journée de la jupe*, (Lilienfeld 2009) ou le féminisme instrumentalisé par l'Islamophobie,' 'Ses yeux bleus et sa peau blanche, ainsi que sa formation classique ... et la totalité de ses rôles sont là pour acréditer l'image de sa francité.' The essay 'Don't touch the white woman' was published in English in Sylvie Durmelat,

Vinay Swamy Eds., *Screening Integration: Recasting Maghrebi Immigration in Contemporary France*. University of Nebraska Press, 2012 http://bader.lejmi. org/2009/10/01/touche-pas-la-femme-blanche-journee-de-la- jupe/. Web. 9 August 2014.

34. The film has not been released commercially in the USA.
35. 'J'ai grandi à Colombes et à St.Cyr-l'Ecole.' 'Zaïda Ghorab-Volta, réalisatrice de 'Jeunesse dorée': 'Je hais les ghettos.' Interview by Anne Diatkine.
36. Franck Nouchi. Preface. DVD *Jeunesse dorée*. MK2 découverte (2002).
37. Martin O' Shaughnessy, trans. 'The Experience of a Maghrebi-French Filmmaker: The Case of Zaïda Ghorab-Volta.' *Cineaste*. Vol. XXXIII, no. 1, Winter 2007: 52–53.
38. Rev. of *Jeunesse dorée/Wesh Wesh, qu'est-ce qui se passe?* *Jeune Cinéma* 275 (May 2002): 57–59.
39. Although I do not particularly subscribe to this term, 'beur' has been used and applied to such persons as children of migrant workers of North-African descent for the past thirty years.
40. Anne Diatkine. 'Zaïda Ghorab-Volta, 'Je hais les ghettos,'' *Libération*, 27 March 2002: 31–32.
41. Ghorab-Volta. 'The Experience of a Maghrebi-French Filmmaker: The Case of Zaïda Ghorab-Volta.' *Cineaste*. Vol. XXXIII 1 (winter 2007): 52. Her filmography stops in 2001.
42. 'Il faut croire au cinéma pour oser nous conter cette histoire de femme qui découvre peu à peu que rien n'était comme elle avait prévu, immergée dans un destin qu'elle ne contrôle plus. Comme ce réalisateur qui retourne trente ans plus tard en Algérie et renonce au film qu'il s'était fait dans sa tête pour prendre le sujet qui s'impose à lui. Cet homme va parler des femmes plutôt que de la guerre, des femmes oubliées dans des coins les plus reculés, des femmes qui ne peuvent que se taire et se sacrifier'.
43. ' ... on attendra Keltoum, la mère, et l'on comprendra avec sa fille qu'elle ne viendra pas, qu'il faut donc partir et que, quelle que soit l'issue, *l'important est le voyage*'. Michel Guilloux. http://www.humanite.fr/node/263448. Web. 28 July 2014.
44. 'Chacun de ces films se penchant sur les difficultés qu'ont eues ces femmes à trouver un espace à elles dans une réalité construite par d'autres, pour d'autres. Car il apparaît clairement dans ces films qu'il n'y a pas d'espace public pour elles. Dans les cafés maghrébins, espace public par excellence, les seules femmes que l'on voit sont considérées comme des femmes publiques'. Ida Kummer. 'Colonisée, maghrébine, beurette: le parcours de la combattante.' *CELFAN*: Cinéma (2002): 49–55.

7 Dérives

1. Michel Tournier. 'Je fais une opposition entre les écrivains inspirés par l'histoire et les écrivains inspirés par la géographie. Et je suis nettement du côté des géographes.' 97.
2. 'C'est ainsi que j'ai abandonné, à l'âge de six ans, une magnifique carrière de peintre ... J'ai donc dû choisir un autre métier et j'ai appris à piloter des avions. J'ai volé un peu partout dans le monde. Et la géographie, c'est exact,

m'a beaucoup servi. Je savais reconnaitre du premier coup d'oeil, la Chine et l'Arizona. C'est très utile si l'on est égaré pendant la nuit.' Saint-Exupéry *Le petit Prince*, 2.

3. Françoise Giroud coined the expression to designate the new youth age in *L'Express* magazine. It did not refer to film at first.
4. Stéphane Bouquet. In Emmanuel Burdeau, Sébastien Bénédict, Stéphane Bouquet et al, eds. *Jacques Rozier. Le Funambule*. Paris: Cahiers du cinéma.
5. With the name Jean-Arthur, we are close to Rimbaldian first names. There is a term in French for people who work in the travel agency field: *'voyagistes'* which is untranslatable into English.
6. Tourism studies may have been overlooked and underrated. They are attached to Parks and Recreations in academia; however the field has a much more serious understanding of travel culture.
7. An interesting ethnographic book on the topic, *Façons de dire, façons de faire* by Yvonne Verdier, develops the historical function of women's work in rural France.
8. Ella Maillart. *Croisières et caravanes* has been reedited six times since 1951.
9. Nicole and Raymond Leininger's book garnered the first prize for outdoor sports literature in 1946 (1er prix de littérature sportive du comité national du sport du plein air).
10. The famous slogan back in the 1970s was 'Le Camping c'est Trigano' (Camping is Trigano!). The Trigano company still exists, and advertises its services as 'Hotellerie de plein air' or great outdoor hotels.
11. http://www.advertisingarchives.co.uk/en/asset/show_zoom_window_ popup.html?asset =13309&location=grid&asset_list=87516287,56156,55 566,17554,15645,46121,4 6120,45082,35878,35877,27551,26555,25911,2 5910,25907,25906,13733,13309,1 3308,13307,13306,6552&basket_item_ id=undefined. Web. 11 August 2014. 'Club Med invites you to spend your holidays in a little grass hut.'
12. The show *Survivor* premiered in 2000 and is still running. http://www. tv.com/survivor/show/4742/summary.html. Web. 11 August 2014.
13. Jacques Villeret. Interview. *Les Naufragés de l'île de la Tortue*, DVD Coffret Jacques Rozier. Supplement. Arcades vidéo, 2008. 'On a avancé dans la brousse au propre et au figuré.'
14. Rozier. 'Inventaire I. Propos de Jacques Rozier.' *Jacques Rozier. Le funambule*. 44.
15. Yves Afonso plays the unforgettable role of a fisherman from l'Ile d'Yeu and had to adopt speech patterns from the l'Ile d'Yeu inhabitants, whereas he is from the Morvan, a region northeast of the Massif Central.
16. Rozier was assistant to Renoir on *French Can-Can* when he returned to France and claims that he was a great admirer of the director. 'Inventaire I. Propos de Jacques Rozier.' *Jacques Rozier. Le funambule*. 22–49.
17. There is a passing homage to Alain Fournier's *Le Grand Meaulnes* in this episode at night, through its total mystery.
18. Wolfgang Schivelbusch. 'The Railway: Industrialization of Time and Space in the 19th century.' http://www.suu.edu/faculty/ping/pdf/TheRailwayJourney. pdf. Web. 22 July 2014.
19. Entretien avec Rozier. *Le Matin*, 16 April 1986.
20. CEE = Communauté Economique Européenne, the precursor to the EU, the European Union.

Conclusion

1. Official site of the festival of travelers in Saint-Malo. http://www.etonnants-voyageurs.com. Web. 22 July 2014.
2. Michel Maffesoli. *L'Instant éternel* 10.
3. Pascal. 'Tout le malheur des hommes vient d'une seule chose, qui est de ne savoir pas demeurer en repos, dans une chambre.' Cited in Pierre Sansot's incipit.
4. *'nomade aventure'* is one of the first French-based sites to be found via Internet search that offers original trips for families.
5. One of the most recent films to perform this scenario is Pascale Ferran's *Bird People* (2014). Yet most of the critiques of the film immediately locate it within the supernatural genre. It takes place at the Roissy airport. Another recent film is Sólveig Anspach, *Lulu femme nue* (2013), based on a comic strip by Etienne Davodeau.
6. *The Vanishing* is a Dutch-French film adaptation with a Franco-Dutch cast.
7. Films like *Saint-Jacques … La Mecque* (Coline Serreau), and *Le Grand voyage* (Ismaël Ferroukhi) are pilgrimage films, but so are others that do not necessarily have a visible pilgrimage marker, such as *Gadjo Dilo* or *Exils* (Gatlif).

Bibliography

Abbeele, Georges Van den. 'Sightseers: The Tourist as Theorist.' *Diacritics* 10.4 (1980): 3–14.

Ahmed, Samira. 'From Casablanca to Calais: Refugees on film.' *Samira Ahmed.* blog. 30 March 2011.

Ajar, Maurice. *La vie devant soi.* Paris: Mercure de France, 1975.

Altman, Rick. *Film/Genre.* London: British Film Institute, 1999.

Ameur-Zaïmeche, Rabah. 'Etre vivant et faire du cinéma.' *Critikat.com.* Audrey Jeamart. 20 June 2006.

André, Agathe. '"Welcome" dans un pays de merde.' *Charlie-hebdo* 18 March 2009.

Andrew, Dudley. *Film in the aura of Art.* Princeton: Princeton UP, 1984.

———. *Mists of regret. Culture and Sensibility in Classic French Film.* Princeton: Princeton UP, 1995.

Angot, Christine. 'Je préférerais qu'ils y fassent attention.' *Epok* 27 (2002): 91.

Appadurai, Arjun. 'Disjuncture and Difference in the Global Cultural Economy.' *Theory, Culture & Society* 7.295 (1990). 295–310.

Archer, Neil. *The French Road Movie Space, Mobility, Identity.* New York: Oxford: Berghahn Books, 2012.

Arnaud, Alain. *Little Senegal. Un film de Rachid Bouchareb.* Paris: La bibliothèque du film- CNC, 2002. 1–24.

Audrey-Foster, Gwendolyn. *Identity and Memory: The Films of Chantal Akerman.* Carbondale: Southern Illinois UP, 2003.

Augé, Marc. *L'Impossible voyage. Le tourisme et ses images.* Paris: Payot & Rivages, 1997.

———. *Un ethnologue dans le métro.* Paris: Hachette littératures, 1986.

Aumont, Jacques. 'Tailler la route. Le plein de super (Alain Cavalier, 1976).' Jacques Aumont, ed. *Les voyages du spectateur. De l'imaginaire au cinéma.* Paris: Léo Scheer, Cinémathèque française, 2004. 221–231.

Austin, Guy. *Contemporary French Cinema- An Introduction.* Second Edition. Manchester: Manchester UP, 2008.

Baeque, Antoine de. 'Drôle de voyage pour une rencontre.' *Libération* 26 May 2004.

———. 'Dupeyron dans la clandestinité.' 26 May 2004. *Libération.* Web. http://next.liberation.fr/cinema/0101490181-dupeyron-dans-la-clandestinité.

Balibar, Etienne. 'At the Borders of Europe.' *Make Worlds.* Freedom movement, 22.2 (2004).

———. 'The Borders of Europe.' Pheng Cheah, and Bruce Robbins, eds. *Cosmopolitics. Thinking and Feeling beyond the Nation.* Trans. J. Swenson. Minneapolis, London: University of Minnesota Press, 1998. 216–229.

Barlet, Olivier. 'La Fille de Keltoum.' *Africultures* (2002).

Barthes, Roland. "On Language." *Empire of Signs.* New York: MacMillan, 1983. 9.

Baudot, François, and Jean Demachy. *Elle Style: The 1980s.* US Edition. Philipacchi Publishing, 2003.

Bauman, Zigmunt. 'Europe of Strangers.' 1998. Web. http://www.transcomm. ox.ac.uk/working%20papers/bauman.pdf

Baurez, Thomas. 'Portrait Romain Duris.' Nouvelle dimension.' *Studio* June 2005: 58–64.

Begag, Azouz. *Le Gône du Chaâba*. Paris: Seuil, 1986.

Benjamin, Walter. *One-Way Street and Other Writings*. London: Penguin, 2009.

——. *The Storyteller. Reflections on the Works of Nicolai Leskov*.II. Web. http:// slought.org/files/downloads/events/SF_1331-Benjamin.pdf. 6 June 2012.

Beugnet, Martine. 'French Cinema of the Margins.' Ezra, Elizabeth, ed. *European Cinema*. Oxford: Oxford UP, 2004. 283–298.

Biro, Yvette. 'Two Irregular Fairy Tales.' *Anachronia* 11 (2012): 106–112.

Blum-Reid, Sylvie. 'Gatlif's Manifesto: Cinema is Music.' Michael Gott, and Thibaut Schilt, eds. *Open Roads, Closed Borders. The Contemporary French-Language Road Movie*. Bristol, Chicago: Intellect, 2013. 203–217.

——. 'The Elusive Search for Nora Luca: Tony Gatlif's Adventures in Gypsy Land.' *Portal: A Journal of Multidisciplinary International Studies* July 2005.

Botton, Alain de. *The Art of Travel*. 2nd edition. London: Penguin, 2003.

Bouvier, Nicolas. *L'Usage du monde*. Paris : Payot & Rivages, 2001.

——. *L'Usage du monde. The Way of the World*. Genève: Droz, 1963.

——. *Oeuvres*. Quarto. Paris: Gallimard, 2004.

Bowles, Paul. *The Sheltering Sky*. New York: John Lehman, 1949.

Brassaï, *Henry Miller: The Paris Years*. Trans. Timothy Bent. New York: Arcades, 1995.

Bruno, Giuliana. *Atlas of Emotion: Journeys in Art, Architecture, and Film*. London: Verso, 2007.

Cailler, Bernadette. *Carthage ou la flamme du brasier. Mémoire et échos chez Virgile, Senghor, Mellah, Gachem, Augustin, Ammi, Broch et Glissant*. Amsterdam: Rodopi, 2007.

Cojean, Annick. 'Rebel Heart Beats to a Different Drum.' *Guardian Weekly* 34 (2001): 8–14.

Coletta, Cristina della. *When Stories Travel: Cross-Cultural Encounters Between Fiction and Film*. Baltimore: Johns Hopkins UP, 2012.

Conley, Tom. *Cartographic Cinema*. Minneapolis: University of Minnesota Press, 2007.

Copperman, Annie. *Review Maine-Océan*. Paris: Les Echos. 18 April 1986.

Corrigan, Timothy. *A Cinema Without Walls. Movies and Culture After Vietnam*. Rutgers: Rutgers University Press, 1991.

Daenincks, Didier. *La Repentie*. Vendôme: Verdier, 1999.

Daney, Serge. *Ciné-Journal*. Vol. 2. Paris: Cahiers du cinéma, 1986.

Debord, Guy. 'Theory of the dérive.' *Lettres Nues* 9 November 1956. Web. http:// www.larevuedesressources.org/theorie-de-la-derive,038.html

Debray, Régis. *Eloge des frontières*. Paris: Gallimard, 2010.

Delerm, Philippe. *La première gorgée de bière et autres plaisirs minuscules*. Paris: Gallimard, 1997.

Delerm, Pierre. *Les Chemins nous inventent*. Paris: Stock, 1997, 1998.

Deleuze, Gilles. *Cinéma 1. L'Image-Mouvement* . Paris: Editions de Minuit, 1983.

Derrida, Jacques, and Catherine Malabou. *La Contre-Allée: Voyager avec Jacques Derrida*. Voyager avec. Paris: Quinzaine Littéraire/Louis Vuitton, 1999.

Dormoy, Nadine, and Liliane Lazar. *A Chacun sa France. Une certaine idée de l'homme*. American Universities Series. Vol. 129. New York, Bern, Frankfurt, Paris: Peter Lang, 1990.

Downing, Lisa, and Sue Harris. *From Perversion to Purity. The Stardom of Catherine Deneuve*. Manchester UP, 2008.

Dupeyron, François. *Inguélézi*. Arles: Actes Sud, 2004.

Dupont-Monod, Claire. 'Enfin le cinéma français se mouille.' *Marianne* 7 March 2009.

Eng, Ian. 'Hegemony-in-Trouble.' Duncan Petrie, ed. *Screening Europe: Image and Identity in Contemporary European Cinema*. London: British Film Institute, 1992. 21–31.

ERASMUS. Web. http://www.erasmus.ac.uk/. 22 November 2012.

Everett, Wendy. 'Leaving Home: Exile and Displacement in Contemporary European Cinema.' Wagstaff, Peter and Wendy Everett, eds. *Cultures of Exiles, Images of Displacement*. New York, Oxford: Berghahn books, 2004: 17–32.

Fassin, Didier. 'Compassion and Regression: The Moral Economy of Immigration Politics in France.' *Cultural Anthropology* 20.2 (2005): 362–387.

Férenczi, Aurélien. 'L'Europtimiste.' *Télérama* 15 June 2005: 48.

Fernandez, Bernard. *Identité nomade. De l'expérience d'Occidentaux en Asie*. Paris: Anthropos, 2002.

Flitterman-Lewis, Sandy. *To Desire Differently: Feminism and the French Cinema*. Expanded 2nd edition. New York: Columbia UP, 1996.

Fogg, Shannon. *The Politics of Everyday Life in Vichy France: Foreigners, Undesirables, and Strangers*. Cambridge: Cambridge UP, 2009.

Fonseca, Isabel. *Bury Me Standing. The Gypsies and Their Journey*. New York: Vintage, 1995.

Frappat, Hélène. 'La Repentie.' *Cahiers du cinéma* 568 (2002): 121–122.

Frodon, Jean-Michel. 'Bled Number One. A l'aventure.' *Cahiers du cinéma* 613 (2006): 30–31.

Galt, Rosalind. *The New European Cinema*. New York: Columbia UP, 2006.

Gatlif, Tony. 'Ceux qui nous quittent.' *Exils*. Prod. Pyramide distribution, Naïve Princes Films. Paris, 2004. CD.

Gervais, Ginette. 'Entretien avec Tony Gatlif.' *Jeune Cinéma* 155 (1983): 30–31.

Gilroy, Paul. *The Black Atlantic. Modernity and Double Consciousness*. Cambridge: Harvard UP, 1993.

Glissant, Edouard. *Poétique de la relation*. Paris: Gallimard, 1990.

Goldmann, Annie. *L'Errance dans le cinéma contemporain*. Paris: Henri Veyrier, 1985.

Gonzague, Arnaud. 'Changer de pays.' *Le Nouvel Observateur* 22–28 September 2005: 6–8.

Gott, Michael. 'Under Eastern Eyes: Displacement, Placessness and the Exilic Optic in Emmanuel Finkiel's Nulle part terre promise.' Michael Gott, and Thibaut Schilt, eds. *Open Roads, Closed Borders. The Contemporary French-Language Road Movie*. Bristol, Chicago: Intellect, n.d. 137–153.

Gracq, Julien. 'Les Yeux bien ouverts.' *Oeuvres Complètes*. Vol. 1. Paris: NRF, Gallimard, 1989: 843–856.

Gratton, Johnnie. 'Experiment and Experience in Sophie Calle phototextual projects.' Gill Rye, and Michael Worton, eds. *Women's Writing in Contemporary*

France: New Writers, New Literatures in the 1990s. Manchester: Manchester UP, 2002. 157–170.

Guilloux, Michel. 'Par la grâce du cinémascope.' *L'Humanité* (2002). Web. (no longer accessible)

Halbertstadt, Michèle. *Adjani aux pieds nus: journal de la "repentie"*. Paris: Calmann-Lévy, 2002.

Hall, Stuart. 'European Cinema on the Verge of a Nervous Breakdown.' Duncan Petrie, ed. *Screening Europe*. London: British Film Institute, n.d. 45–53.

Hargreaves, Alec. 'Perceptions of Place among writers of Algerian Immigrant Origin in France.' John Connell, Russell King, and Paul White, eds. *Writing Across Worlds: Literature and Migration*. London, New York: Rouledge, 1995.

Hayward, Susan. *French National Cinema*. London, New York: Routledge, 1993.

Heyman, Danièle. *Le Monde* 25 May 1993.

———. 'Conte de la ville vague.' *Le Monde* 6 Apr. 1989.

Higbee, Will. 'Displaced audio: Exploring Soundscapes in Maghrebi-French filmmaking.' *Studies in French Cinema* 9.3 (2009): 225–241.

Hirschberg Lynn. 'Lover Boys.' *New York Times Style Magazine* 17 September 2006: 190–193.

Hofmann, Michael. 'Introduction.' Joseph Roth, ed. *Report from a Parisian Paradise: Essays from France 1925–1939*. Trans. Michael Hofmann. New York, London: W.W. Norton and Company, 2003.

Holmlund, Chris. 'Stars and Stardom in French Cinema.' *Screen* 43.4 (2002): 452–455.

Hottell, Ruth A. 'Flying through Southern France: Sans Toit ni loi by Agnès Varda.' *Women's Studies: An Inter-disciplinary Journal* 28.6 (1999): 675–696.

Huston, Nancy. *Tombeau de Romain Gary*. Arles: Actes Sud, 1995.

Huston, Nancy, and Leïla Sebbar. *Lettres parisiennes. Histoires d'exil*. Paris: Bernard Barrault, 1986.

Jurij M. Lotman, Julian Graffy. 'The Origins of Plot in the Light of Typology.' *Poetics Today* 1.1/2 (Autumn 1979): 161–194.

Klapisch, Cédric. *L'Auberge espagnole*. Presskit. Mars Distribution, 2002.

Kracauer, Siegfried. 'Le Chemin de fer.' Siegfried Kracauer, ed.. *Le Voyage et la danse. Figures de ville et vues de films*, ed. Philippe Despoix. Trans. Sabine Cornille. Saint-Denis: Presses Universitaires de Vincennes, 1996.

Kummer, Ida. 'Colonisée, maghrébine, beurette: le parcours de la combattante.' *CELFAN: cinéma Maghrébin* I.1–2 (2002): 49–55.

Laffan, Brigid. 'The European Union: A Distinctive Model of Internationalization.' *Journal of European Public Policy* 5.2.18 (1998): 235–253.

Laffeter, Anne. 'Les sans-papiers. Nouveaux héros de cinéma.' *Les Inrockuptibles* 31 March 2009.

Lapierre, Nicole. *Pensons ailleurs*. Paris: Stock, 2004.

Laronde, Michel. *Autour du roman beur: Immigration et identité*. Paris: L'Harmattan, 1993.

Lasalle, Mick. *The Beauty of the Real: What Hollywood can learn from Contemporary French Actresses*. Stanford: Stanford General Books/Stanford UP, 2012.

Leininger, Nicole and Raymond. *La Route sans borne. En campant, de France, aux Indes, à bicyclette*. Paris: J. Susse, 1947.

'Le Matin du cinéma. Entretien avec Rozier.' *Le Matin* (1986).

Levieux, Michèle. 'Entretien avec le cinéaste Aki Kaurismäki.' *L'Humanité* 19 May 2011.

Levieux. Michèle. 'Sur fond de colère sourde.' *L'Humanité* 30 September 2009.

Lewis, Paul. 'Vacation Innovator: Gilbert Trigano.' *New York Times* 21 July 1985. Web. http://www.nytimes.com/1985/07/21/business/vacation-innovator-gilbert-trigano-redefining-the-club-med-formula.html

Liandrat-Guigues, Suzanne. *Modernes Flâneries du Cinéma*. Paris: De l'incidence 2009.

Lioret, Philippe. 'Welcome, Philippe Lioret, réalisateur.' *L'Humanité dimanche* 12 March 2009: 1.

Lorrain, Francois-Guillaume. 'Le Havre, mon amour.' *Le Point* 15 December 2011.

Loshitzky, Yosefa. *Screening Strangers. Migration and Diaspora in Contemporary European Cinema*. Bloomington, Indianapolis: Indiana UP, 2010.

MacCannell, Dean. *The Tourist. A New Theory of the Leisure Class*. Berkeley, Los Angeles: University of California Press, 1999.

MacOrlan, Pierre. *Quai de tous les départs*. Paris: Phébus, 1999.

Maffesoli, Michel. *Du Nomadisme. Vagabondages initiatiques*. Paris: Librarie Générale Française, 1997.

——. *Le Voyage ou la conquête des mondes*. Paris: Editions Dervy, 2003.

Maillart, Ella. *Croisières et caravanes*. Paris: Payot & Rivages, 2001.

——. *Croisières et Caravanes (Cruises and Caravans)*. Trans. Gabrielle Rives. Paris: Seuil, Payot & Rivages, 1951, 2001.

——. *The Cruel Way: Switzerland to Afghanistan in a Ford, 1939*. n.d.

Maistre, Xavier de. *Voyage autour de ma chambre*. Turin/Paris: Editions d'aujourd'hui, 1794/ 1984.

Mandelbaum, Jacques. 'Rabah Ameur-Zaïmeche, le cinéma est un puissant outil de transformation et d'ouverture.' *Le Monde* 7 June 2006.

Maximoff, Matéo. *Le Prix de la liberté*. Aubenas: Wallada, 1996.

——. *Les Ursitory*. 2eme. Romainville, 1980.

Mazierska, Ewa, and Laura Rascaroli. *Crossing New Europe. Postmodern Travel and the European Road Movie*. London: Wallflower Press, 2006.

Memmi, Albert. *La Statue de sel*. Paris: Gallimard, 1966.

Mendelson, Edward. 'Baedeker's Universe.' *Yale Review* 74 (1985): 386–403.

Mérigeau, Pascal. 'Au départ, ce n'était pas un film, mais un piège d'amour.' Interview. *Le Monde* 18 January 1995: 24.

Modiano, Patrick. *Dora Bruder*. Paris: Gallimard, 1997.

Moine, Raphaëlle. *Les Genres du cinéma*. Paris: Armand Colin, 2002.

Monbron, Fougeret de. *Margot la Ravaudeuse* . Paris: Jean-Jacques Pauvert, 1958.

Montaigne, Michel de. *Journal de voyage*, ed. Claude Pinganaud. Paris: Arléa, 1998.

Morand, Paul. *Le Voyage*. Paris: Editions du Rocher, 1994.

Morin, Edgar. *Le Cinéma ou l'homme imaginaire*. Paris: Minuit, 1956.

Moudileno, Lydie. 'The Postcolonial Provinces.' *Francospheres* 1.1 (2012): 53–68.

Mühlethaler, Jacques, Hervé Dumont, and Maria Tortajada. *Histoire du cinéma suisse de 1962 à 2000*. Vol. 2007. Editions Cinémathèque Suisse, Gilles Attinger S.A., n.d.

n/a. 'De simples valeurs humaines ne sont pas respectées.' *Le Monde* 11 March. 2009.

n/a. *Le Havre*. cndp. Web. http://www.cndp.fr/ag-film/films/le-havre/paroles. html.

n/a. The Innovators: 1970–1980: Keeping a distance.' (na). BFI. *Film Forever*. Web. http://old.bfi.org.uk/sightandsound/feature/196

Naficy, Hamid. *An Accented Cinema. Exilic and Diasporic Filmmaking*. Princeton: Princeton UP , 2001.

Onfray, Michel. *Théorie du voyage. Poétique de la géographie*. Paris: Librairie Générale de France, 2007.

O'Shaughnessy, Martin. 'The Experience of a Maghrebi-French Filmmaker: The Case of Zaïda Ghorab-Volta.' *Cineaste* XXXIII.1 (2007): 52–53.

Pélegrin, Dominique Louise. 'Tous les détours du monde.' *Télérama* 30 December 1992: 52–53.

Perec, Georges, and Robert Bober. *Récits d'Ellis Island. Histoires d'errance et d'espoir* . Paris: INA/Editions du Sorbier, 1980.

Perret, Roger. 'Mon existence, condamnée à l'exil et à l'aventure.' Schwarzenbach, Annemarie. *Où est la terre des promesses? Avec Ella Maillart en Afghanistan (1939–1940)*. Paris: Payot & Rivages, 2004. 179–195.

Peters, John Durham. 'Exile, Nomadism, and Diaspora. The Stakes of Mobility in the Western Canon.' Hamid Naficy, ed. *Home, Exile, Homeland*. New York, London: Routledge, 1999. 17–41.

Petit, Sarah. *Entretien avec Sarah Petit*. Web. http://www.commeaucinema.com/film/le-lac-et-la-riviere,16789.

Pidduck, Julianne. 'Travel with Sally Potter's Orlando: Gender, Narrative, Movement.' *Screen* 38.2 (Summer 1997): 172–189.

Portuges, Catherine. 'French Women Directors Negotiating Transnational Identities.' *Yale French Studies* 115 (2009): 47–63.

Powrie, Phil. *French Cinema in the 1980s. Nostalgia and the Crisis of Masculinity*. Oxford: Oxford UP, 1997.

Rapold, Nicolas. 'Trapped in a Jungle and a State of Mind.' *New York Times* 9 August 2012. Web. http://www.nytimes.com/2012/08/10/movies/almayers-folly-directed-by-chantal-akerman.html?_r=0

Raspiengeas, Jean-Claude. 'Welcome.' *La Croix* 11 March 2009.

Rebichon, Michel. 'Tony Gatlif en transe.' *Studio* June 2006: 134–135.

Reid, Mark A. 'Many Rivers to Cross with Christian and Muslim Flow.' SCMS annual conference. Boston. 21–25 March 2012. Lecture.

Remy, Vincent. 'Maine-Océan.' *Télérama* 6 July 1994: 30

Rosello, Mireille. *Postcolonial Hospitality: The Immigrant as Guest*. Stanford: Stanford UP, 2001.

Rosenberg, Matt. 'Grand Tour of Europe. The Travels of 18th and 19th Century Twenty Somethings. ' Geography about.com. Web. 12 June 2012.

Roth, Joseph. *La Légende du Saint Buveur/ Die Legende von Heilige Trinker*. Trans. Claude Riehl, Dominique Dubuy. First Edition: 1939. Paris: Seuil, 1986.

Rousso, Henry. 'Comparer les clandestins de Calais aux juis est une preuve d'ignorance.' *20 minutes fr*. http://www.20minutes.fr/cinema/309573-henry-rousso-comparer-clandestins-calais-juifs-preuves-ignrance.

Roux, Hervé. 'Mascaret.' *Cahiers du cinéma* 382 (1986): 17–19.

Rozier, Jacques. *Jacques Rozier. le Funambule*. Paris: Editions du Centre Pompidou, 2001.

Ruff, Frederick J. 'Mr. Ibrahim'. Film Review. *Journal of Religion and Film* 8.1 (April 2004). Web. https://www.unomaha.edu/jrf/Vol8No1/vol8no1.htm, 25 April 2015.

Sadoul, Georges. *Dictionnaire des films*. Paris: Seuil, 1965.

Saint-Exupéry, Antoine de. *Le Petit Prince*, ed. John Richardson Miller. New York, London: Houghton Mifflin Company, 1970.

Sand, George. *L'histoire de ma vie*. Paris: Stock, 1960.

Sansot, Pierre. *Du bon usage de la lenteur*. Paris: Payot & Rivages, 1998, 2000.

Scherzer, Dinah. *Cinema, Colonialism, Postcolonialism. Perspectives from the French and Francophone World*. Austin: Texas UP, 1996.

Schmitt, Eric Emmanuel. *Monsieur Ibrahim et les fleurs du Coran/ Monsieur Ibrahim and the Flowers of the Koran*. Paris: Albin Michel, 1999.

Schulman, Peter. *The Sunday of Fiction. The Modern French Eccentric*. Purdue: Purdue UP, 2003.

Seghers, Anna. *Transit*. Trans. Christa Wolf. Paris: Autrement, 1995.

Sellier, Geneviève. 'Don't touch the white woman.' Swamy Vinay, and Sylvie Durmelat, eds. *Screening Integration: Recasting Maghrebi Immigration in Contemporary France*. Lincoln, London: U. Nebraska Press, 2012. 144–160.

———. 'French Actresses: From Nymphettes to Mummy via the Woman Woman.' *Sites: Journal of French and Francophone Studies* 4.1 (2000): 15–17.

Silverman, Max. *Facing Postmodernity*. New York: Routledge, 1999.

Skira-Breteau, Gisèle. *Cinéastes de la mélancolie- Les entretiens de Zeuxis*. Biarritz: Seguier, 2010.

Smith, Alison. *French Cinema in the 1970s: The Echoes of May*. Manchester: Manchester UP, 2005.

'Sotigui Kouyaté: The Wise Man of the Stage.' *The UNESCO Courier* (2001): 47–48. Web. http://unesdoc.unesco.org/Ulis/cgi-bin/ulis.pl?catno=123776& set=502D3EC4_0_16&database=ged&gp=0Use%20of%20uninitialized%20 value%20in%20concatenation%20(.)%20or%20string%20at%20D:%5CWeb-Root%5CUlis%5CCgi-bin%5Culis.pl%20line%204225.&mode=e&lin=1&ll=f, 6 August 2013.

Spaas, Lieve. *The Francophone Film: A struggle for Identity*. Manchester, New York: Manchester UP, 2000.

Stam, Robert. 'The Subversive Charm of Alain Tanner. Jonah who will be 25 in the year 2000.' *Jump Cut. A Review of Contemporary Media* 15 (1977): 1, 5–7.

Steiner, George. *Une certaine idée de l'Europe*. Trans. Christine Le Boeuf. Paris: Actes Sud, 2005.

Steinert-Borella, Sarah. *The Travel Narratives of Ella Maillart: (en) gendering the quest*. New York, Bern, Berlin: Peter Lang, 2006.

Stora, Benjamin. *Le Transfert d'une mémoire. De l'Algérie française au racisme anti-arabe*. Paris: La Découverte, 1999.

Tabucchi, Antonio. *Indian Nocturne*. Trans. Tim Parks. Sellerio editore 1984. New York: New Directions, 1989.

———. *Petits Malentendus sans importance*. Paris: Christian Bourgois, 1987.

Tarr, Carrie. 'Franco-Arab Dialogues in/Between French, Maghrebi-French and Maghrebi cinema(s).' *Contemporary French and Francophone Studies* 13.3 (2009): 291–303.

———. *Reframing Difference. Beur and banlieue filmmaking in France*. Manchester: Manchester UP, 2005.

Tarr, Carrie, and Brigitte Rollet. *Cinema and the Second Sex. Women's Filmmaking in France in the 1980s and 1990s.* New York: Continuum, 2001.

Thierry Guichard, Philipp. 'Nocturne Indien.' *Le Matricule des Anges* 007.133 (1994). Web. http://www.lmda.net/din/tit_lmda.php?id=3363

Thomas, Dominic. 'Into the European Jungle: Migration and Grammar in the New Europe.' Thomas, Dominic, ed. *Africa and France: Postcolonial Cultures, Migration and Racism.* Bloomington: Indiana University Press, 2013.

Tournier, Michel. 'J'écris pour être lu, pas pour le plaisir'- Entretien de François Busnel. *Lire* Summer 2006: 94–99.

Tranchant, Marie-Noel. 'André Wilms, entre Marx et Jesus.' *Le Figaro* 21 December 2011.

Trémois, Claude-Marie. *Les enfants de la liberté. Le jeune cinéma français des années 90.* Paris: Seuil, 1997.

Tuozzi, Silvia Angrisani and Carolina. *Tony Gatlif: Un cinéma nomade.* Lindau s.r.l. Torino: Il Pesce Volante, 2003.

Turner, Jack. 'Antonioni's The Passenger as Lacanian Text.' *Other Voices* 1.3 (199). Web. http://www.othervoices.org/1.3/jturner/passenger.php

Ungar, Steven. *Cléo de 5 à 7.* London: BFI-Palgrave MacMillan, 2008.

Vigo, Luce. 'Régler leur compte aux normes. Jacques Rozier.' *Révolution* 322 (1986): 2–5.

Vincendeau, Ginette. *Stars and Stardom in French Cinema.* London, New York: Continuum, 2002.

Virilio, Paul. *Open Sky/La Vitesse de Libération.* Trans. Julie Rose. Paris/London: Galilée/Verso Press, 1995, 1997.

Voituret, Denis. 'Ella Maillart, un nouveau "genre de voyageuse": 1923–1935.' 29.2 (2010): 119–127.

White, Jerry. *Revisioning Europe: The Films of Alain Tanner and John Berger.* Calgary: University of Calgary Press, 2012.

Wideman, Dominique. 'Entretien avec Emmanuel Finkiel.' *L'Humanité* 1 April 2009.

Wiener, Bernard. 'Return from Africa. The Long Way Home.' *Jump Cut: A Review of Contemporary Media* 4 (1974): 3–4.

Filmography

Karin Albou

La petite Jérusalem. d. Karin Albou. Script Karin Albou. Perf. Bruno Todeschini, Fanny Valette, Elsa Zilberstein. Prod. Gloria Films, Films par Films, 2005. 96 min.

René Allio

Transit. d. René Allio. Script René Allio, Jean Jourdheuil, adapted from Anna Seghers. Perf. Sebastian Koch, Claudia Messner, Rüdiger Vogler. Prod. Action Film, France 3, La September, Paris Classics Productions, Société Française de Production, Zweites Deutsches Ferhnsehen, 1991. 125 min.

Rabah Ameur-Zaïmeche

Bled Number One/Back Home. d. Rabah Ameur-Zaïmeche. Script Rabah Ameur-Zaïmeche, Louise Therme. Perf. Meriem Serbah, Amel Jafri, Rabah Ameur-Zaïmeche. Prod. Sarrazink Productions, CNC, Films du Losange, 2006. 100 min.

Wesh Wesh, qu'est-ce qui se passe? Wesh Wesh, what's going on? d. Rabah Ameur-Zaïmeche. Script Rabah Ameur-Zaïmeche. Perf. Rabah Ameur-Zaïmeche, Ahmed Hammoudi. Prod. Sarrasink Productions, 2001. 83 min.

Sólveig Anspach

Lulu femme nue. d. Sólveig Anspach. Script Sólveig Anspach, Jean-Luc Gaget. Perf. Karin Viard, Bouli Lanners. Prod. Arturo Mio, Le Pacte, Orange cinéma séries, Cinémages 7. 2013. 90 min.

Michelangelo Antonioni

Profession Reporter/The Passenger. d. Michelangelo Antonioni. Script Peter Wollen, Michelangelo Antonioni, Mark Peploe. Perf. Maria Schneider, Jack Nicholson. Prod. CIPI Cinematografica SA, Les Films Concordia, Compagna Cinematografica Champion, 1975. 119 min.

Chantal Akerman

Demain on déménage/Tomorrow we move. d. Chantal Akerman. Script Akerman, Eric De Kuyper. Perf. Aurore Clément, Jean-Pierre Marielle, Sylvie Testud. Prod. Prod. Gemini films, Paradise Films, 2004. 100 min.

De l'autre côté./From the other side. d. Chantal Akerman. Script Chantal Akerman. Documentary. Prod. AMIP, Carré noir, RTBF. Paradise Films, 2002. 99 min.

Les Rendez-vous d'Anna/The Meetings of Anna. d. Chantal Akerman. Script Chantal Akerman. Perf. Aurore Clément, Helmut Griem, Magali Noel, Lea Massari, Jean-Pierre Cassel. Prod. Hélène Films, Paradise Films, Unité Trois, Zweites Deutsches Fernsehen ZDF, 1978. 120 min.

Yamina Benguigui

Inch' Allah Dimanche/ Inch' Allah Sunday. d. Yamina Benguigui. Script Yamina Benguigui. Perf. Fejria Deliba, Sinedine Soualem, Marie-France Pisier. Prod. Bandits, ARP sélection, 2001. 98 min.
Mémoires d'Immigrés, l'héritage maghrébin. d. Yamina Benguigui. Script Yamina Benguigui. Documentary. Prod. Bandits Films, Canal +, 1997. 160 min.

Edmond Bensimon

Emmenez-moi. d. Edmond Bensimon. Script Edmond Bensimon. Perf. Zinedine Soualem, Gérard Darmon, Lucien Jean-Baptiste. Prod. Vendredi films, France 2, Norimages, Canal +, Région Nord Pas de Calais, 2005. 98 min.

Bernardo Bertolucci

The Sheltering Sky. d. Bertolucci. Script John Peploe, B. Bertolucci, adapted from Paul Bowles' novel. Perf. John Malkovich, Debra Winger. Prod. Warner Bros., 1990. 138 min.

Julie Bertucelli

Depuis qu'Otar est parti/Since Otar Left. d. Julie Bertucelli. Script Julie Bertucelli, Bernard Renucci, Adapted from Roger Bohbot. Perf. Esther Gorintin, Nino Komasuridze. Prod. Les Films du Poisson, Arte France cinéma, 2003. 103 min.

Bertrand Blier

Les Valseuses/Going Places. d. Bertrand Blier. Script Bertrand Blier, Philippe Dumarçay. Perf. Gérard Depardieu, Patrick Dewaere, Miou Miou. Prod. C.A.P.A.C., SN Prodis, Universal Pictures France, 1974. 115 min.

Robert Bober

Récits d'Ellis Island. Histoires d'errance et d'espoir/Ellis Island Tales. d. Robert Bober. script Georges Perec. Documentary. Dist. INA, 1979. 116 min.

Carole Bonstein

Une Suisse rebelle: Annemarie Schwarzenbach 1908–1942, dir. Carole Bonstein. Script Carole Bonstein. Prod. Troubadour films, 2000. 56 min.

Rachid Bouchareb

London River. d. Rachid Bouchareb. Script Zoe Galeron, Olivier Lorelle, Rachid Bouchareb. Perf. Brenda Blethyn, Roshdy Zem, Sami Bouajila, Sotigui Kouyaté. Prod. Rachid Bouchareb, 2009. 88 min.
Silver Bear Best Actor Sotigui Kouyaté Berlin 2009.

Indigènes/ Days of Glory. d. Rachid Bouchareb. Script Rachid Bouchareb, Olivier Lorelle. Perf. Roshdy Zem, Samy Naceri, Sami Bouajila, Jamel Debbouze. Prod. Tessalit Productions, France 2 cinéma, France 3 cinéma, Studio Canal, 2006. 120 min.

Little Senegal. d. Rachid Bouchareb. Script Rachid Bouchareb, Olivier Lorelle. Perf. Roshdy Zem, Sharon Hope, Sotigui Kouyaté. Prod. 3B, Canal Plus, 2001. 97 min.
Best Actor Sotigui Kouyaté, Cologne Mediterranean Film Festival 2001, ACCT Promotional Award, & Best actor of the South Sotigui Kouyaté, Namur International Festival of French Speaking Films 2001.

Serge Bozon

De l'autre côté de la mer La France. d. Serge Bozon. Script Serge Bozon. Perf. Sylvie Testud, Pascal Greggory, Guillaume Verdier. Prod. Les Films Pelléas, Centre Images, CNC, CinéCinéma, Cinémage, coficup, Région Ile de France, Soficas, Soficinéma 3, 2007. 102 min. Prize Jean Vigo.

Dominique Cabrera

L'autre côté de la mer/The Other Shore. d. Dominique Cabrera. Script Nidam Abdi, Dominique Cabrera, Louis Mathieu de Vienne. Perf. Roshdy Zem, Marthe Villalonga, Ariane Ascaride, Claude Brasseur. Prod. Bloody Mary Productions. France 2, 1997. 89 min.

Sophie Calle

No sex last night/Double Blind. d. Sophie Calle, Greg Shepard. Script Sophie Calle. Perf. Sophie Calle, Greg Shepard. Prod. Paulo Branco, 1992, 1996. 76 min. Georges Sadoul Prize.

Mehdi Charef

La Fille de Keltoum/Bent Keltoum/Daughter of Keltoum. d. Mehdi Charef. Script Mehdi Charef. Perf. Baya Belal, Celia Malki. Prod. Canal Horizon, Canal +, CNC, Eurimages, 2001. 106 min.

Au pays des Juliets/In the country of Juliets. d. Mehdi Charef. Script Mehdi Charef. Perf. Laure Duthilleul, Claire Nebout, Maria Schneider. Prod. Centre européen cinématographique Rhône-Alpes, Erbograph Co, France 3 cinema, Investimage 3, 1992, 92 min.

Le Thé au harem d'Archimède/Tea in the Harem. d. Mehdi Charef. Script Mehdi Charef. Perf. Rémi Martin, Khader Boukhanef, Laure Duthilleul. Prod. Michèle Costa-Gavras, 1985. 110 min.
Chicago International Festival, Cannes Youth Award., special Jury Award, César Award, Prize Jean Vigo (France).

Patrice Chéreau

Ceux qui m'aiment prendront le train/Those who love me can take the train. d. Patrice Chéreau. Script Patrice Chéreau, Danièle Thomson, Pierre Trividic. Perf. Pascal Greggory, Valeria Bruni-Tedeschi, Charles Berling, Vincent Perez, Jean-Louis Trintignant. Prod. Téléma, Canal +, France 2 cinéma, France 3 cinéma, Azor Films, CNC, Procirep, 1998. 122 min.

César Award 1999.

Alain Corneau

Nocturne Indien. d. Alain Corneau. Script Alain Corneau, adapted from Antonio Tabucchi's novel. Perf. Jean-Hughes Anglade, Clémentine Célarié, Otto Tausig. Prod. AFC, Sara Films, Ciné 5, Christian Bourgois, 1989. 110 min.
César Best Cinematography (Yves Angelo), 1990, FIPRECI award: Montreal World Film Festival 1989.

Benoît Delépine and Gustave de Kervern

Mammuth. d. Benoît Delépine and Gustave de Kervern. Script Benoît Delépine and Gustave de Kervern. Perf. Gérard Depardieu, Isabelle Adjani, Yolande Moreau, Miss Ming. Prod. GMT Productions, No Money Productions, Arte France cinéma, 2010. 92 min.

Costa-Gavras

Eden à l'Ouest/Eden is West. Dir. Costa Gavras. Script Jean-Claude Grumberg, Costa Gavras. Perf. Riccardo Scamarcio, Eric Caracava. Prod. Michèle Ray-Gavras, Costa Gavras, 2009. 110 min.

Julie Delpy

2 days in New York. d. Julie Delpy. Script Julie Delpy, Alexia Landeau. Perf. Julie Delpy, Chris Rock, Albert Delpy. Prod. Polaris Film Production & Finance, Tempête sous un crâne, Senator Film Produktion, Saga Film, Alvy Productions, In

Production, TDY Filmproduktion, BNP Paribas Fortis, Protozoa Pictures, Senator Film, 2012. 96 min.

2 days in Paris. d. Julie Delpy. Script Julie Delpy. Perf. Julie Delpy, Albert Delpy, Daniel Brühl, Adam Goldberg, Marie Pillet. Prod. Polaris Film Production & Finance, Tempête sous un crâne, 3L Filmproduktion, Back Up Media, Rézo Films, 2007. 96 min.

André Delvaux

Un soir, Un train. d. André Delvaux. Script André Delvaux, based on novel by Johan Daisne. Perf. Anouk Aimée, Adriana Bogdan,Yves Montand. Prod. Parc Films, Les productions Fox Europa, Les films du siècle, 1968. 86 min.

Jacques Demy

Model Shop. d. Jacques Demy. Script Jacques Demy, Carole Eastman. Perf. Anouk Aimée, Gary Lockwood. Prod. Columbia Pictures Corporation, 1969. 95 min.

Les Parapluies de Cherbourg. d. Jacques Demy. Script Jacques Demy. Perf. Catherine Deneuve, Nino Castelnuovo, Marc Michel, Anne Vernon. Prod. Parc Film, Madeleine Films, Beta Film, 1964. 91 min.

Claire Denis

Chocolat. d. Claire Denis. Script Claire Denis, Jean-Pol Fargeau. Perf. Isaach de Bankolé, Giulia Boschi, François Cluzet, Mireille Perrier. Prod. Caroline Productions, Cerito Films, Cinémanuel, La Sept Cinéma, Le F.O.D.I.C. Cameroun, MK 2 Productions, TF1 Film Productions, Wim Wenders Productions, 1988.105 min.

Fosco and Donatello Dubini

The Journey to Kafiristan/Die Reise nach Kafiristan. d. Fosco & Donatello Dubini. Script Fosco & Donatello Dubini, Barbara Marx. Perf. Jeanette Hain, Nina Petri. Prod. Dubinifilmproduktion, ARTE, 2001. 101 min.

Olivier Ducastel, Jacques Martineau

Drôle de Félix/The Adventures of Felix. d. Olivier Ducastel, Jacques Martineau. Script Ducastel & Martineau. Perf. Sami Bouajila, Patachou, Ariane Ascaride, Pierre Loup Rajot. Prod. Canal +, C.N.C., la Sofica Gimages 2, Les Films Pelléas, Pyramide Productions, arte france cinéma, 2001. 95 min.

François Dupeyron

Inguélézi. d. François Dupeyron. Script François Dupeyron. Perf. Marie Payen, Eric Caravaca, Françoise Lebrun. Prod. Les Films en hiver, 2004. 100 min.

Monsieur Ibrahim et les fleurs du Coran/Monsieur Ibrahim. d. François Dupeyron. Script Eric-Emmanuel Schmitt, François Dupeyron. Perf. Omar Sharif, Pierre Boulanger, Gilbert Melki. Prod. ARP, France 3 cinéma, 2003. 95 min.

Ismaël Ferroukhi

Le Grand voyage. d. Ismaël Ferroukhi. Script Ismaël Ferroukhi. Perf. Mohammed Majd, Nicolas Cazalé. Prod. Humbert Balsan, 2004. 108 min.

Emmanuel Finkiel

Nulle part, terre promise. d. Emmanuel Finkiel. Script Maurizio Lozi, Emmanuel Finkiel. Perf. Elsa Amiel, Nicolas Wanczycki. Prod. Les films du Poisson, Sophie Dulac Prod, 2008. 94 min.

Voyages/Tracks. d. Emmanuel Finkiel. Script Emmanuel Finkiel. Perf. Shulamit Adar, Liliane Rovère, Esther Gorintin. Prod. Les films du Poisson, Canal +, 1999. 115 min.

César award: best first film, best editing, 2000, Louis Delluc prize 1999.

Madame Jacques sur la Croisette. d. Emmanuel Finkiel. Script Emmanuel Finkiel. Perf. Shulamit Adar, Films du Poisson, 1995. 36 min.

Stephen Frears

Dirty Pretty Things. d. Stephen Frears. Script Steven Knight. Perf. Chiwetel Ejiofor, Audrey Tautou, Sergio Lopez, Sophie Okonedo. Prod. BBC, Celador Productions, Jonescompany Production, 2002. 97 min.

American Black Film Festival, best performance by an actor: Chiwetel Ejiofor 2003, Black Reel: Best Performance Chiwetel Ejiofor, 2004. British Independent Film Award 2003.

Tony Gatlif

Liberté/Korkoro/Freedom. d. Tony Gatlif. Script Tony Gatlif, Lucy Allwood. Perf. Marc Lavoine, Marie-Josée Croze, James Thiérrée. Prod. Princes Films, France 3 cinéma, Rhône- Alpes Cinéma, TPS, 2009. 111 min.

Grand Prix des Amériques, Montreal World Film Festival 2009.

Transylvania. d. Tony Gatlif. Script Tony Gatlif. Perf. Asia Argento, Birol Unel, Amira Casar. Prod. Les Princes Films, Pyramide prod., 2006. 103 min.

Georges Delerue Prize, Ghent International Film Festival 2006.

Exils/ Exiles. d. Tony Gatlif. Script Tony Gatlif. Perf. Lubna Azabal, Romain Duris. Prod. Princes Films, Pyramide prod., 2004. 104 min.

Best Director, Cannes 2004.

Gadjo Dilo/The Crazy Stranger. d. Tony Gatlif. Script Tony Gatlif. Perf. Romain Duris, Rona Hartner, Isidor Serban. Prod. Canal +, CNC, Princes Films, 1997. 102 min.

Cesar Best Music, Tony Gatlif 1999.

Mondo. d. Tony Gatlif. Script Tony Gatlif, Jean-Marie Le Clézio. Perf. Ovidiu Balan. Prod. Canal +, CNC, KG Prod., 1995. 80 min.

Chicago International Children's Film Festival: Adult's Jury Award. 1998.

Haile Gerima

Sankofa. d. Haile Gerima. Script Haile Gerima. Perf. Kofi Ghanaba, Oyafunmike Ogunlano, Alexandra Duah. Prod. Channel Four Films, Diproci, Ghana National Commission on Culture, Mypheduh Films, 1993. 125 min.

Khaled Ghorbal

Un si beau voyage /Such a beautiful Journey. d. Khaled Ghorbal. Script Khaled Ghorbal. Perf. Asumpta Serna, Farid Chopel. Prod. Yoko Films, Shilo Films, Les films bleus, 2008. 137 min.

Zaïda Ghorab-Volta

Jeunesse dorée/Gilded Youth. d. Zaïda Ghorab-Volta. Script Zaïda Ghorab-Volta. Perf. Alexandra Laflandre, Alexandra Jeudon. Prod. Bénédicte Mellac. Arte France Cinéma, 2001. 85 min.

Fiona Gordon (& Bruno Romy, Dominique Abel)

La Fée/The Fairy. d. Fiona Gordon, Bruno Romy, Dominique Abel. Script Fiona Gordon, Bruno Romy, Dominique Abel. Perf. Fiona Gordon, Dominique Abel. Prod. Courage mon amour MK2, 2011. 93 min.

Robert Guédiguian

Le Voyage en Arménie/Armenia. d. Robert Guédiguian. Script Robert Guédiguian. Perf. Ariane Ascaride, Gérard Meylan, Simon Abkarian. Prod. AGAT Films @ Cie, France 3 Cinéma, Canal +, Cine Cinema, 2006. 125 min.

Jean-Claude Guiguet

Les Passagers/The Passengers. d. Jean-Claude Guiguet. Script Jean-Claude Guiguet. Perf. Fabienne Babe, Bruno Puzulu, Stéfane Rideau, Véronique Silver. Prod. Little Bear, CNC, Lancelot Films, 1999. 93 min.

Golden Precolumbian Circle.

Philippe Harel

Les Randonneurs/Hikers. d. Philippe Harel. Script Eric Assous, Philippe Harel. Perf. Karin Viard, Vincent Elbaz, Philippe Harel, Géraldine Pailhas, Benoît Poelvoorde. Prod. Canal +, Lazennec Films Studio Images 3, TF1 Film Productions, 1997. 95 min.
Special Jury Award, Alpes d'Huez International Comedy Film Festival 1997.

Alejandro González Iñárritu

Biutiful. d. Alejandro González Iñárritu. Script Alejandro González Iñárritu, Nicolas Giacobone, Armando Bo. Perf. Javier Bardem, Maricel Alvarez, Hanaa Bouchaib. Prod. Menageatroz, Mod Producciones, Focus Features, Television Española, Televisió de Catalunya, Ikiru films, 2010. 148 min.

Marc Isaacs

Calais: The Last Border. d. Marc Isaacs. Diverse Productions, UK. 2003. 60 min.

Cédric Kahn

Feux Rouges/Red Lights. d. Cédric Kahn. Script Georges Simenon, Laurence Ferreira Barbosa, Cédric Kahn, Gilles Marchand. Perf. Jean-Pierre Darroussin, Carole Bouquet. Prod. Alicélo, France 3 cinéma, CNC, 2004. 105 min.

Aki Kaurismäki

Le Havre. d. Aki Kaurismäki. Script Aki Kaurismäki. Perf. Kati Outinen, André Wilms, Blondin Miguel. Prod. Sputnik, Pyramide Productions, Pandora Filmproduktion, 2011. 93 min.

Les lumières du faubourg/Lights in the Dusk. d. Aki Kaurismäki. Script Aki Kaurismäki, Sakke Jarvenpaa. Perf. Kati Outinen, Matti Pellonpää. Prod. Sputnik, 2006. 78 min.

Tiens ton foulard Tatiana/Hold on to your scarf, Tatiana. d. Aki Kaurismäki. Script Aki Kaurismäki. Perf. Kati Outinen, Matti Pellonpää. Prod. Finnish Film productions, Pandora Filmproduktion, Sputnik, 1993. 60 min.

La Vie de Bohème. d. Aki Kaurismäki. Script Aki Kaurismäki, based on Henri Murger. Perf. Matti Pellonpää, Evelyne Didi, André Wilms. Prod. Sputnik, Pyramide Productions, Films A2, Pandora Filmproduktion, Svenska Film Institutet, Canal +, 1992. 100 min.

Cédric Klapish

Casse-tête chinois/Chinese Puzzle. d. Cédric Klapisch. Script Cédric Klapisch. Perf. Romain Duris, Audrey Tautou, Kelly Reilly, Sandrine Holt, Zinedine Soualem.

Prod. Opposite Field pictures, Belgacom, Ce qui me meut Motion pictures, La Compagnie cinématographique, Panache Productions, 2013. 117 min.

Les Poupées russes/Russian Dolls. d. Cédric Klapisch. Script Cédric Klapisch. Perf. Romain Duris, Audrey Tautou, Kelly Reilly, Kevin Bishop, Aïssa Maiga, Cécile de France. Prod. Lunar, Studio Canal, France 2, Canal Plus, Ce qui me meut motion pictures, TPS cinéma, 2005. 125 min.

Cesar Best Support Actress, Cécile de France 2006.

L'Auberge espagnole/The Spanish Inn/The Spanish Apartment/Euro Pudding. d. Cédric Klapisch. Script Cédric Klapisch. Perf. Romain Duris, Audrey Tautou, Cécile de France, Judith Godrèche, Kelly Reilly, Zinedine Soualem, Pablo Klapisch. Prod. BAC films, Ce qui me meut Motion Pictures, France 2 Cinéma, Mate films, 2002. 122 min.

Audience Award, Brisbane International Film Festival 2003. Cesar Most promising actress, Cécile de France 2002. Lumière Award, Best Screenplay 2003.

Chacun cherche son chat/When the Cat's Away. d. Cédric Klapisch. Script Cédric Klapisch. Perf. Romain Duris, Zinedine Soualem, Renée Le Calm, Garance Clavel. Prod. Aïssa Djabri, Manuel Munz, Farid Lahouassa, 1996. 91 min.

Xavier Koller

Journey of Hope/Reise der Hoffnung. d. Xavier Koller. Script Xavier Koller, Feride Çiçekoglu. Prod. Antea Cinematografica, Catpics, Channel Four Films, Cineverde, Condor Films, Dewe Hellteiler, Eurimages, Schweizer Ferhnsehen, Schweizerische Radio und Ferhnsehgesellshaft, Département Fédéral de l'intérieur, Télévision Suisse Romande, 1990. 110 min.

Bronze Leopard, Locarno International Film Festival 1990.

Bouli Lanners

Eldorado. d. Bouli Lanners. Script Bouli Lanners. Perf. Bouli Lanners, Fabrice Adde, Philippe Nahon. Prod. Casa Kafka Pictures, CNC, Centre du cinéma et de l'audiovisuel de la communauté française de Belgique, Eurimages, 2008. 80 min.

André Cavens award for Best Film. (Belgian Film Critics Association).

Patrice Leconte

Les Bronzés/French Fried Vacation. d. Patrice Leconte. Script Patrice Leconte. Perf. Josiane Balasko, Luis Rego, Michel Blanc, Christian Clavier, Gérard Jugnot, Dominique Lavanant, Thierry Lhermitte. Prod. Compagnie Commerciale Française cinématographique, Concorde Film, Studio Canal, 1978. 87 min.

Sarah Léonor (Petit)

Au voleur/A Real Life. d. Sarah Léonor. Script Emmanuelle Jacob, Sarah Léonor. Perf. Florence Loiret Caille, Jacques Nolot, Guillaume Depardieu. Prod. Les Films Hatari. Le Studio Orlando, CNC, Région Ile de France, 2009. 100 min.

Jean-Paul Lilienfeld

La Journée de la jupe/Skirt Day. d. Jean-Paul Lilienfeld. Script Jean-Paul Lilienfeld. Perf. Isabelle Adjani, Denis Podalydès. Prod. Mascaret films, ARTE France. Rezo films, 2009. 87 min.

Cesar award 2010.

Richard Linklater

Before Midnight. d. Richard Linklater. Script Richard Linklater, Julie Delpy, Ethan Hawke. Perf. Ethan Hawke, Julie Delpy. Prod. Faliro House, Venture Forth, Castle Rock Entertainment, Detour Filmproduction, 2013. 109 min.

Hollywood Film Award 2013.

Before Sunset. d. Richard Linklater. Script Richard Linklater, Julie Delpy, Ethan Hawke, Kim Krizan. Perf. Julie Delpy, Ethan Hawke. Prod. Warner Independent Pictures, Castle Rock Entertainment, Detour Filmproduction, 2004. 80 min.

Before Sunrise. d. Richard Linklater. Script Richard Linklater, Kim Krizan. Perf. Julie Delpy, Ethan Hawke. Prod. Castle Rock Entertainment, Detour Filmproduction, Filmhaus Wien Universa Filmproduktions, Sunrise, Columbia Pictures Corporation, 1995. 105 min.

Silver Berlin Bear 1995.

Philippe Lioret

Welcome. d. Philippe Lioret. Script Philippe Lioret, Emmanuel Courcol, Olivier Adam, Serge Frydman, Simone Chiossi. Perf. Vincent Lindon, Firat Ayverdi, Audrey Dana. Prod. Christophe Rossignon. Nord Ouest Productions, Studio 37, France 3 cinéma, Fin Août Productions, Canal +, 2009. 110 min.

Label Europa Cinema, Berlin International Film Festival 2009.

Gillies MacKinnon

Hideous Kinky. d. Gillies MacKinnon. Script Esther Freud, Billy MacKinnon. Perf. Kate Winslet, Bella Riza, Said Taghmaoui. Prod. AMLF, Arts Council of England, BBC, The Film Consortium, Greenpoint Films, L Films, 1998. 98 min.

Chris Marker

Sans Soleil. d. Chris Marker. Script Chris Marker. Perf. Florence Delay, Arielle Dombasle, Riyoko Ikeda, Documentary. Prod Argos Film, 1983. 100 min.

Cinema Eye Honors Award 2014, 2015.

La Jetée. d. Chris Marker. Script Chris Marker. Perf. Hélène Châtelain, Jean Négroni. Prod. Argos Films, 1962. 28 min.

Prix Jean Vigo 1963

Laetitia Masson

La Repentie/The Repentant. d. Laetitia Masson. Script Laetitia Masson, loosely based on Didier Daenincks' novel. Perf. Sami Frey, Samy Naceri, Isabelle Adjani. Prod. Michèle Halberstadt. ARP Selection, Canal +, France 3 cinéma, 2002. 125 min.

A vendre/For Sale. d. Laetitia Masson. Script Laetitia Masson. Perf. Sandrine Kiberlain, Sergio Castellitto, Jean-François Stévenin. Prod. Canal +, La Cuel Lavelette prod., La 7 cinéma, 1998. 100 min.

Yolande Moreau

Quand la mer monte/When the sea rises. d. Yolande Moreau and Gilles Portes. Script Yolande Moreau and Gilles Portes. Perf. Yolande Moreau, François Morel, Jackie Berroyer. Prod. Ognon Pictures, Stromboli Pictures, R.T.B.F., 2004. 90 min.

Ermanno Olmi

La Légende du Saint-Buveur/The Legend of the Holy Drinker. d. Ermanno Olmi. Script based on Joseph Roth, by Tullio Kezich, Olmi. Perf. Rutger Hauer. Prod. Cecchi Gori Group Tiger, RAI, Aura films, Telemax, 1988. 127 min.

Golden Lion, Venice 1989.

Rithy Panh

Un barrage contre le Pacifique/The Seawall. d. Rithy Panh. Script Marguerite Duras, Rithy Panh, Michel Fessler. Perf. Isabelle Huppert, Gaspard Ulliel, Astrid Bergès-Frisbey. Prod. Diaphana, 2008. 115 min.

Sarah Petit (Léonor)

Le lac et la rivière. d. Sarah Petit. Script Sarah Petit. Perf. Thomas Cerisola, Mona Heftre. Prod. Elena Films, Les Films Hatari, 2002. 56 min.

L'Arpenteur/The Land Surveyor. d. Sarah Petit. Script Sarah Petit. Perf. Ovanatan Avékidian, Pierre François Laks. Prod. Don Films, Point de repères, Sesame Films, 2001. 45 min.

Prix Jean Vigo (short) 2002.

Manuel Poirier

Western. d. Manuel Poirier. Script Manuel Poirier. Perf. Sergi Lopez, Sacha Bourdo, Elizabeth Vitali. Prod. Salomé, Diaphana Films, Canal +, C.N.C., 1997. 124 min.

Prix Michel Simon: Sacha Bourdo 1998, Cannes Jury Prize Manuel Poirier. 1997.

Jean Renoir

La Bête humaine. d. Jean Renoir. Script Jean Renoir based on Emile Zola's novel. Perf. Simone Simon, Jean Gabin, Julien Carette, Fernand Ledoux. Prod. Paris Film, 1938. 100 min.

Pierre Rissient

Cinq ou la peau/Five and the Skin. d. Pierre Rissient. Script Lucie Albertini, Alain Archambault, Eugène Guillevic, Fernando Pessoa, Pierre Rissient. Perf. Féodor Atkin, Eiko Matsuda. Prod. Bancom audiovision, G.P.F.I. , Les Films de l'Alma, 1982. 95 min.

Roberto Rossellini

Journey to Italy/Viaggio in Italia. d. Roberto Rossellini. Script Roberto Rossellini, Vitaliano Brancati. Perf. Ingrid Bergman, George Sanders. Prod. Adolfo Fossatoro, 1954. 97 mn.

Jean Rouch

Petit à Petit. d. Jean Rouch. Script Jean Rouch. Perf. Damouré Zika, Lam Dia, Illo Goudal, Safi Faye. Prod. Les Films de la Pléiade, 1970. 90 min.

Jacques Rozier

Maine-Océan. d. Jacques Rozier. Script Jacques Rozier. Perf. Lydia Feld, Luis Rego, Bernard Menez, Rosa Maria Gomes, Abdel Kedadouche. Prod. France 3 cinéma, France Line, Les Films du Passage, 1986. 130 min.

Prix Jean Vigo.

Les Naufragés de l'île de la tortue/The castaways of Turtle Island. d. Jacques Rozier. Script Jacques Rozier. Perf. Jacques Villeret, Patrick Chesnais. Prod. Callipix, 1976. 140 min.

Du Côté d'Orouët. d. Jacques Rozier. Script Jacques Rozier, Alain Raygot. Perf. Bernard Menez, Caroline Cartier, Danièle Croisy, Françoise Guégan. Prod. V.M. Productions, Antinéa, 1973. 150 min.

Adieu Philippine. d. Jacques Rozier. Script Jacques Rozier, Michèle O'Glor. Perf. Jean-Claude Aimini, Daniel Descamps, Stefania Sabatini. Prod. Rome Paris Films, Euro International Film, Alpha Productions, United, 1962. 106 min.

Rentrée des Classes/Back to School. d. Jacques Rozier. Script Jacques Rozier, Michèle O'Glor. Perf. René Boglio, Marius Sumian, the teacher and the pupils of Correns. Prod. Dovidis, Films du Colisée, 1955. 24 min.

Christophe Ruggia

Le Gône du Chaâba/The Kid from Chaaba. d. Christopher Ruggia. Script Azouz Begag. Perf. Bouzid Negnoug, Mohamed Fellag. Prod. Films Christiani- Orly Films, Vertigo, 1998. 96 min.

Djamila Sahraoui

Barakat! Enough! d. Djamila Sahraoui. Script Djamila Sahraoui, Cécile Wargaftig. Perf. Rachida Brakni. Prod. Les Films d'Ici, Arte Productions. 2006. 95 min.

Coline Serreau

Saint-Jacques...La Mecque. d. Coline Serreau. Script Coline Serreau. Perf. Artus de Penguern, Muriel Robin, Jean-Pierre Daroussin. Prod. Téléma, France 2 Productions, Eniloc films, TPS Star, 2005. 110 min.

Siegfried

Sansa. d. Siegfried. Script Siegfried. Perf. Ivry Gitlis, Roschdy Zem. Prod. Vagabondages films Arte, 2003. 116 min.

Youth Jury Award, Ghent International Film Festival 2003.

Alain Tanner

Fourbi. d. Alain Tanner. Script Alain Tanner, Bernard Comment. Perf. Karin Viard, Jean-Quentin Châtelain. Prod. Filmograph, Noé Productions, 1996. 114 min.

Messidor. d. Alain Tanner. script Alain Tanner. Perf. Clémentine Amouroux, Catherine Rétoré. Prod. Citel Films, Gaumont, Société suisse de radiodiffusion et télévision, 1979. 123 min.

Jonas qui aura 25 ans en l'an 2000/Jonah who will be 25 in the year 2000. d. Alain Tanner. Script John Berger Alain Tanner. Perf. Raymond Bussières, Miou Miou, Myriam Boyer, Jean-Luc Bideau. Prod. Citel, SFP, Action Films, télévision suisse-romande, 1975. 116 min.

La Salamandre/The Salamander. d. Alain Tanner. Script John Berger, Alain Tanner. Perf. Jean-Luc Bideau, Jacques Denis, Bulle Ogier. Prod.Filmograph SA, Forum Films, Svocine, 1971. 125 min.

OCIC Award, Forum of New Cinema, Berlin International Film Festival 1971.

Jacques Tati

Trafic/Traffic. d. Jacques Tati. Script Jacques Tati, Jacques Lagrange. Perf. Jacques Tati, Marcel Fraval, Maria Kimberly. Prod. Les Films Corona, Les Films Gibe, Océania Films, Selenia films, 1971. 96 min.

Jean-Marc Vallée

Wild. d. Jean-Marc Vallée, script Nick Hornby, Cheryl Strayed. Perf. Reese Witherspoon, Laura Dern. Prod. Fox Searchlight, Pacific Standard, 2014. 115 min.

Agnès Varda

Les Plages d'Agnès/The Beaches of Agnès. d. Agnès Varda. Script Agnès Varda. Perf. Agnès Varda, Mathieu Demy. 2008. Prod. Lisa Blok-Linson, Thomas E. Taplin, Agnès Varda, 2008. 110 min.

EDA Female Focus Award, Women Film Journalists, 2009. Cinema Eye Honors Award, 2010. Cesar Award: Best Documentary Film 2010. Chlotrudis Award 2009.

Les Glaneurs et la Glaneuse/The Gleaners and I. d. Agnès Varda. Script Agnès Varda. Perf. Alain Wertheimer, Agnès Varda, Chris Marker, Documentary. Prod. Ciné Tamaris, 2000. 82 min.

Chicago International Film Festival Award, European Film Award, Montréal Festival of New Cinema, National Society of Film Critics Awards 2000.

Sans toit ni loi/Vagabond. d. Agnès Varda. Script Agnès Varda. Perf. Sandrine Bonnaire, Macha Méril, Yolande Moreau. Prod. Ciné Tamaris, Films A2, Ministère de la Culture, 1985. 105 min.

Cesar Best Actress Sandrine Bonnaire 1986, FIPRESCI. Golden Lion, Venice 1986.

Documenteur. d. Agnès Varda. Script Agnès Varda. Perf. Mathieu Demy, Sabine Mamou. Prod. Ciné Tamaris, 1981. 65 min.

Cléo de 5 à 7. d. Agnès Varda. Script Agnès Varda. Perf. Corrine Marchand, Antoine Bourseiller, Dorothy Blanck, Michel Legrand, José Luis de Villalonga. Prod. Ciné Tamaris, Rome Paris Film, 1962. 90 min.

Jean Vigo

L'Atalante. d. Jean Vigo. Script Jean Vigo, Jean Guinée. Perf. Dita Parlo, Michel Simon, Jean Dasté, Gilles Margaritis. Prod. Jean-Louis Nounez, 1934. 89 min.

Patrick Volson

Le voyage de Louisa. d. Patrick Volson. Script Azouz Begag. Perf. Mélèze Bouzid, Jamal Hadir. Prod. France 2, Pampa Prod., RAI, 2005. 105 min.

Laura Waddington

Border. d. Laura Waddington. Prod. Love Streams Production, 2004. 27 min.
Grand Prix experimental essai art video. Côté Court, France 2005.

Yolande Zauberman

Moi Ivan, toi Abraham/Ivan & Abraham. d. Yolande Zauberman. Script Yolande Zauberman. Perf. Roma Alexandrovitch, Aleksandr Yakoviev. Prod. Belarus Films, Hachette Première, VITT, 1993. 105 min.

Erick Zonca

Julia. d. Erick Zonca. Script adapted from Emile Bohbot, Michael Collins, Aude Py and Erick Zonca. Perf. Tilda Swinton, Saul Rubinek. Prod. Les Productions Bagheera, France 3, Le Bureau, Studio Canal, 2008. 144 min.

Best Actress, International Cinephile Society Award, Tilda Swinton, 2010.

Index